Mozi
A Modern Translation and Contemporary Interpretation

墨子今譯時析

目錄

2

Table of Contents

兼愛

戰爭與和平

All-embracing Love

War and Peace

民主集中

Democratic Centralization

簡樸生活

修身

Living a Simple Life

Self-edification

治學做人

On Study and Conduct

墨家復興的啟示

春秋戰國時代，墨家繼儒家而起，儒墨並雄，與主張「貴己」、「為我」的楊朱之說成為一時顯學。墨家兼愛觀、義政觀、義利一元論、非命和邏輯，對後起的儒家（如孟子）、名家、法家都有影響，道家的《莊子》中亦充滿了對墨家或辯或駁的回聲。但自漢朝以後，墨家就幾乎從思想界消失了。

直至近代，中國又在內在外進入類似於列國紛爭的春秋戰國時代，知識份子與仁人志士對墨子再度發生興趣，希望以其思想解決時代的問題。而今天的中國內外處境已與一二百年前的有所不同，我們還有需要重讀《墨子》嗎？

或許從探討墨家在近兩千年歷史中沉寂的原因，我們更能回答為甚麼要重讀《墨子》這問題。學者任繼愈在其《墨子與墨家》書中指出：秦漢

The Revival of Mohism: What It Teaches Us

Mohism arose after Confucianism during the Spring and Autumn period, and together with Yangism, which contended that human actions are and should be based on self-interest, the three became the prominent schools of thought of the time. Mohist views on all-embracing love, righteous governance, a righteousness-interest monism, anti-fatalism and logic made an impact on the later Confucians (like Mencius), the School of Names and also the Legalists. The Daoist _Zhuangzi_, meanwhile, is filled with refutations of Mohist claims. However, after the Han dynasty, Mohism almost disappeared from the intellectual world until the modern era, when China again entered an internal and external period of a rivalry, similar to that of the Spring and Autumn period, so that intellectuals and people with lofty ideas have again become interested in Mozi's thought, hoping to find solutions from it for the problems of more recent times. But as China's domestic and international circumstances are now so different from those of one or two hundred years ago, is there any point in reading _Mozi_ again?

Perhaps if we look at what caused Mohism to fade into oblivion over the past two thousand years, we will be able to see why we _should_ read _Mozi_ again. Scholar Ren Jiyu points out in his _Mozi and the Mohists_ that the unification of China brought about in the Qin and Han dynasties put an end to the violent battles

以後，中國一統，消弭了春秋戰國列國廝殺的亂象，墨子「兼愛」、「非攻」已無針對性；漢初七王之亂後，取消了貴族世襲制，建立了官吏選拔制，墨子「尚賢」的主張實現了；中央集權，「尚同」也實現了。

在春秋戰國列國紛爭的形勢中，墨家人物尚有遊說各國，在一些國家實踐其主張的空間（如耕柱到楚，許行由楚到齊，秦國亦有墨家活動）。但秦漢大一統之後，國君只有一個，知識份子主張的「買家」只有一個了，而秦只買法家的賬，漢初是黃老之術，漢武帝時董仲舒提出「罷黜百家，獨尊儒術」，此後兩千年都是儒家壟斷了官方意識形態，墨家就此失去試用的機會。

進一步說明墨家幾近消失的原因，可將之分為內外兩種。就內在思想而言，墨家確實太具有時代針對性（如「非攻」、「節葬」），所以，當那個時代及其政治社會問題消失之後，它的存

among states during the Spring and Autumn and Warring States periods, making Mozi's ideas of "all-embracing love" and "anti-aggression" no longer of relevance. In the beginning of the Han dynasty, the Revolt of the Seven Princes led to the abolition of hereditary succession and the establishment of a system of selecting officials; thus realizing Mozi's idea of "valuing virtuous people." With this system, political power was centralized, and Mozi's idea of "valuing unity" was also fullfilled. During the earlier Spring and Autumn and Warring States periods when inter-state rivalry was dominant, there was still room for the Mohists to peddle their political ideas to different states (for example, Gen Zhu visited Chu; Xu Xing went from Chu to Qi; there were also Mohist activities in Qin). Yet after the unification under the Qin and Han, there was only one ruler, thus only one "buyer" of the ideas proposed by intellectuals. In the Qin dynasty, only Legalism was recognized; at the beginning of the Han, the Huang-Lao method (Daoism) prevailed; during the reign of Emperor Wu of Han, Dong Zhongshu proposed "to dismiss the hundred schools and revere only the Confucian method," since when Confucianism has monopolized the official ideology, denying any chance of Mohism being tried out.

In order to elaborate on the causes of Mohism's near disappearance, we need to discuss the internal and external factors. Internally speaking, the ideas of Mohism were too

在價值也就消失了。它不像儒家和道家那樣，對於人性和存在本身有着深入的思考，值得任何時代的人反復琢磨。

墨家的思想亦存在粗糙與矛盾的一面：在「天志」、鬼神的賞罰上，墨家就難以回答「約伯問題」（為何好人不得好報，惡人反得好報）；在「節葬」與「明鬼」中，如後來漢代的王充所指出的，其主張是矛盾的（因為既然承認人死後成鬼有靈，則會指望其子孫厚祭他，而不樂見薄葬）；在「兼愛」、「非攻」的問題上，一方面反對殺人，另一方面為了保護弱者又不得不參加慘烈的戰鬥；「尚賢」擴大了統治階層的基礎，但「尚同」卻又可能使壞天子能夠實行集權統治⋯⋯這些矛盾使墨家思想的吸引力難以維持。

在內容表達的方式上，如果說「非攻」、「尚賢」等「十論」過分樸實重複而無簡約之美，那麼《墨經》卻又過分簡約難以令人領會，前者使

specifically targeted at issues of a certain period (e.g., "anti-aggression," "simple funerals"). Therefore, when these social and political problems disappeared, the existential value of the school vanished. Mohism lacked what Confucianism and Daoism possessed: profound thoughts on humanity and human existence, which are worth pondering for people in any age. Mohism is also rather crude and contradictory in certain respects. In "Tian Zhi," when talking about the rewards and punishments of spirits and gods, Mohists could not give a satisfactory answer for "Job's question" of why good people aren't rewarded while bad people may get rewarded. In "Jie Zang" and "Ming Gui," as Wang Chong from the Han dynasty pointed out, the claims are contradictory (because, as it asserts, a man becomes a spirit after death, then it is certain for him to expect his descendants to give him a lavish funeral instead of a simple one); on issues of "all-embracing love" and "anti-aggression," despite Mohists' opposition to killing people, they could not avoid fighting brutal battles in order to protect the weak; and while "valuing virtuous people" did help expand the governance base, "valuing unity" might have made it possible for an evil Son of Heaven to implement centralized governance. These contradictions have made the attractiveness of Mohism unsustainable. Content-wise, if we say the "ten arguments" such as "anti-aggression" and "valuing virtuous people" sounded overly unsophisticated and repetitive and thus lacked the beauty of simplicity, then "Mo Jing" would be considered

人覺得墨家質樸無文，後者則使之難以傳承。因此到了後來，墨家談治世不如儒家詳細，談心性不如佛教細膩，談養生不如道家明白，講宗教又不如道教玄虛，沒有了「賣點」。

墨家思想主張知行合一，要求大公無私，「為義」不惜赴火蹈刃，死不旋踵，這使得加入墨家的要求過高，起碼普通人是難以成為墨家的。像墨子本人和禽滑厘那樣為天下之義整日奔走、過着極端簡樸的生活，非常人所能及，墨家的軍事化的嚴密組織和嚴格訓練，也嚴重地限制了普通人加入墨家的可能性，使得其後繼乏人。

從外在環境來說，秦漢以後，墨家除了給官方定於一尊的意識形態排斥外，其信徒的行事特質也不容於統治者。墨家性格在春秋戰國的亂世，有着鮮明的呈現。比如秦國的一個墨家鉅子（首領），他的獨生兒子犯了罪，按墨家戒律當死，秦國國君看他只有這麼一個兒子，就為他兒

too brief to be understood; the former made Mohism appear simplistic while the latter made it hard to pass on. This explains why it later turned out that Mohists' discussion of governance was not as thorough as Confucians'; on heart and mind not as meticulous as Buddhists'; on the way to remain in good health not as clear as Daoists'; and on religion not as subtle as Daoists'. Hence gradually it lost its "selling point."

Mohist philosophy advocated putting knowledge into action and demanded fairness and impartiality. "For the sake of righteousness" Mohists were willing to tread on fire and blades, willing to sacrifice themselves without regret. Such extreme commitments made the Mohist school too hard to follow — at least it would not be easy for an ordinary man to become a Mohist. Like Mozi and Qin Huali, they bustled around every day for the sake of righteousness and led an extremely frugal and simple life, a lifestyle that was probably too challenging for most people. Besides, the tight organization and strict training required by the Mohist military system also discouraged ordinary people from joining the Mohist school. This made it difficult for the movement to find successors.

As a consequence, since the Qin and Han dynasties, the rejection of Mohism by the official authoritarian ideology has meant its followers' conduct being unacceptable to the ruling elite. During the disorderly Spring and Autumn and Warring States

子求情，但鉅子仍舊處死了自己的兒子。（如按儒家思想，鉅子是可以讓兒子活的。）另一個在楚國的鉅子孟勝率一百八十名墨家為一名違抗國君的大夫守城，全軍覆滅，可謂被大夫利用，是「愚忠」。（換了別人可能不會這麼頭腦簡單。）而當亂世結束，進入秦漢大一統之後，這種半軍事化半宗教化的非政府組織，只會威脅到統治者，在公開層面無法存在，而只能潛入地下，成為「地下社會」或「會黨」了。

到了近代，隨着基督教（新教）東漸，以及從晚清開始中國進入一個長達二百年的「過渡」期，動亂頻仍，「皇帝」失權，軍閥崛起。同時中國又被捲入世界圖景之中，「中國之中國」成了「世界之中國」，而十九世紀後期、二十世紀的初期，世界又類似於列國紛爭的春秋戰國，帝國主義、殖民主義橫行，弱肉強食，因此，中國人一下子感覺回到了春秋戰國時代，墨子的「尚義」精神，又有了提倡的必要。墨子對於絕對正

periods, Mohism did make a vivid impression. For example, in the Qin state, when the only son of one of the Mohist moguls (chiefs) committed a crime, Mohist discipline affirmed that he deserved the death penalty. However, despite the ruler of Qin making a plea for leniency, knowing the culprit was the only son of the mogul, the mogul still chose to have him executed. (According to Confucian thought, the mogul would have been able to choose not to execute his son.) Another mogul in the state of Chu, Meng Sheng, led a hundred and eighty Mohist members to defend the city for a minister who revolted against the ruler; the action ended in total defeat. Apparently, he was being used by the minister, and the mogul's act was a case of "mindless loyalty." (Others might not have been as simple-minded.) Once the chaos ended and the world was unified under the Qin and Han dynasties, such semi-military and semi-religious non-governmental organizations would only become a threat to those in power. As a result, they were no longer able to survive openly and were forced to go into hiding and become "underground societies" or "secret parties."

In the recent, era when Christianity (Protestantism) came to the East and when China began a two hundred-year-long "transition" period in the late Qing dynasty, unrest was frequent: "emperors" lost their power and warlords emerged. At the same time, China was being drawn into the world whirlpool — "the China of China" became "the China of the

義「天志」的呼喚、「非攻」的主張，有了用武之地。「兼愛」的主張，使人們感到與基督教的「博愛」精神一致。

《墨經》中的科技與邏輯知識，又讓人覺得墨子與西方現代科學和哲學的一致。「天志」對於「天」的強調，則使不少的中國基督徒感到墨子有類似基督教的「上帝」觀念，值得重視。因此從譚嗣同、梁啟超這樣的儒家，到王治心這樣的基督徒，都對墨子思想發生興趣，墨子終於成為復興的「諸子學」當中的一個「顯學」了。

但這一波墨學復興卻是曇花一現。彼時知識界認為主流儒家的「通經致用」不敷應對民族危亡和西學衝擊，故致力從中國傳統文化中找尋能夠與西方「民主與科學」等精神對接的資源，折射出國人的文明挫敗感、對以西方為指標的現代化的寄望。

world." On the other hand, the world in the late nineteenth and early twentieth centuries resembled the Spring and Autumn and Warring States periods when inter-state rivalries were the norm: imperialism and colonialism dominated, and the weak states became the prey of the powerful ones. The Chinese, unsurprisingly, felt they had returned to the Spring and Autumn and Warring States periods and once more advocated the Mohist principle of "valuing righteousness." The way Mozi called upon the absolutely righteous "will of heaven" and argued for "anti-aggression" was again deemed useful for tackling the issues of the time. People felt the congruence between the doctrine of "all-embracing love" and the spirit of "agape" advocated by Christianity. People also found consistency between the scientific-technological and logical knowledge discussed in "Mo Jing" and the modern science and philosophy of the West. In addition, the emphasis on "heaven" in the "will of heaven" grabbed the attention of many Chinese Christians who likened it to the idea of "God" in Christianity. Therefore, from Confucians such as Tang Sitong and Liang Qichao to Christians such as Wang Zhixin, all were interested in Mozi's thought, and finally Mohism succeeded in reappearing as one of the "prominent schools" among the "hundred schools of thought."

However, this wave of Mohism revival was short-lived. At that time, it was commonly held among academics that the

　　從思想角度而言，墨家是比較能比附西方先進文明的學說，但墨家自漢代中絕之後只有「死掉的文本」《墨子》，而沒有「活的傳統」，放在現實的政治、經濟與社會環境，只是一種空談，遠不及西方已見成效的學說來得可行，無論是資本主義抑或共產主義。到國族危亡之秋，仁人志士與各種政治力量，也無暇在故紙堆中大做文章，只好找現成的有巨大動員能力的理論來匡世。墨學經歷過內戰與對日抗戰又消沉了，在中共建國後的革命思想狂飆年代，也不用說了。

　　時至當代，全球化使世界上近二百個主權國家的關係越趨緊密，並形成了全球經濟、科學與生態。但由於多個國家膨脹的國族主義與它們基督教、伊斯蘭教、儒家或印度教等信仰結合，導致文明之間或隱或顯的競爭，甚至戰爭。

　　整體而言，全球獲得長足的進步，但許多地方，貧者彌貧，富者彌富，各種不平等在加劇。

mainstream Confucians' stress on "being proficient in classics and putting them into practice" was not enough to cope with the national crises and the impact of Western knowledge; they therefore made efforts to uncover resources in traditional Chinese culture that might reconcile with the Western ideas of "democracy and science." This reflects Chinese people's frustration with Chinese culture and the hope they pinned on modernization based upon the Western model. Although as a philosophy Mohism is relatively more compatible with the advanced Western civilizations, after its disappearance in the Han dynasty, only "a text that lost its life" — _Mozi_ — remained and there was no "living tradition" of the doctrine to follow.

If we were to put _Mozi_ into the political, economic and social contexts of the real world then, it would come across as mere empty talk and far less credible than the Western doctrines that had already shown results, whether capitalism or communism. At a time when the life and death of the nation was at stake, people with lofty ideas and the various political forces could spare no time to dig into old books. They turned instead to the influential theories at hand to try to rectify the world. Once again, Mohism faded away during the period of the civil war and the war against the Japanese invasion, and even more so when China entered the whirlwind of radical revolutionary thought after the Chinese communists founded the People's Republic of China.

這依然是一個春秋戰國時代。墨子思想對於「正義」的強調，令人對當代國際及國家內弱肉強食的狀況關注；對於「兼愛」、「天志」的重視，跟各大文明中的宗教底蘊相合；對於「非攻」、「節用」的強調，則對當代霸權主義、好大喜功與奢侈浪費的風氣，具有很強的針對性。

而墨子的「尚賢」、「尚同」的主張也有其參考價值。「尚賢」就是舉拔賢人，並要打破等級制度，不用人唯親，這對在許多社會盛行的「裙帶主義」，依然不失為一種警示。「尚同」是統一天下的是非標準，以統一天下的行動，有人會詬病這違反民主、多元的原則，但民主不等於沒有主流意見（共識），問題是如何把民心民意集中起來；而多元發展至極端，令信息越來越碎片化，群組更形對立，社會陷入嚴重分裂，則會窒礙社會的發展。

「尚賢」加「尚同」把各級優秀領導推舉出

Globalization has now tightened the ties between nearly two hundred sovereign countries of the world, forming a global entity of economies, science and ecology. Yet at the same time, the rise in nationalism in various countries combined with their religious beliefs (Christianity, Islam, Confucianism, Hinduism, etc.) has led to implicit or explicit competition among civilizations, sometimes even to wars. In general, the world has made significant progress, but in many places, the poor have become poorer, the rich have become richer, and all kinds of inequalities rankle. This represents yet another situation like the Autumn and Spring and Warring States periods. Mohism's emphasis on "righteousness" can be directed against the predatory behaviors seen among and within countries in the present-day world. Its stress on "all-embracing love" and the "will of heaven" is a perfect match with the spirit of the religions of all great civilizations. Its emphasis on "anti-aggression" and "frugality" can counter the hegemonic, grandiosity-seeking and extravagant trends of the present age. Besides, Mozi's doctrines on "valuing virtuous people" and "valuing unity" are useful references. "Valuing virtuous people" means recruiting and promoting the virtuous as a means to break away from the hierarchical system and favoritism. This still works as a caution against the "nepotism" prevalent in many societies. "Valuing unity" means unifying the moral standards of the world to bring about global actions. While some might suggest this idea violates the principles of democracy and

來，由他們代表天下百姓的意志，他們又一層一層地向上統一意志，但同時有義務指出上面的錯誤，到達天子（國家主席、總統）這頂級，最後以「天志」（自然法）來制約，形成統一的是非標準。證諸於 2020 年對抗新冠肺炎的經驗，有沒有統一的是非標準，簡單如戴口罩的效用，是成敗關鍵之一。如上所論，墨子的一些主張對當代國際及國家內的突出問題仍可提供解決的思路。

墨子重視實踐和實驗，在科技研究上有所成就。他有關「行」的一些主張，符合現代教育「動手」的理論，對匡正國人輕實踐與技能的傾向，有所裨益。今天的中國，整個教育制度對學生社會實踐與技術能力的培養仍然不足，而這種動手的能力正是中國向前邁進時所需的。墨子的有關學說，對中國人講的「知行合一」的「行」的方面，是一個有力的補充。

近年，中國官方推行「中華民族偉大復興」

pluralism, democracy does not necessarily imply the absence of mainstream opinions (consensus), but it can be difficult to unify the wishes and opinions of people. What is more, pluralism in its extremes might make information fragmentary, groups hostile to each other and split society, and in the end inhibit social development. "Valuing virtuous people" and "valuing unity" aim at promoting outstanding leaders at all levels and allowing them to represent the wills of the people of the world. If people's wills can be unified level by level right to the top, and at the same time each stratum can be responsible for pointing out the mistakes committed by its superiors until the topmost Son of Heaven (the president of state) is reached, whose actions are dictated by the "will of heaven" (natural law), this system can create a unified standard of right and wrong. The experience in the fight against Covid-19 has shown us that the existence of a unified standard of right and wrong is a crucial factor for success, even in a simple issue such as the effectiveness of wearing a mask. As suggested above, some of Mozi's arguments can still offer ways to solve today's urgent international and domestic problems.

Mozi valued practice and experiment and made achievements in scientific and technological research. His thought on "practice" matches well with the modern educational theory of "practice" and is thus beneficial in reorienting Chinese people's tendency towards overlooking practice and techniques. In modern China,

理念，較為重視傳統文化以及經典學習，這種國學熱潮與前述其他內外因素結合，也催生了一批現代新墨家。他們認為墨家經過現代化的詮釋，以及原典義理的重光，可以開出超越政治儒學的兼具中國特色與普世價值的政治哲學，諸如平等、人權、社會契約、法治、言論自由、結社自由等方面。

「普世性」和「時代性」，是當今探討墨家的重要着眼點，但也應注意其「中國特色」。以民主制度為例，有論者說墨子在《尚同上》闡述了民主選舉產生政府的觀點，但若以墨家思想脈絡來看，其主張更近似中國現今實行的民主集中制。其實，中國的民主集中制和西方的自由民主制不一定截然對立，而是可以互補長短。

以世界和平（中國古稱「天下太平」）理想為另一例，墨家的「兼愛」、「非攻」加上「交利」似乎包含了儒家金律的「消極無傷害原則」（己

the educational system still provides insufficient nurturance of students' social participation and skills. Such hands-on competence, however, is necessary for China to move forward. Mozi's idea in this respect can make a significant contribution to the meaning of "practice" in "unity of knowledge and practice" as understood by Chinese people.

In recent years, the Chinese government has vowed to bring about "the great revival of the Chinese nation" and put more emphasis on studying traditional culture and classics. This boom in cultural studies, together with the internal and external factors mentioned above, have inspired a batch of modern neo-Mohists. They think that Mohism can be given an updated interpretation and with the rediscovery of the doctrines in the classics, Mohism can surpass political Confucianism and create a political philosophy that can preserve a uniquely Chinese character while promoting universal values. They see these values as equality, human rights, social contract, rule of law, freedom of speech and freedom of association. While "universality" and "timeliness" are two focuses of the current study of Mohism, we should also pay attention to the "uniquely Chinese character." We can take the democratic system as an example. Some scholars have said Mozi elaborated in "Shang Tong I" on how a democratic election system forms a government; yet if we read it in the context of Mohist thought, its claims appear closer to the centralized system practiced in

所不欲，勿施於人），又規避了基督教金律的「潛隱地強加於人」（你們願意別人怎樣待你們，你們也要怎樣待別人），能夠為全球倫理金律提出第三條進路，有助於人類追求崇高的目標。這墨家金律對中國倡導的「構建和諧社會」、「人類命運共同體」理念，也可以提供有力的文化支撐。

現代新墨家與一個世紀前籌謀復興墨學的知識界，在對待中國自身文化態度上不盡相同，現今的學者一定程度上恢復了文化自信，可以較平衡的心態對比中西文化，也一定程度上擺脫了本質主義的窠臼（如把墨家描繪為代表底層向代表貴族的儒家在學術主張上的階級鬥爭），用人類文明史觀超越階級鬥爭史觀。

知識界在文化態度上的改變，對包括墨家在內的傳統文化的探討肯定有好處。墨家的再生對中國整體傳統文化的復興和再造自有其歷史意義。墨家是儒家最早的反對派，非儒可糾正這主

China nowadays. In fact, the Chinese centralized system and the Western liberal democratic system may not be as antagonistic as they seem: they may form a complementary relationship. Take the ideal of world peace (it was called "peace of the whole world" in ancient China) as another example. "All-embracing love," "anti-aggression" as well as "mutual interests" espoused by Mohism seem to have implied the Confucian golden rule of "negative no harm principle"(do not do to others what you would not like done to yourselves) while avoiding the golden rule of Christianity — "impose on others discreetly"(do to others what you would have them do to you). Thus, it can offer a third approach to a golden rule that is applicable to global ethics, which can facilitate the pursuit of the noble human aim. The Mohist golden rule can also offer a powerful cultural basis for the ideas of "building a harmonious society" and "the community with a shared future for mankind" now advocated by China.

Contemporary neo-Mohists differ in their attitude towards Chinese culture from the academics who planned to revive Mohism a century ago. At present, scholars have regained confidence in their own culture, and therefore can compare Chinese and Western cultures in a more balanced way. They are also relatively free from the dogmas of essentialism (such as regarding the Mohists as the representatives of the lower class who, in class struggles, fought against Confucianism,

流傳統文化的一些流弊、補充其不足。

當然，儒家還是有不少墨家不及以及可以借鑑的地方。在新的歷史條件、沒有「官方」儒家的情況下，若能再現儒墨並雄，我們對傳統文化的前景，或可持較樂觀的期待。

上世紀末蘇聯等多個共產黨執政國家垮台後，世界至今並沒有進入一些學者與政治人物預測的以美國為首的西方自由民主制度下的大一統「天下」，反而進入了多極化的格局，種種國際問題更加突出。在意識形態與政治制度對立加劇的情形下，「老二」的中國與「老大」的美國如何避免因競爭而引起不可收拾的後果，是當務之急。

中國自身由於高速發展等原因造成眾多社會問題，要付出極大努力去解決，才能建成一個公平、公正、良政善治、可持續發展的社會。在國

which represented the aristocracy in the academic realm) so as to be able to replace the class-struggle view of history with a human cultural development view of history. This change of academics' cultural perspectives is certainly advantageous to the study of traditional culture, and Mohism is no exception. The revival of Mohism is historically relevant to the rejuvenation and regeneration of the overall traditional Chinese culture. Mohists were the earliest opponents of Confucians, and as non-Confucians they helped overcome some of the shortcomings of the mainstream traditional culture, at the same time providing remedies for its insufficiency. Certainly, there are many aspects of Confucianism that are complementary to or exemplary for Mohism. Under a new historical condition where there is no "official" Confucian doctrine, if Confucianism and Mohism can rise and lead together again, then there will be reasons for us to remain optimistic about the future development of Chinese traditional culture.

Since the downfall of the Soviet Union and other communist states at the end of the last century, the whole world, despite predictions made by some scholars and politicians, has not become "unified" under the Western liberal democratic system spearheaded by the United States. Instead, the world has become very polarized, and international disputes of various kinds have escalated. In view of the rising confrontation over ideologies and political systems, it is of utmost urgency for

際與國內新的情勢下，中國人或許可從墨子學說
的古老智慧中，找出有針對性的方法回應時代的
需求。

the world's No. 2 and No. 1 powers — China and the United States — to seek to avoid contests that may lead to devastating consequences. In China, factors such as high-speed development has created many social problems. The country needs to make a tremendous effort to solve these problems, and only then can it build a society with equality, justice, good governance and sustainable development. In the new international and domestic circumstances, Chinese people inspired by the ancient wisdom of Mohist doctrine may find specific solutions to the needs of our time.

宗教 *Religion*

一

順天意者，兼相愛，交相利，必得賞。

【原文】

子墨子曰：「然則天亦何欲何惡？天欲義而惡不義。然則率天下之百姓以從事於義，則我乃為天之所欲也。我為天之所欲，天亦為我所欲。然則我何欲何惡？我欲福祿而惡禍祟。若我不為天之所欲，而為天之所不欲，然則我率天下之百姓，以從事於禍祟中也。然則何以知天之欲義而惡不義？曰天下有義則生，無義則死；有義則富，無義則貧；有義則治，無義則亂。然則天欲其生而惡其死，欲其富而惡其貧，欲其治而惡其亂，此我所以知天欲義而惡不義也。」

故天子者，天下之窮貴也，天下之窮富也，故於富且貴者，當天意而不可不順，順天意者，兼相愛，交相利，必得賞。反天意者，別相惡，交相賊，必得罰。然

One

Those who obey the will of heaven, love each other all-embracingly and act out of mutual interest will certainly be rewarded.

Translation:

Master Mozi said, "What does heaven want and what does it abhor? Heaven seeks righteousness and rejects unrighteousness. In this case, if I lead the people of the world to do righteous things, I will be doing what heaven wants. If I do what heaven wants, heaven will do what I want. If this be so, what do I want and what do I want to avoid? I want good fortune and prosperity, and I want to avoid any calamity inflicted by the spirits. If instead of doing what heaven wants, I seek to do what heaven rejects, then I will be leading the people of the world down a path of calamity inflicted by the spirits. That being the case, how can one know that heaven wants righteousness and rejects unrighteousness? To reply: if there is righteousness, the world will flourish; without righteousness, the world will perish. If there is righteousness, there will be wealth; without righteousness, there will be poverty. If there is righteousness, the world will remain orderly; without righteousness, the world will find itself in chaos. In this case, heaven wants the people to flourish and

則是誰順天意而得賞者？誰反天意而得罰者？子墨子言曰：「昔三代聖王禹湯文武，此順天意而得賞也。昔三代之暴王桀紂幽厲，此反天意而得罰者也。」然則禹湯文武其得賞何以也？子墨子言曰：「其事上尊天，中事鬼神，下愛人，故天意曰：『此之我所愛，兼而愛之；我所利，兼而利之。愛人者此為博焉，利人者此為厚焉。』故使貴為天子，富有天下，業萬世子孫，傳稱其善，方施天下，至今稱之，謂之聖王。」然則桀紂幽厲得其罰何以也？子墨子言曰：「其事上詬天，中詬鬼，下賊人，故天意曰：『此之我所愛，別而惡之，我所利，交而賊之。惡人者此為之博也，賊人者此為之厚也。』故使不得終其壽，不歿其世，至今毀之，謂之暴王。」

順天意者，義政也。反天意者，力政也。然義政將奈何哉？子墨子言曰：「處大國不攻小國，處大家不篡小家，強者不劫弱，貴者不傲賤，多詐者不欺愚。此必上利於天，中利於鬼，下利於人，三利無

does not want to see them perish; it wants the people to be wealthy and does not want them to be poor; it wants the people to live in order and does not want them to suffer chaos.

"This is how I know heaven wants righteousness and abhors unrighteousness.

"Therefore, the Son of Heaven is the most honorable person in the world, he is the wealthiest person in the world. Hence, one who is wealthy and honorable cannot but obey the will of heaven. Those who obey the will of heaven love each other all-embracingly and act out of mutual interest; these people will certainly be rewarded. Those who disobey the will of heaven despise each other and harm each other; these people will certainly be punished. In this case, who then are the ones who obey the will of heaven and are rewarded? Who are the ones who disobey the will of heaven and are punished?"

Master Mozi said, "In the past, the sage kings of the Three Dynasties — Yu, Tang, Wen and Wu — these were the men who obeyed the will of heaven and were rewarded. The tyrannical kings of the Three Dynasties — Jie, Zhou, You and Li — these were the men who disobeyed the will of heaven and were punished."

This being so, why were Yu, Tang, Wen and Wu rewarded?

所不利，故舉天下美名加之，謂之聖王。力政者則與此異，言非此，行反此，猶倖馳也。處大國攻小國，處大家篡小家，強者劫弱，貴者傲賤，多詐欺愚。此上不利於天，中不利於鬼，下不利於人。三不利無所利，故舉天下惡名加之，謂之暴王。」

子墨子言曰：「我有天志，譬若輪人之有規，匠人之有矩，輪匠執其規矩，以度天下之，曰：『中者是也，不中者非也。』今天下之士君子之書，不可勝載，言語不可盡計，上說諸侯，下說列士，其於仁義則大相遠也。何以知之？曰：我得天下之明法以度之。」（《天志上》）

【今譯】

墨子說：「上天喜愛甚麼，厭惡甚麼呢？上天愛好義而憎惡不義。那麼率領天下的百姓去做符合義的事，便是在做上天所愛好的事了。我做上天所喜歡的事，上天也就會做我所喜歡的事。那麼我又愛好甚麼、憎惡甚麼呢？我喜歡福祿而厭惡禍患，如果我不做上天所喜歡的事，而去做

Master Mozi said, "They revered heaven above, paid tribute to the spirits and gods in the middle and loved the people below. Hence the will of heaven states: 'For those whom I love [people], their love is all-embracing; for those I benefit, the benefit they give is all-embracing. Their acts of love are generous, their services are substantial.' Therefore, they were honorably made Sons of Heaven and acquired the wealth of the whole world, their descendants inherited their kingdoms for generations and promoted their virtues throughout the world; even now they are applauded and called sage kings."

This being so, then why were Jie, Zhou, You and Li punished?

Master Mozi said, "What they did insulted heaven above, insulted the spirits and gods in the middle, and harmed the people below. Hence the will of heaven states: 'For those whom I love, they hate them with disdain; for those I benefit, they make them harm each other. Their evil deeds are widespread, their damage is substantial.' Therefore, they were short-lived and their kingdoms were even shorter-lived; even now they are condemned and called tyrannical kings."

Those who obey the will of heaven practice righteous governance; those who disobey the will of heaven impose governance by force. Then how should righteous governance be carried out?

上天所不喜歡的事，那麼就是率領天下的百姓，從事於禍患災殃中了。那麼，怎樣知道上天喜愛義而憎惡不義呢？回答：天下有義，就能生存，天下無義，就只有死亡；有義，就能富有，無義，就會貧困；有義，就有秩序，無義，就陷入混亂。上天喜歡人們孳生而討厭他們死亡，喜歡人們富有而討厭他們貧困，喜歡人們有秩序而討厭他們陷入混亂，這就是我知道的上天愛好義而憎惡不義的原因。

天子是天下極尊貴的人，天下極富有的人，所以尊貴且富有的人，對天意就不可不順從。順從天意的人，就會兼相愛，交相利，必定得到賞賜；違反天意的人，互相交惡，互相殘害，必定得到懲罰。那麼誰順從天意而得到賞賜？誰違反天意而得到懲罰？墨子說：「從前三代的聖王禹、湯、文王、武王，是順從天意而得到賞賜的；從前三代的暴王桀、紂、幽王、厲王，是違反天意而得到懲罰的。」既然如此，禹、湯、文王、武王得到賞賜的原因是甚麼？墨子說：「他們所做的事，上尊天，中敬奉鬼神，下愛人民。所以天意說：『對我所愛的，他們兼而愛之；對我所利

Master Mozi said, "The people of a big state do not attack a small state; the members of a big clan do not seize control of a small clan; the mighty do not rob the weak; the honorable do not despise the inferior; nor do the shrewd deceive the unintelligent. In this way, one is certainly serving the interests of heaven above, serving the interests of the spirits in the middle, and serving the interests of the people below. Serving the interests of these three parties is like serving the interests of all. Hence the whole world glorifies them as sage kings.

"Those who govern by force take a different path, they speak a different language, act in an opposite way, and seem to be running in the opposite direction. The people of a big state attack a small state; the members of a big clan seize control of a small clan; the mighty rob the weak; the honorable despise the inferior; and the shrewd deceive the unintelligent. In this way, such a person is harmful to heaven above, harmful to the spirits in the middle, and harmful to the people below. Being harmful to all three parties is like serving no one's interest at all. Hence the whole world condemns them as tyrannical kings."

Master Mozi continued, saying "I have the will of heaven, just as the wheelwright has the compass, or the carpenter has the try [carpenter] square. The wheelwright and the carpenter make measurements of circles and squares with their compass

的，他們兼而利之。愛人的事做得最廣博，利人的事做得最厚重。」所以使他們貴為天子，富有天下，子孫基業傳萬世，傳揚他們的美德，教化遍施於天下，到現在還受人稱道，被稱為聖王。」

那麼，桀、紂、幽王、厲王得到懲罰，又是因為甚麼呢？墨子說：「他們做事，上辱罵上天，中辱罵鬼神，下殘害人民。所以天意說：『對我所愛的，他們全都憎惡；對我所利的，他們交相殘害。惡人的事他們做得最多；害人的事他們做得最嚴重。』所以使他們不得壽終，基業身前便不能保全。至今人們還在唾罵他們，稱他們為暴王。」

順從天意，就是實行仁義政治；違反天意，就是實行暴力政治。那仁義政治應該怎麼做？墨子說：「居於大國地位的不攻打小國，居於大家族地位的不掠奪小家族，強者不強迫弱者，貴人不傲視賤人，狡詐的不欺壓愚笨的。這樣就必然上利於天，中利於鬼，下利於人。做到這三利，就會無所不利。所以將天下的美名加給他們，稱他們為聖王。暴力政治則與此不同，他們的言論

and try square, and will say, 'That which matches is correct, that which doesn't is not.' Nowadays, books written by scholars and gentlemen are voluminous and their speeches are countless. They try to persuade the vassal rulers above and the officials below, yet they are so far away from benevolence and righteousness. How do I know? To reply: I have obtained the most distinctive standard of the world to measure them with." ("Tian Zhi I")

Contemporary interpretation:

At the time of Mozi, "lord" and "heaven" as concepts were both regarded as having a will. This idea had been handed down from ancient traditions of centuries earlier, as far back as at least the Shang, and was still believed by common people at the time. Mozi held that the order of the human world was inconceivable without being guaranteed by a righteous lord of heaven. Since people could not conceal their evil thoughts and mistakes from heaven, they had to pursue goodness and keep themselves away from evil so that heaven would not be displeased. According to Mozi, even though the "spirits and gods" belong to a lower class of existence when compared with "heaven," they are beings with will, feelings and wisdom, and they are able to reward good deeds and punish evil ones.

Perhaps from a Mohist point of view, the saying "Look up and you will find a god three feet above" is indeed true.

不是這樣，行動也跟這相反，猶如背道而馳。居於大國地位的攻伐小國，居於大家族地位的掠奪小家族，強者搶奪弱者，貴者傲視賤者，狡詐的欺壓愚笨的。這上不利於天，中不利於鬼，下不利於人。三者都不利，就沒甚麼利了。所以將天下惡名加給他們，稱他們為暴王。」

墨子說：「我有天的意志，就好像製車輪的有了圓規，木匠有了方尺。製輪人和木匠拿着他們的圓規和矩尺來量度天下的圓和方，說：『符合規矩的就是對的，不符合的就是錯的。』現在天下士君子的書多得載不完，言語多得不能全都記下，對上遊說諸侯，對下遊說有名之士，但他們對於仁義，則相差很遠。我怎麼知道的？回答：我得到天下的明法來衡量他們。」

【時析】

在墨子時代，上古的傳統和當時普通人的傳統仍舊保留着，保留了上古的「帝」和「天」的意志性。對於墨子來說，沒有帝或天來保證最終正義，人間的秩序乃是不可想像的。在天的面前，人們不能隱瞞自己的惡念和過錯，因此必須積極

Mozi always put "heaven," "spirits," which he considered agents or intermediaries of heaven, and "man" together so as to caution rulers to serve the interests of all three, otherwise they would be punished. During that time, the several dozen states in China, big or small, were all under autocratic rule and no one was able to restrict the power of the autocrats. Mozi could only caution them that evil actions might bring about dire consequences, the gravest one of which would be to offend heaven, for which they would be forsaken and punished.

The Old Testament describes the relationship between the Israeli chiefs, the kings and Jehovah as this: if they do not obey Jehovah's commands, they will be punished; if they do, they will be blessed.

Mozi's idea of a proper relationship between the vassal state rulers and heaven is similar.

During the Spring and Autumn and Warring States periods, the sole aim of the Chinese philosophers was to persuade the rulers of the various states to practice benevolent governance, to turn away from tyrannical rule, to kill fewer people and let more live, so as to follow the way of heaven. This is the way for the rulers to please heaven and the spirits above and to gain support from the people below, and the only way to become unbeatable and win the world over.

向善，克己棄惡，以免為天所不喜。墨子的「鬼神」雖然是較「天」低一級的存在，但仍是有意志、感情和智慧的，他們也能夠進行獎善罰惡的工作。可以說，在墨子的觀念中，「舉頭三尺有神明」不是虛言。

墨子的「天」、「鬼」總是跟「人」三者並出，用來警告統治者做事做人，都要符合這三者的利益，否則就會遭報應。當時中國尚存在幾十個大大小小的國家，一國的國君都是專權者，沒有人能制約他們的權力，墨子只能借他們行事的嚴重後果來警告他們，而最嚴重的後果，當然就是得罪於天，被天所拋棄，被天所懲罰。《舊約》中描述了以色列諸酋長、列王跟耶和華的關係，如果他們不聽耶和華的話，就會受到懲罰，聽話，就會得到祝福。從墨子的主張，可看到合理的諸侯與天的關係與此類似。

春秋戰國的中國思想家，他們的根本旨趣仍在於遊說各國的國君實行仁政，減少暴政，少殺人，多生人，符合天道。這樣上得天鬼喜歡，下得人民擁護，才能無往不勝，得到天下。

Among pre-Qin philosophers, Mozi was the one who inherited the ideas of "heaven," "lord" and "spirits and gods" from the Xia-Shang-Zhou period. He put the ideas into a system that can be applied to different realms in our social-political life. Perhaps the idea of "adopting heaven's principles" can be considered the fulcrum of the system. "To adopt heaven's principles" means one should look up to heaven as the standard and undertake to unify the perspectives of heaven and man.

There are two dimensions of relationship to be pursued. One is the vertical relationship between heaven and man, the other is the parallel relationship between individual humans. In the vertical relationship, heaven creates and cultivates all things (including mankind), the lord of heaven mandates that man should love and care about each other in the same way as he does; those who comply will be rewarded and those who defy him will be punished. Besides, man should follow the example and model set up by heaven and obey heaven's commands, otherwise he will suffer the calamities sent from heaven. In the parallel relationship, since heaven is full of loving kindness towards man, those who adopt heaven's principles should also be full of loving kindness towards each other.

In "Fa Yi," Mozi mentions that one should not look upon his parents, scholars or rulers of the world as standards, for even

　　墨子是先秦諸子中，明確地繼承了夏商周「天」、「帝」、鬼神觀念的思想家，他把這種觀念系統化，並且運用到社會政治生活各個方面。如果要找出其中的樞紐，大概是「法天」一說。「法天」是指人要以天為法則，將人與天統一起來看問題。

　　這裏有兩個維度的關係。一個是天與人的垂直關係，一個是人與人的水準關係。就垂直關係說，天生養萬物（包括人類），天對人有要求，它要求人們像它那樣愛人利人，符合它要求的它就獎賞，違背它要求的它就懲罰；人也要以天為效法的典範和楷模，聽天的話，否則就會得到天降的災禍。就水準關係說，既然天是充滿愛人利人之心的，那麼效法天的人也應該有愛人利人之心。

　　在《法儀》中，墨子說，人世間的父母、學者、君王不可法，因為他們雖然人不少，但「仁者寡」，好的少，不足以法。在墨子看來，天是大公無私，施而不誇耀，光明經久不衰的，同時天又是有意志和情感的，從天生有萬物，養育萬

though there are a lot of them, "few are benevolent." As not many are good, we should not look upon their principles as standards. Mozi sees heaven as fair and unselfish; it gives but does not flaunt, and its light never dies. At the same time, heaven has a will and emotions; the lord of heaven creates all things, nurtures all things and loves all things. Heaven wishes that humans will follow in loving and benefiting each other instead of hating and doing harm to each other.

Heaven offers the prototype and standard by saying, "love each other all-embracingly and act out of mutual interests." Mozi thought that those who could best adopt heaven's principles were the sage kings, sages or benevolent men, the next best were the big-hearted people, the last were the ordinary or small-hearted people.

Mozi said, "I have the will of heaven, just as the wheelwright has the compass, or the carpenter has the try square. The wheelwright and the carpenter make measurements of circles and squares with their compass and try square, and say, 'That which matches is correct, that which doesn't is not.'" Some people take "compass and try square" to mean "tools," but in fact they should be interpreted as referring to the implied principles and standards by which Mozi lived. Mozi, who differed from the Daoists and Confucians, always took heaven as a personal god upon whom judgments of the

物，兼愛萬物，利益萬物來看，天是希望人們也跟祂一樣，兼相愛，交相利，而不是相反的兼相惡、交相賊。

天是「兼相愛、交相利」的原型和標準，「法天」「法」得最好的人是聖王、聖人或仁人，其次是大人，最後才是普通人或小人。

墨子說，「我有天的意志，就好像製車輪的有了圓規，木匠有了方尺。製輪人和木匠拿着他們的圓規和矩尺來量度天下的圓和方，說：『符合規矩的就是對的，不符合的就是錯的。』」

有些人將這裏的「規矩」解釋為「工具」，其實應當是指規和矩所代表的原則和標準。跟道家、儒家不同的是，墨子始終是從作為人格神的「天」及其「天意」的層面來衡量和判斷當時的社會現象，這使他有濃厚的神學意味。

「法天」也就是「效法天」，從垂直維度說就是「順天」，順從天的意願。天的意願是甚麼？概括地講就是「兼相愛、交相利」，具體地講，

social phenomena at the time could be based. This made him a thinker with a strong theological nuance.

To adopt heaven's principles is the same as "to emulate heaven," speaking from the vertical dimension this means to "obey heaven" — to comply with the will of heaven. What is the will of heaven? In broad terms it means to "love each other and act out of mutual interest." In concrete terms, it means what Mozi coined as "the three interests," "the eight don'ts," "the three dos," "the two capabilities" and "the three to-becomes."

The three interests meant serving the interest of heaven above, serving the interest of spirits in the middle and serving the interest of people below. Serving the interests of these three parties amounted to serving the interests of all; in other words, serving the interest of the state, serving the interest of the common people and serving the interest of people of the world. The eight don'ts meant that big states do not attack small states; big clans do not disturb small clans; the mighty do not plunder the weak; the many do not bully the few; the shrewd do not deceive the unintelligent; the honorable do not despise the inferior; the rich do not insult the poor; and the young do not rob the elderly. The three dos said those with power should help others swiftly; those with wealth share it with others persistently; those who have understood

就是墨子所謂「三利」（上利乎天、中利乎鬼、下利乎人，三利無所不利；或利國家、利百姓、利人民）、「八不」（大國不攻小國、大家不亂小家、強不劫弱、眾不暴寡、詐不欺愚、貴不傲賤、富不侮貧、壯不奪老）、「三有」（有力者疾以助人、有財者勉以分人、有道者勸以教人）、「兩強」（上之強聽治、下之強從事）、「三之」（國家之富、人民之眾、刑政之治）。與這些行為和狀態相反的當然就是「逆天」或「反天意」了。法天順天的就是聖王，他們奉行的是義政，不法天反天的就是暴王，他們奉行的是力政。

應機地說，墨子所謂「擇務而從事」，就是根據當時各個國家的不同情況開出不同的藥方。《魯問》記載：墨子出外遊歷，魏越問他：「如果能見各地的諸侯，您將說甚麼呢？」墨子說：「凡到一個國家，一定要選緊要的事去做。假如國家昏亂，就告訴他們尚賢尚同的道理；假如國家貧窮，就告訴他們節用節葬的道理；假如國家喜好聲樂、沉迷於酒，就告訴他們非樂非命的道理；假如國家荒淫怪僻、不講究禮節，就告訴他們尊天事鬼的道理；假如國家專門掠奪侵略別國，

the Way teach others devotedly. The two capabilities was an exhortation to those who governed to be capable of listening to those they governed, and to those being governed to be capable of taking orders. Finally, the three to-becomes urged the state to become wealthy, the people to become numerous and governance to become secured by the administration of punishments. Those actions and situations which violated the principles described above would be defined as "disobeying heaven" or "acting against the will of heaven." If a ruler strove to emulate or obey heaven, then he would be seen as a "sage king" who practices "righteous governance." If a ruler did not emulate heaven but instead disobeyed heaven and was autocratic, then he would be seen as a "tyrannical king" who practices "governance with might."

Depending on the circumstances, Mozi "picked important tasks to undertake" and gave different counsels to different states according to their problems.

As seen in "Lu Wen," As Master Mozi was about to travel, Wei Yue asked, 'When you meet with the rulers of different states, what will you say?' Mozi said, "Whenever someone visits a state, he must choose which important tasks to undertake. If the state is in chaos, then tell the state about the worthiness of virtue and unity; if the state is poor, then tell it about the principles of frugality and having simple funerals; if the state

就告訴他們兼愛非攻的道理。所以說要選擇緊要的事去做。」

儘管「尊天事鬼」在這裏被作為擇務而行事的一項，實際上，既然這些出了大問題的國家都是因為在做不符合天志、天意的事，從而需要墨家去加以糾正和幫助，那麼，根本的原因還是這些國家逆天而非順天，沒有法天，成了天的「不肖子」。

「法天」的思想，在道家那裏也能看到。老子就說過，「人法地，地法天，天法道，道法自然」。只不過跟墨子相比，道家的「天道」是清淨無為，老子和莊子的聖人、真人、至人、神人都是從消極意義上說的，安安靜靜地過淡泊的日子，不亂折騰就可以。而墨子的「法天」所法之「天」卻是主動的、積極的、熱情的愛人利人者，因此分享了這樣的「天」的墨家聖人，就是大禹和墨子式的興天下之利、除天下之害，「墨突不黔」式的人民公僕。

在「天」與「民」的關係上，後人很容易將

indulges in music and alcohol, then tell it about the demerits of music and the falsehood of fatalism; if the state is unregulated and depraved, then tell it about honoring heaven and serving the spirits; if the state takes other states by force and oppression, then tell it about the worthiness of reciprocal love and the falsehood of aggression. That is what I mean by picking which important tasks to undertake."

Even though "to revere heaven and pay tribute to gods" was considered in this passage as one of the important tasks to be carried out, most of the states that got into serious trouble were those that did not comply with the will of heaven. Instead of telling these states to adopt heaven's principles, Mozi found it necessary to correct them and save them from the mistaken path, for the root of their problem lay in their disobeying heaven rather than obeying heaven, which had turned them into "deviant" Sons of Heaven.

The idea of "adopting heaven's principles" can be seen in Daoist thought. Laozi once said, "Man adopts Earth's principle, Earth adopts Heaven's principle, Heaven adopts the Way's principle, the Way adopts Nature's principle." Nonetheless, the Daoists took "heaven's way" as quiet inaction. Thus, according to Laozi and Zhuangzi, the sage, the pure man, the perfect man and the godly man were all icons of passivity — all chose to lead a simple and quiet life without

墨子的天民觀與孟子據《周書泰誓》中「天視自我民視，天聽自我民聽」引申出的民本論混同起來。其實，在墨子那裏，天是天，民是民，民在君王的率領下做了錯事，一樣要受到的天的警告和懲罰。

並非民（百姓）的任何「視」、「聽」都能跟天一致，在有些情況下，即使舉國的百姓都贊成國君，跟國君一致，但在天看來國君仍是不義的話，天照樣會懲罰國君，給他降災。在這一點上，墨子的天與《舊約》裏的耶和華有些相似，只要以色列人背離了上帝（如拜偶像），上帝就會讓以色列人吃苦頭，比如上帝發動周圍民族打擊以色列人，讓他們輸得很慘。或者倘若有城市違背了上帝的律法，做上帝討厭的事，上帝就會毀滅或破壞那城市，如所多瑪。

墨子的天跟這個耶和華一樣，並不一味地遷就百姓。孟子經由「天視自我民視，天聽自我民聽」走向了民本論，但在墨子這裏，由於對天的主權特別強調，因此，帶有更濃厚的「神學」色彩，天不僅有天下土地所有權、天下萬民擁有

any agitations. In contrast, the "heaven" that Mozi asked us to follow was conceived as an active and enthusiastic altruistic being. The Mohist sage, therefore, is one like the legendary Yu the Great or Mozi who both strove to promote the interests of the world and to save the world from calamities. He is the true public servant of people and acts like Mozi — who constantly ran around serving people.

As for the relationship between "heaven" and "people," later generations often confused Mozi's view with the people-oriented philosophy of Mencius that originated from Zhou Shu Tai Shi — "Heaven sees through my people's sight; heaven hears through my people's ears." For Mozi, heaven is heaven and people are people. If people are led by their rulers to act wrongly, it is certain that they will be warned and punished. It is simply not true that whatever people (the common people) "see" or "hear" is always consistent with heaven. In some cases, even when all the people of the state share the same opinion as the ruler, if heaven considers it unrighteous, the ruler will be punished by heaven and suffer hardship. On this point, Mozi resembles Jehovah of the Old Testament: as when the people of Israel betrayed God (by worshipping idols), God caused them to suffer adversity: God mobilized the surrounding tribes to attack the people of Israel and made sure they lost miserably. Another example is seen in the city of Sodom: when the city betrayed the Law of God

權、天下萬民獎懲權、天下萬民監督權,還對天子有監察和領導權。實際上,墨子把天子的幾乎所有權力都剝奪了,把它們給了「天」。這無疑是在用「神權」限制「君權」(見《天志》、《明鬼》),在一定意義上也限制了「民權」(見《尚同》)。難怪胡適要說,倘若墨家掌握了政權,就相當於羅馬教皇了,因為墨家自認為能領會「天意」代表天來治理國家。

我們看到,墨子的神學是粗糙的。在墨子的時代,就遭到不少的反駁和質疑。在墨子的後學那裏,就漸漸地向着唯物論的方向發展了。(見孫中原《墨子及其後學》,159-161頁)在墨子的時代,中國人尚沒有「輪回」的觀念,也沒有聽說過「末日審判」這回事,因此墨子的「報」的觀念,主要還是停留在實打實的「現世報」上。

墨子只能根據他的「三表法」,根據古書所記載的鬼神出沒報仇的事以及民間鬼神故事來說好人好報、惡人惡報,而這是很容易被「證偽」的,因為現實經驗中好人沒有好報、惡人反有好報的事情太多了。

and did things that displeased God, God destroyed the city. The heaven depicted by Mozi acts like Jehovah, who will not always yield to people's wishes. Mencius however followed the path of: "Heaven sees through my people's sight; heaven hears through my people's ears" and developed it into a people-oriented philosophy. Mozi in contrast emphasized the sovereignty of heaven and had quite a strong "theological" leaning. He ascribed to heaven not only the ownership of all the lands, but also the ownership of all the people. With this he included the right of heaven to punish and monitor the people, as well as the right to monitor and lead the Son of Heaven. In fact, Mozi deprived the Son of Heaven of nearly all his powers and ascribed them to "heaven" instead. It seems that he used "the right of heaven" to restrict "the right of the ruler" (see "Tian Zhi" and "Ming Gui"), and to a certain extent he also restricted "the right of the people" (see "Shang Tong"). No wonder Hu Shi said, if Mohists came to power, they would act like the Pope of Rome. For Mohists believed that they could comprehend the will of heaven and govern the state on heaven's behalf.

We can see that Mozi's theological stance is rather unpolished. During his time, he received several rebuttals and reservations. Later, Mozi's disciples gradually directed Mohist philosophy towards materialism. (See Sun Zhongyuan, _Mozi and his Disciples_, pp.159-161.)

二

偌若信鬼神之能賞賢而罰暴也，則夫天下豈亂哉！

【原文】

子墨子言曰：「逮至昔三代聖王既沒，天下失義，諸侯力正，是以存夫為人君臣上下者之不惠忠也，父子弟兄之不慈孝弟長貞良也，正長之不強於聽治，賤人之不強於從事也，民之為淫暴寇亂盜賊，以兵刃毒藥水火，退無罪人乎道路率徑，奪人車馬衣裘以自利者。並作由此始，是以天下亂。此其故何以然也？則皆以疑惑鬼神之有與無之別，不明乎鬼神之能賞賢而罰暴也。今若使天下之人，偌若信鬼神之能賞賢而罰暴也，則夫天下豈亂哉！」（《明鬼下》）

【今譯】

墨子說：「及至當初三代聖王死後，天下喪失了義，諸侯用暴力相互征伐，因此就存在種種亂象：君對臣沒有恩惠，臣對君沒有忠誠，父兄

In Mozi's time, the idea of "reincarnation" was unheard of by Chinese people, and neither did they learn about "Judgment Day." Therefore, the Mohist idea of "bearing the consequences" was mainly limited to those that one would receive during his "lifetime." Mozi could only refer to his own "three criteria method" and drew on the legends of spirits and gods as recorded in ancient documents as well as the folklore about spirits and gods in order to illustrate how good consequences come to good people and bad consequences come to those who are wicked. However, it is too easy to "falsify" such a claim, for in reality there are good people who are never rewarded with good consequences, while too often we see bad people who enjoy good fortune.

Two
If we could convince people that spirits and gods are able to reward good conduct and punish what is wicked, then would the world be in such chaos?

Translation:
Master Mozi said, "With the passing away of the sage kings of the Three Dynasties [Xia, Shang and Zhou], the world

對子弟不慈愛，子弟對父兄不孝悌，官長不能勤勉治政，平民不願努力勞動，人們做出淫暴、寇亂、盜賊之事，還拿着兵器、毒藥、水火，在大小道路上阻遏襲擊無辜的人，搶奪別人的車馬衣裘，為自己謀利。從那時開始，這些事一併發作，搞得天下大亂。這是甚麼緣故呢？都是因為人們對鬼神的有無疑惑不定，不明白鬼神能夠賞賢罰暴。現今若能使天下之人都信鬼神能夠賞賢罰暴，天下豈能混亂？」

【時析】

有些人認為墨子在這裏所說的話邏輯不通。對墨子所說的話，如果從「社會共識」或「公民宗教」的角度來看，就比較容易理解。一個時代、一個社會要維持其存在和秩序，就需要有一些共同的信念和信條，不管這些信念是不是「正確」。比如在中世紀的歐洲，人們都相信上帝的存在，相信上帝所頒佈的一系列法律並按照它們去生活，宗教改革後，由於出現了跟舊教不同的新教，社會共識出現問題，這一個共識的人群（教派）跟那一個共識的人群（教派）無法相處，就發生爭拗和戰爭。在現代社會，有所謂「公民宗教」

lost righteousness. The vassal state rulers now govern by force and have caused the world to become out of order. Rulers and superiors are not gracious to their ministers and subordinates, while ministers and subordinates are not loyal to their rulers and superiors; fathers and elder brothers are not caring of their sons and younger brothers, while the sons and younger brothers are neither filial nor faithful to their fathers and elder brothers; officials are not diligent at government affairs, while the common people are lazy at work; people are debauched, wicked, become thieves or robbers, threatening innocent passersby with weapons, poisons, water and fire, and looting others' carriages, horses, clothes and furs for their own interests. Because of this conduct, the world has dissolved into chaos. Why does this happen? This happens because people are skeptical about the existence of spirits and gods, and they don't accept that spirits and gods are able to reward good conduct and punish what is wicked. If we could convince people that spirits and gods are able to reward good conduct and punish what is wicked, then would the world be in such chaos?" ("Ming Gui III")

Contemporary interpretation:

Some people think what Mozi said here is illogical. It may be easier for us to understand his words if we read them from a "social consensus" or "civil religion" perspective. For a society or an era to maintain its existing order, some shared beliefs or

之說，比如美國，人們就普遍相信人權、自由、愛國主義等等，這相當於以前的基督教，為了這些價值，美國人民覺得鬥爭是值得的。

社會共識是一個社會賴以建立互信和秩序的前提之一。它就像共同的軌道一樣，使人們能夠彼此往來、交通，減少「交易費用」。比如清教徒嚴格地按照基督教倫理規範從商，明清時期的徽商和晉商能夠按照儒家倫理從商，促進商業文明的發展。交易的各方都預設一些基本的價值（如清教或儒家的），如誠信、不欺詐、不做假等；如果連這些基本共識都沒有了，就會出現三聚氰胺毒奶粉、地溝油這些沒有基本底線的事故。

墨子認為，他那個時代之所以出現大問題，一個主要原因就是人們對天鬼失去了信仰，懷疑天鬼的賞罰作用。如果人人都能恢復對天鬼的信仰，相信天鬼也會對自己的行為進行監督和獎罰，「舉頭三尺有神明」，自覺約束自己的行為，天下也就不會大亂了。可以說，天鬼信仰是墨子的「公民宗教」。

doctrines, whether they are "correct" or not, must be in play. For example, in the Middle Ages, Europeans believed in the existence of God and the set of laws that He mandates; thus they lived in compliance with those laws. It was only after the Reformation that Protestant beliefs rose against the old Catholic doctrines. Once social consensus falls apart, people who share a common set of beliefs (sects) can no longer live in peace with people who share a different set of beliefs. This invariably results in confrontation and war between the groups. In modern society, there exists a so-called "civil religion." For instance, Americans mostly believe in human rights, freedom, patriotism, etc., just as the Protestants did in the past. Americans think that these values deserve to be fought for.

Social consensus is a prerequisite for a society wishing to build trust and order. It is like a shared track on which people can interact and communicate with a reduced "transaction cost." For example, Protestants complied strictly to Christian ethical norms in their trades, while similarly, merchants of Hui and Jin during the Ming and Qing dynasties followed Confucian ethics when they did business with each other. In their own ways, both groups facilitated the development of a civilized business culture. In this culture, all business partners shared some basic values (such as Protestant or Confucian), e.g. integrity, honesty and truthfulness, etc. If this sort of basic consensus is lacking

三

上以交鬼之福，下以合驩聚眾，
取親乎鄉里。

【原文】

今執無鬼者曰：「意不忠親之利，而
害為孝子乎？」子墨子曰：「古之今之為
鬼，非他也，有天鬼，亦有山水鬼神者，
亦有人死而為鬼者。今有子先其父死，弟
先其兄死者矣，意雖使然，然而天下之陳
物曰『先生者先死』，若是，則先死者非
父則母，非兄而姒也。今絜為酒醴粢盛，
以敬慎祭祀，若使鬼神請有，是得其父母
姒兄而飲食之也，豈非厚利哉？若使鬼神
請亡，是乃費其所為酒醴粢盛之財耳。
自夫費之，非特注之污壑而棄之也，內者
宗族，外者鄉里，皆得如具飲食之。雖使
鬼神請亡，此猶可以合驩聚眾，取親於鄉
里。」

今執無鬼者言曰：「鬼神者固請無有，
是以不共其酒醴粢盛犧牲之財。吾非乃今

in society, dreadful abuses will occur. This was seen in recent years in China in the adulteration of infants' milk powder with melamine and the distribution of gutter oil.

Mozi believed that the predicament of his time was caused by people's lack of faith in the existence of heaven and spirits, and their doubt about the ability of heaven and spirits to administer rewards and punishments. If everyone restored their faith in heaven and spirits and could believe that these two "bodies" monitor human actions and administer rewards and punishments accordingly, and that if you look up "you will find a god three feet above," then people would regulate their own behaviors and the world would not dissolve in chaos. We can say that a faith in heaven and spirits plays the role of "civil religion" in Mozi's mind.

Three
To receive the blessings of spirits from above, gather people together to enjoy themselves below, thus strengthening the ties between villagers.

Translation:
Lately, some people who denied the existence of spirits said:

愛其酒醴粢盛犧牲之財乎？其所得者臣將何哉？」此上逆聖王之書，內逆民人孝子之行，而為上士於天下，此非所以為上士之道也。是故子墨子曰：「今吾為祭祀也，非直注之污壑而棄之也，上以交鬼之福，下以合驩聚眾，取親乎鄉里。若神有，則是得吾父母弟兄而食之也。則此豈非天下利事也哉！」

是故子墨子曰：「今天下之王公大人士君子，中實將欲求興天下之利，除天下之害，當若鬼神之有也，將不可不尊明也，聖王之道也」。（《明鬼下》）

【今譯】

現在堅持沒有鬼神的人說：「你的意思也許不符合雙親的利益，而有害於做孝子吧？」墨子說：「古往今來所說的鬼神，沒有別的，有天上的鬼，也有山水的鬼神，也有人死後變成的鬼。現在有兒子比父親先死、弟弟比兄長先死的情況，即使如此，按天下常理來說，還是說『先生的先死』。按照這說法，則先死的不是父親就是

"Isn't this detrimental to parents and thus harmful to filial sons?"

Master Mozi said, "Spirits, then and now, are no different; there are spirits of heaven, spirits of mountains and rivers, as well as those spirits of the dead. Now there are cases when sons die before their father, and younger brothers die before their elder brothers. Nevertheless, as the common saying goes, 'He who is born first dies first.' If this is the case, then the first to die should either be the father or the mother, the elder brother or the elder sister. Now we prepare cleansed wine, rice and sacrifices and offer them with reverence. If spirits and gods do exist, then the sacrifices will be offered to fathers, mothers, elder brothers and sisters; how can it not be of benefit to them? Even if spirits and gods do not exist, it will just be a matter of spending some money on the wine, rice and sacrifices. What is more, if we have spent money on the offerings, we will not afterwards dump them in ditches, we will share them among kinsmen and fellow villagers. Even if spirits and gods do not exist, the offerings can be used to gather people together for a feast, thus strengthening the ties between villagers."

Lately, those who denied the existence of spirits said, "Since it is true that spirits and gods do not exist, it is unnecessary to waste money offering wine, rice and sacrifices. We are not unwilling to spend on the wine, rice and sacrifices, but

母親，不是哥哥就是姐姐。現在準備好潔淨的酒食祭品，用以恭敬謹慎地祭祀。假使鬼神真有的話，這是讓父母兄姐得到飲食，豈不是大大的好處嗎？假使鬼神確實沒有的話，這不過是浪費他製作酒食祭品的一點資財罷了。而且所謂花費，也不是把祭品倒進污水溝，而是內而宗族、外而鄉親，都可以請來飲食的。即使鬼神真不存在，也可以用來聯歡聚會，聯絡鄉里感情。」

現在堅持沒有鬼神的人說：「鬼神本來就不存在，因此不必供給那些酒醴、米飯、犧牲之財。我們並非愛惜那些財物，〔問題只在於〕祭祀能得到甚麼呢？」這種說法上違背聖王之書，內不合民間孝子之行，卻想去做天下的精英 —— 這實在不是精英之道呀。所以墨子說：「現在我們去祭祀，並不是（把食物）倒進污水溝裏，而是上以邀鬼神之福，下以集合民眾歡會，聯絡鄉里的感情。假若鬼神存在，那就是將我們的父母兄弟請來共食。這豈不是對天下都有利的事情嗎？」

所以墨子說：「現在天下的王公大人士君子，如果確實想興天下之利，除天下之害，那麼對於

what we can gain from this?" This attitude betrays what was written by the sage kings of the past and offends those filial sons among our people, and yet those who hold it want to rise above others. But this is obviously not the way to become higher than others.

In answer, Master Mozi said, "Now when we are done with worship, we will not immediately dispose of the offerings in ditches; what we do instead is to receive the blessings of spirits and gods from above, and gather people together to enjoy themselves below, thus strengthening the ties between fellow villagers. If spirits and gods do exist, then we will be offering the sacrifices to our parents and siblings. How can it not be beneficial to the world?"

Master Mozi continued, "For all the kings, dukes, great men, officials and gentlemen of the world, if they really want to promote the interests of the world and save the world from calamities, then they should take the existence of spirits and gods seriously and be respectful to them. This is indeed the Way of the sage kings." ("Ming Gui III")

Contemporary interpretation:

In this passage, Mozi argues that even if spirits and gods do not exist no harm or waste will result from offering sacrifices to them. The offerings can be shared and enjoyed afterwards

鬼神的存在，將不能不重視確信它，這才是聖王
之道。」

【時析】

墨子在這裏是在退一步講，即使鬼神不存
在，祭祀鬼神也沒有害處，不會造成浪費，因為
在食用撒下來的祭品時，可以跟一起來祭神的同
宗同鄉聯絡感情，起到團結的作用。

這令人想起法國思想家巴斯卡著名的打賭
說。巴斯卡是虔誠的冉森派（天主教中相信加爾
文主義的派別）教徒，他認為，理性無法證明上
帝是否存在，但是，理性能夠告訴我們，不把賭
注押在上帝存在上的人是愚蠢的。因為，如果你
打賭上帝存在，而上帝真的存在，你便能得到永
生之樂，進天堂而免下地獄；如果你打賭上帝存
在，而上帝並不存在，那你因為相信上帝具備一
些美德（如虔誠、愛心），不會失去任何東西。
如果你打賭上帝不存在，而上帝也的確不存在，
雖然你是對的，但你也一無所獲；最慘的是，你
打賭上帝不存在，但上帝卻真實地存在，那麼，
你就不僅得不到永生進天堂，還得下地獄永受

among kinsmen and fellow villagers, strengthening the ties between those involved.

This reminds us of what is known as Pascal's wager. French thinker Blaise Pascal was a devout Jensenist (a group of Catholic followers who believed in Calvinism) who held that human reason alone cannot decide whether God exists or not. Nonetheless, reason can disclose to us how foolish it would be for us to live as though God does not exist.

He said that if you wager on the existence of God and God really exists, then you would be rewarded with eternal happiness in heaven and thus saved from hell. If on the other hand, you wager on the non-existence of God and God really does not exist, then you would gain nothing even if you are right. However, if the contrary is true and God does exist, then the most miserable prospects await you: you would not only miss the chance of eternal life in heaven, you would also have to suffer eternal punishment in hell!

Through such probability analysis, Pascal was convinced that because of such two equally possible scenarios, it is always beneficial for us to believe in the existence of God.

Mozi's lines of argument are similar to those of Pascal's. In order to argue against the then skepticism about the existence

苦！通過這一番可能概率的計算，巴斯卡論證了在可能性相等的情況下，相信上帝存在是無論如何不會吃虧的。

墨子的這個論證跟巴斯卡的打賭說有點相似，他針對當時人對鬼神的懷疑說，在相信鬼神存在和不相信鬼神存在之間，還是相信鬼神存在合算。因為，假如鬼神真的存在，那你祭鬼神就能讓你的親人（父母兄姐之靈）得到飲食；假如鬼神並不存在，你祭祀鬼神也不會吃虧，因為祭品最終還是被你和親友鄉人一起食用，你們聯絡了感情，增進了和諧。

中國人所謂的「社會」，是由「社」發展而來的，「社」就是土地神的意思，人們在祭祀土地神的過程中聚會，來自不同血緣家族的人們一起飲食、活動、做生意，形成同一鄉土地域的生活共同體。發展到後來又有佛教、道教的廟會等，可見宗教活動是社會形成的起源和核心。古代西方社會也是以神廟、教會為核心逐漸形成的。墨子正確地看到宗教活動能夠增強社會凝聚力的功能，確實是有獨到之處。

of spirits and gods, he pointed out that it would always be more favorable to believe in the existence of spirits and gods rather than not. Because if spirits and gods do exist, then the sacrifices offered to them will also feed members of your family (parents and siblings who have passed away). If spirits and gods do not exist, then the offerings will not be wasted because they can be shared as food among your kinsmen and fellow villagers, and in doing so help strengthen emotional ties and promote harmony.

For Chinese people, a "society" (*she hui*) is built from "*she*," which in Chinese means the god of the earth. When people gathered together (*hui*) for worshipping the god of the earth, they came from different families to enjoy food together, hold activities and do business, gradually forming a regional network of livelihoods. In later times, the network was developed into temple fairs with Buddhist or Daoist influence.

We can see that religious activities were the origin and the core of a society in China. Likewise, ancient Western societies also formed around temples and churches.

Mozi correctly identified the social function of religious activities in forging social ties. In doing this, Mozi indeed made a unique contribution to societal thinking.

四

入則孝慈於親戚，出則弟長於鄉里，坐處有度，出入有節，男女有辨。

【原文】

是故古之聖王，發憲出令，設以為賞罰以勸賢，是以入則孝慈於親戚，出則弟長於鄉里，坐處有度，出入有節，男女有辨。是故使治官府，則不盜竊，守城則不崩叛，君有難則死，出亡則送。此上之所賞，而百姓之所譽也。執有命者之言曰：「上之所賞，命固且賞，非賢故賞也，上之所罰，命固且罰，不暴故罰也。」是故入則不慈孝於親戚，出則不弟長於鄉里，坐處不度，出入無節，男女無辨。是故治官府則盜竊，守城則崩叛，君有難則不死，出亡則不送。此上之所罰，百姓之所非毀也。執有命者言曰：「上之所罰，命固且罰，不暴故罰也，上之所賞，命固且賞，非賢故賞也。」以此為君則不義，為臣則不忠，為父則不慈，為子則不孝，為兄則

Four

The people were filial to their parents at home and deferential to seniors when they were away from home; they observed propriety in manner, moderation in movement, and distinction between men and women.

Translation:

The ancient sage kings issued laws and orders and carried out a system of rewards and punishments to encourage good conduct. As a result, the people were filial to their parents at home and deferential to seniors when they were away from home; they observed propriety in manner, moderation in movement, and distinction between men and women. Therefore, when they administered the government, there was no theft; when they guarded the city, there was no unrest. If their ruler was under attack, they defended him with their own lives; if their ruler was forced into exile, they escorted him out. These people were rewarded by their superiors and praised by the common people. Those who believed in fatalism said, "He who has been rewarded by his superior is fated to be rewarded, and it has got nothing to do with his good conduct; he who has been punished by his superior is fated to be punished, and it has got nothing to do with his wicked

不良，為弟則不弟，而強執此者，此特凶言之所自生，而暴人之道也。（《非命上》）

【今譯】

　　所以古時候的聖王頒佈法令，設立賞罰制度以鼓勵賢人，因此人們在家裏對雙親孝順慈愛，在外面尊敬鄉里長輩。舉止有節度，出入有規矩，能區別對待男女，讓他們治理官府則沒有盜竊，守城則沒有叛亂，君有難則可以殉職，君逃亡則會護送。這些人都是上司所讚賞，百姓所稱譽的。主張「有命」的人說：「上司所讚賞，是命裏本來就該讚賞，並不是因為賢良才讚賞；上司所懲罰，是命裏本來就該懲罰，不是因為凶暴才懲罰。」所以，在家裏對雙親不孝順慈愛，在外面對鄉里長輩不尊敬，舉止沒有節度，出入沒有規矩，不能區別對待男女，讓他們治理官府則會盜竊，守城則會叛亂，君有難不會殉職，君逃亡也不會護送。這些人都是上司所懲罰，百姓所譭謗的。主張「有命」的人說：「上司所罰是命裏就該罰，不是因為他凶暴才罰；上司所賞，是命裏就該賞，不是因為他賢良才賞。」用這種觀點來

conduct." As a result, the people were unfilial to their parents at home and insolent to seniors when they were away from home; they showed no propriety in manner, no moderation in movement, and no distinction between men and women. Therefore, when they administered the government, there were thefts; when they guarded the city, there was unrest. If their ruler was under attack, they would not die for him; if their ruler was forced into exile, they would not escort him out. These people were punished by their superiors and despised by the common people. Those who believed in fatalism said, "He who has been punished by his superior is fated to be punished, and it has got nothing to do with his wicked conduct; he who has been rewarded by his superior is fated to be rewarded, and it has got nothing to do with his good conduct." When a person holding such a stance became a ruler, he would be unrighteous; if he became a father, he would be uncaring; if he became the elder brother, he would be bad; if he became the young brother, he would be insolent. Those who are obsessed with such thoughts are responsible for planting malicious language and taking the malevolent path. ("Fei Ming I")

Contemporary interpretation:

In this passage, Mozi wanted to confront a then popular doctrine of fatalism (it was particularly popular in local communities where Mozi lived). According to this doctrine,

做國君就會不義，做臣下就會不忠，做父親就會
不慈愛，做兒子就會不孝順，做兄長就會不良，
做弟弟則會不悌。頑固主張這種觀點，簡直是壞
話的根源，是凶暴者的道理。

【時析】

　　這裏墨子所針對的，是當時社會上（尤其墨
子所處的民間社會）所流行的命定論。這種命定
論認為，一些人享有高官厚祿，跟其人品無關，
而是由他的命決定的；一些人遭受困厄磨難，也
跟其人品無關，亦是由他的命決定的。墨子看出
這種命定論會導致很嚴重的社會後果，那就是助
長人的惰性，讓人消極無為地等待命運的安排，
而不去發揮能動性，同時，這種命定論還會使人
推卸自己的責任，不肯為自己的行為負責，因為
反正一切事都是由命運而不是他自己決定的。命
定論認為，一個人的受賞受罰都是由命運而不是
由他的品德和才能決定的，即命運與德行無關，
那就會掏空道德，人的一切道德努力都不必要，
這就會嚴重破壞社會秩序，使君臣父子兄弟都不
必要按照道德（惠、忠、慈、孝、悌、友等）來
彼此相待，搞得天下大亂。

those who enjoy high positions and a generous salary do not earn them by their good conduct; rather, they are destined to be so rewarded. Similarly, those who suffer difficulties and hardships do not bear them because of their bad conduct; rather, they are destined to be punished. Mozi was aware of the dire social consequences such fatalistic thoughts would bring. He knew it would result in inertia and have people passively waiting for fate to befall them instead of being proactive. Fatalistic thoughts also encourage people to shirk their responsibilities and deny accountability for their actions; they claim that all happenings are predestined and therefore totally out of their control. Since fatalism asserts that the rewards and punishments we get are predestined by fate rather than being in our own hands, how our lives turn out has nothing to do with our own moral conduct. Such a belief suggests moral practice is meaningless and moral effort unwarranted, and it significantly damages social order. When people no longer are willing to treat each other morally (with virtues of benefit, loyalty, care, filial behavior, deference, friendship, etc.), chaos results in the world.

In the past, some people thought that Mozi's arguments in "Fei Ming" (Against Fatalism) were contradictory to those in "Tian Zhi" (Heaven's Will). This is because traditional interpretations of the texts rested on a kind of theism that equated the will of God (heaven's will) with a preassigned plan for everyone,

　　以前有人認為，墨子的「非命」與他的「天志」說自相矛盾，因為按照傳統的有神論理解，既然有神的旨意（天志），那麼神就會給人做出安排，包括每一個人的命運。但實際上，墨子的「天」及其旨意（天志），強調的只是天的公正無私的審判者的性格，而不是像基督教的上帝那樣的控制者的角色。在墨子看來，天的存在最終保證了每個人的行為會得到該得的賞罰，保證最終的公義。如上面所說，墨子由於缺乏來世和輪回的觀念（他只是模糊地有一點後來道教的子孫報應的觀念），只能將賞罰落實在此生，因此其神學存在着重大的理論缺陷。若在用一個上帝（天志）來保證最終正義的實現這一點上，他跟基督教倒是一致的。按照墨子的「天」的觀念，天並不會在人的行為之前就決定人的命運，只會在人的行為之後，根據該行為的好壞善惡，予以相應的賞罰。從這一點說，墨子的「非命」說，不但不和「天志」說自相矛盾，反而是相輔相成，能夠自圓其說的。

　　決定論（包括預定論）跟自由意志論的矛盾，是哲學永恆的主題之一。就墨子的「非命」觀來

including his fate. Nonetheless, in understanding Mozi's use of "heaven" and "heaven's will," heaven's role should be interpreted as that of a just and impartial judge, instead of a controller like God in Christianity. For Mozi, the existence of heaven serves as the assurance of ultimate justice, enabling people to receive the rewards or punishments that they deserve. As already mentioned, the ideas of a "next life" and "reincarnation" were lacking in Mozi's system; he had only a vague idea of retribution visiting descendants (similar to Daoism), so unavoidably rewards and punishments would happen in this life. This belief is seen as a significant flaw in his theology. Yet in assigning God (heaven's will) to the promising role in the realization of ultimate justice, his point of view matches well with that of Christianity. According to the Mohist idea of "heaven," man's fate will not be decided before he takes any action. Instead, man's fate will only be decided upon what he has done, when rewards or punishments will match with the goodness or badness of his deeds. If we read *Mozi* in this light, we should be able to find his arguments in "Against Fatalism" and "Heaven's Will" as not contradictory but as complementary to and coherent with each other.

Whether determinism (including the doctrine of predestination) is compatible with the doctrine of free will is a never-ending philosophical issue. As to Mozi's arguments against fatalism, we should acknowledge his correct emphasis

看，我們應該承認，他強調人要積極努力有德行是完全正確的，但同時也應該承認，人確實會受到自然與社會環境、時代局限、遺傳因素、機遇等各方面的限制，其努力並不一定能完全得到相應的報償，有德不必然有福，無德不必然無福，人的遭遇總是有一些「不可預測」的因素，傳統上就把這個因素叫作命。也許，這正是「做人」的一個「渾沌」之處吧。

在當代，由於科技的快速發展，發現許多與人的自由意志相關的事情背後其實有種種生理的、環境的因素，這也很容易導致決定論。比如學生打機上癮，損害了眼和腦，導致「後天閱讀障礙」，這時，到底應該由誰來負責？是學生自己，還是「後天閱讀障礙」這種新興的疾病？如果承認學生是有自由意志的，他應該負多少責任？再比如網癮或毒癮，長期發展下去可能導致上癮者大腦中某一部位發生畸變，這種由自由意志導致物質性損傷的例子真是太多了，這種在後期越來越由腦部畸變部位決定的行為（幾乎成了一種本能的、天生的行為），到底還算不算是自由意志下做出的行為？上癮者要不要負責任以及

on encouraging people to keep up their moral effort. On the other hand, we should also admit that as human beings are subject to constraints arising from natural and social environments, generational preconceptions, hereditary factors, as well as opportunities etc., their efforts might not be matched perfectly with reward or punishment. There is no certainty that a good person will be blessed and a bad person not blessed. For human encounters often involve "contingent" factors, something we are used to calling "fate." Perhaps this is where our quest to "become human" has always become "muddled."

In our own times, the rapid advancement of science and technology has shown us that quite a few actions that were once thought to be self-determining have turned out to be controlled by physiological or environmental factors. Such discoveries have reinforced the popularity of determinism. For example, when a student becomes addicted to computer games and damages his eyes and brain so badly so as to result in "acquired reading disorder," who should be responsible? Is it the student himself, or this emergent condition? If we admit that the student has free will in his actions, to what extent should he be responsible for them? Take another example. Addiction to the internet or to drugs will in the long run cause mutation in some parts of the brain. Given that there are so many cases of physiological damage that are caused by initial

負多大責任？在科學主義者強盛的今天，很容易就用機械論來解釋和解決這些問題。比如前幾年戒除毒癮和消除強姦犯的一個辦法，就是通過腦部手術，割除他們腦中產生「癮」感的某些部位。這麼做的實際效果如何尚無定論，但是在戒「癮」的過程中，在分析問題產生和解決問題的過程中，仍然不能忽視自由意志的因素。

五
不肯曰：「我罷不肖，我為刑政不善。」必曰：「我命故且亡。」

【原文】

今夫有命者言曰：「我非作之後世也，自昔三代有若言以傳流矣。今故先生對之？」曰：「夫有命者，不志昔也三代之聖善人與？意亡昔三代之暴不肖人也，何以知之？初之列士桀大夫，慎言知行，此上有以規諫其君長，下有以教順其百姓，故上得其君長之賞，下得其百姓之譽。列士桀大夫，聲聞不廢，流傳至今，而天下

actions of free will, do we still count such addictive behavior as self-determined if it is the mutation in the brain which gradually determines the person's actions? If it has become an instinctual, or inborn behavior, can we say that addicts are still free to choose what to do? Should they be responsible for their illness? If so, to what extent?

At a time when advocates of scientism are the most powerful voice of today, people are susceptible to mechanistic explanations and solutions to the problem. For instance, a few years ago, one method to treat drug addiction and to eradicate the compulsion to rape was to surgically remove the part of the brain that was responsible for "the addiction." Its effectiveness is still being debated. However, even when such treatment for "addiction" is undertaken, for the sake of causal analysis and solution formulation, we should not undermine free will as one of the many factors involved.

Five

They would never say, "I am negligent and incompetent. I have not set up good rules and do not govern well." They would rather say, "I am fated to perish."

皆曰其力也，必不能曰我見命焉。」

是故昔者三代之暴王，不繆其耳目之淫，不慎其心志之辟，外之敺騁田獵畢弋，內沈於酒樂，而不顧其國家百姓之政。繁為無用，暴逆百姓，使下不親其上，是故國為虛厲，身在刑僇之中。不肯曰：「我罷不肖，我為刑政不善。」必曰：「我命故且亡。」雖昔也三代之窮民，亦由此也。內之不能善事其親戚，外不能善事其君長，惡恭儉而好簡易，貪飲食而惰從事，衣食之財不足，使身至有饑寒凍餒之憂。必不能曰：「我罷不肖，我從事不疾。」必曰：「我命固且窮。」雖昔也三代之偽民，亦猶此也。繁飾有命，以教眾愚樸人久矣。（《非命中》）

【今譯】
現在主張「有命」的人說：「並不是我在後世說這種話的，自古時三代就有這種流傳了。先生為甚麼痛恨它呢？」［墨子］答道：「說『有命』的人，不知是三代的善人，還是三代殘暴無

Translation:

Some people lately, who were adherents to fatalism, have said, "We are not the first to hold such a view. It has been in currency since the time of the Three Dynasties. Master, why do you condemn it?"

Master Mozi said, "Were those who believed in fatalism the sages and good men of the Three Dynasties? Or were they the wicked and deviant men of the Three Dynasties? How do we know? In the beginning, upright officials and distinguished ministers deliberated in their speech and deeds. They were able to advise those above them, their rulers and superiors, and to teach and guide the common people below them. They were therefore rewarded by their rulers and superiors, and they were praised by the common people. The high reputation attached to such upright officials and distinguished ministers never dies and has been handed down to us. People continue to praise them for their efforts; no one would say, 'Fate is on their side.'"

On the other hand, the tyrannical kings of the Three Dynasties of the past indulged themselves in sensual pleasures and let their minds go astray. Out in the wild, they messed around racing and hunting; when they stayed at home, they indulged themselves in wine and music, forgetting all about their governance of the state and the

能的人，怎麼知道呢？古時候有功之士和傑出的大夫，說話謹慎，行動敏捷，對上能規勸進諫君長，對下能教導百姓。所以上能得到君長的獎賞，下能得到百姓的讚譽。有功之士和傑出的大夫聲名不會廢止，流傳到今天。天下人都說是他們的努力，必定不會說『我有好命』。」

所以昔日三代的凶暴君王，不改正他們耳目的聲色享受，不謹慎他們內心的邪僻，外則驅車打獵射鳥，內則耽於酒和音樂，不顧國家和百姓的政事。大量從事無用的事，對百姓凶暴，使下級不敬重上司，所以國家空虛，人民滅亡，自己也受到刑戮的懲罰。他們不肯說「我疲懶無能，我沒做好刑法政事」，卻必說「我命中本來就要滅亡」。即使是昔日三代的窮困人，都是這樣說。內不能好好對待雙親，外不能好好對待君長，厭惡恭敬勤儉，而喜好簡慢輕率，貪於飲食而懶於勞作，衣食財物不足，致使有饑寒凍餒的憂患。他們必不會說「我疲懶無能，不能勤快勞作」，而一定說「我命裏本來就窮」。昔日三代虛偽的人，也都這樣說。他們粉飾「有命」之說，教唆那些愚笨樸實的人，這已經很久了。

people. Much of what they did was either of no use or was oppressive to their people, and made juniors disrespectful of their superiors. As a result, the state became exhausted, the people suffered, and they had to bear punishment and humiliation. Yet those in power would never say, "I am negligent and incompetent. I have not set up good rules and do not govern well." Rather they would say, "I am fated to perish." The miserable people populating the Three Dynasties also shared the same thoughts. They were unable to serve their families well at home, and they were not able to serve their rulers and superiors well at work. They disliked deference and frugality, and they favored quick and easy fixes. They craved food and drink and were lazy at work. As clothing and food became scarce, they became anxious about hunger and cold. Yet they would never say, "I am negligent and incompetent. I am not devoted to my work." They would rather say, "I am fated to be miserable." The dishonest people of the Three Dynasties also shared the same notions. They embellished fatalistic thoughts and drilled them into simple-minded people for a long time." ("Fei Ming II")

Contemporary interpretation:

When a hardworking person achieves notable success, people in general will often think that he has earned the success by his effort. If the successful person is confident, he may give credit to himself. If he is modest, he will be grateful to the

【時析】

通常，一個人勤奮工作獲得成功，人們會認為這是他自己通過努力獲得的，成功者如果自信些，也會將成功歸於自己，如果謙虛些，會感恩於周圍的人和環境，或感恩於上帝（如果是有神論者的話）。而失敗者，如果不能誠實地面對自己的失敗，卻推卸責任，就會總是從別人身上找原因，而不從自己身上找原因。他們的一個藉口，就是說「這是由命決定的」。墨子這裏舉的聖王和暴王的例子，就是這樣的。對於亡國之君，「命」正是他們常用來推卸責任的一個藉口。墨子的「神學」，其實質是「政治神學」，是用來警告、規勸世上國君要順從「天志」，積極主動地興天下之利，除天下之害，做真正成功的「天子」（聖王）；亦是要作為天的「不肖子」的「暴王」戒除殘暴，勿沉湎於歌舞酒色，勿在亡國後反以「命」來推卸責任。

正如我們在前面所說，墨子對於人的自由意志和主觀能動性的強調，是跟他的天鬼賞罰說緊密聯繫在一起的。如果將《非命》跟《天志》、《明鬼》連在一起看，就會很明顯了。

people around him, to the favorable circumstances, or to God (for those who believe in God). Those people who fail, if they cannot admit of their failures, will try to shrug off their responsibilities and put the blame on others instead of on themselves. Sometimes they excuse themselves with: "All is predetermined by fate." The sage kings and tyrannical kings that Mozi refers to in this passage are such examples. For those in power who ruined their states, "fate" was the typical excuse they used to dismiss responsibility.

For Mozi, "theology" in essence is a treatise of "political theology" which he used to caution and advise rulers of the world to submit to the "will of heaven", that is, to try their best to promote the interests of the world and save the world from calamities. As a theology, it encourages the rulers to become successful "Sons of Heaven" (sage kings), and also warns those "deviant" Sons of Heaven or "tyrannical kings" to turn away from cruelty, to break off from indulgence in pleasure, wine and lust, and to abstain from shirking responsibilities when they ruin their states and use "fate" as an excuse.

As we said earlier, Mozi emphasizes that man's free will and initiative are closely related to his doctrine of rewards and punishments by gods. This connection becomes most evident when we read "Fei Ming" (Against Fate), "Tian Zhi" (Heaven's Will) and "Ming Gui" (On Spirits) together.

六
百門而閉一門焉，則盜何遽無從入？

【原文】

　　子墨子有疾，跌鼻進而問曰：「先生以鬼神為明，能為禍福，為善者賞之，為不善者罰之。今先生聖人也，何故有疾？意者先生之言有不善乎？鬼神不明知乎？」子墨子曰：「雖使我有病，何遽不明？人之所得於病者多方，有得之寒暑，有得之勞苦，百門而閉一門焉，則盜何遽無從入？」（《公孟》）

【今譯】

　　墨子生病了，跌鼻進來問他：「先生認為鬼神靈明，能降禍福，做好事的就獎賞，做壞事的就懲罰。現在先生作為聖人，為甚麼還會得病呢？我在想，這是因為先生的言論有不好的地方，還是鬼神並不明智？」墨子答道：「我生病，怎麼可以說鬼神不靈明呢？人得病的原因很多，有因寒暑而得，有因勞苦而得，好像房屋有一百

Six
You are closing only one of a hundred doors; how can you prevent thieves from entering through the other ones?

Translation:

Master Mozi became ill, and Die Bi went to him asking, "Master, you believe that spirits and gods are wise, and they can send fortune or misfortune to people, rewarding those who do good and punishing those who do evil. But then, Master, you are a sage, why do you get sick? Is it because you have said something that is not good? Or are the spirits and gods muddle-headed?"

Master Mozi said, "How come my illness would mean that the spirits and gods are muddle-headed? There are many ways for people to get sick, some due to the heat and the chill, some due to hardships. It sounds as if you are closing only one of a hundred doors; how can you prevent thieves from entering through the other ones?" ("Gong Meng")

Contemporary interpretation:

How was it that Die Bi came to be called "Die Bi" (literally,

個門，只關上一個門，盜賊哪個門不可以進來
呢？」

【時析】

跌鼻同學為甚麼叫「跌鼻」，也許是因為把
鼻子跌壞了，別的同學給他起的外號。看來這個
同學雖然鼻子跌壞了，腦子卻很好使，也很有跟
老師辯論以追求真理的精神。他提出了一個約伯
式的問題：為甚麼好人遭惡報呢？為甚麼有德者
無福報，反要受苦？是不是因為鬼神並沒有那麼
靈呢？這問題可以說是直擊墨子老師的要害啊！
有時提出一個問題甚至比解決一個問題更有價值
呢！

墨子的回答，不僅沒有解決問題，反倒危及
到他的「政治神學」。因為「政治神學」是說，
一個國家亡了，是因為天在懲罰這個國家，而天
懲罰這個國家，是因為它的國君為非作歹。現在，
這些國君聽了墨子老師的自我辯護，會很高興地
說，哈哈，我之所以亡國，並非因為我違逆了天
意，而是因為我用人不當，軍糧不夠多，敵人太
強大，要不乾脆就說，我命不好。總之跟老天沒

"to fall and break one's nose")? Perhaps he did fall and break his nose so that fellow students nicknamed him Die Bi? Even if he had a broken nose, he had a pretty good brain and was a resolute truth-seeker who dared to confront his teacher. He raised a question in the manner of Job: Why do good people suffer misfortunes? Why should virtuous people end up with no reward but just endure suffering? Is it because the spirits and gods are not as smart as they are supposed to be? The question really hit home with Master Mozi. Sometimes it is more important for us to ask a good question than to answer it!

Mozi's answer, unfortunately, did not only leave the question unsolved, but put his "political theology" at risk. For his doctrine saw the downfall of a state as the punishment imposed by heaven, and the reason for the punishment was the malevolent deeds of the ruler. So if the rulers of failing states knew how Mozi defended himself before Die Bi, they would gladly say, "Ha ha, the downfall of my state is not because I betrayed heaven's will. It must either be due to my mismanagement of staff, shortage of army provisions, the intimidation of rivals, or to put it simply that I am ill-fated. Whichever way, it has nothing to do with good old heaven."

In this situation, the "political theology" or doctrine that Mozi saw as the means to keep rulers in check would eventually amount to nothing.

有關係。這樣一來，墨子用天來監督國君的「政治神學」，就落了空。

　　墨子像約伯那樣堅持自己的「義」，認為自己是一個「義人」，沒有甚麼過錯，但他沒有像約伯那樣被上帝帶給他看的宏偉莫測的景象嚇呆，驚歎不已，沒有保持對上帝的絕對信任，而是更像一個理性主義者那樣，從別的地方找原因。倒是後來那個罵墨子「無父無君」的孟子，反而以「天將降大任於斯人也」部份地解答了跌鼻同學提出的這個難題。倘若孟子早生幾十年，他一定會這樣回答跌鼻：「我生病了，是因為老天要磨練我，使我更好地為人民服務啊！」

Mozi, like Job, insisted that he abided by "righteousness" and did nothing wrong, and as such he saw himself as a "righteous man." Yet unlike Job, who was confounded by the unfathomable grandeur that God had shown him and kept his absolute faith in God, Mozi attempted to find a way out like a rationalist. A possible answer to the question Die Bi posed would be offered by Mencius — the philosopher later criticized Mozi as "ignoring one's father and ruler" — who said, "Heaven tests a man before entrusting him with important tasks." If Mencius had been born several decades earlier, he would have answered Die Bi with these words: "I get sick because heaven wants to put me to a test so that I can improve as a person and better serve the people!"

兼愛 *All-embracing Love*

一

天之行廣而無私，其施厚而不德，其明久而不衰。

【原文】

　　然則奚以為治法而可？故曰莫若法天。天之行廣而無私，其施厚而不德，其明久而不衰，故聖王法之。既以天為法，動作有為，必度於天，天之所欲則為之，天所不欲則止。然而天何欲何惡者也？天必欲人之相愛相利，而不欲人之相惡相賊也。奚以知天之欲人之相愛相利，而不欲人之相惡相賊也？以其兼而愛之，兼而利之也。奚以知天兼而愛之，兼而利之也？以其兼而有之，兼而食之也。今天下無大小國，皆天之邑也。人無幼長貴賤，皆天之臣也。此以莫不犓羊牛、豢犬豬，絜為酒醴粢盛，以敬事天，此不為兼而有之，兼而食之邪？天苟兼而有食之，夫奚說以不欲人之相愛相利也？故曰：「愛人利人者，天必福之，惡人賊人者，天必禍之。」曰：「殺不辜者，得不祥焉。夫奚說人為

One
Heaven's acts are encompassing and unselfish; they provide generously. Heaven is modest about what it does; it keeps on shining and its light never dies.

Translation:

Then what can be considered the proper way to govern a state? We may say that there is no better way than adopting heaven's principles. Heaven's deeds are encompassing and unselfish; they provide generously. Heaven is modest about what it does; it keeps on shining and its light never dies. The sage kings therefore adopted its principles. So, when someone endeavors to adopt heaven's principles, his actions and plans need to follow heaven's standards: he will have to do whatever heaven wants and avoid what heaven does not like. Yet what does heaven want and what does it reject? Heaven certainly wants people to love and benefit each other, and dislikes people hating and doing harm to each other. How do we know that heaven wants people to love and benefit each other, and dislikes people hating and doing harm to each other? It is because heaven loves people all-embracingly and benefits people all-embracingly. How do we know that heaven loves people all-embracingly and benefits people all-

其相殺而天與禍乎？是以知天欲人相愛相
利，而不欲人相惡相賊也。」

昔之聖王禹、湯、文、武，兼愛天下
之百姓，率以尊天事鬼，其利人多，故天
福之，使立為天子，天下諸侯皆賓事之。
暴王桀、紂、幽、厲，兼惡天下之百姓，
率以詬天侮鬼。其賊人多，故天禍之，使
遂失其國家，身死為僇於天下。後世子孫
毀之，至今不息。故為不善以得禍者，桀、
紂、幽、厲是也。愛人利人以得福者，禹、
湯、文、武是也。愛人利人以得福者有矣，
惡人賊人以得禍者亦有矣！（《法儀》）

【今譯】

那麼，用甚麼作為治理國家的法則才行呢？
可以說，最好以天為法則。天的運行廣大無私，
它的恩賜豐厚而不自居，它的光耀永遠不衰，所
以聖王以它為法則。既然以天為法則，行動做事
就須依天而行。天所喜歡的就去做，天所不喜歡
的就停止。那麼天喜歡甚麼不喜歡甚麼呢？天肯
定喜歡人相愛相利，而不喜歡人相互厭惡和殘

embracingly? We know this because heaven cherishes people all-embracingly and nurtures people all-embracingly.

All states, big or small, are heaven's cities. All people — young or old, honorable or inferior — are heaven's subjects. People all raise sheep and oxen, dogs and pigs, and having cleansed themselves prepare wine, rice and sacrifices to offer to heaven in reverence. Isn't it obvious that heaven cherishes people all-embracingly and nurtures peoples all-embracingly? If we can see how heaven cherishes and nurtures people all-embracingly, how can we say that heaven does not want people to love and benefit each other? Therefore, it is said, "For those who love and benefit others, heaven will certainly bless them with fortune; for those who hate and harm others, heaven will certainly bring misfortune to them." It is said, "If one kills an innocent person, he will be cursed. How do we know that if people kill each other, heaven will bring misfortune to them? It is because we know that heaven wants people to love and benefit each other, and dislikes people hating and doing harm to each other."

In the past, the sage kings Yu, Tang, Wen and Wu all loved the people of the world all-embracingly. They taught them to revere heaven and pay tribute to the spirits and the gods. The benefit they brought to people was great, so heaven blessed them with fortune and established them as the Sons

害。怎麼知道天喜歡人相愛相利，而不喜歡人相
互厭惡和殘害呢？這是因為天對所有人都愛護，
都有利。怎麼知道天對所有人都愛護和有利呢？
因為天化育所有人，供養所有人。現在天下不論
大國小國，都是天的城邑。人不論長幼貴賤，都
是天的臣民。因此人無不餵牛羊、養豬狗，潔淨
地準備好酒食祭品，以虔誠之心來祭天。這不正
說明了天化育所有人，供養所有人嗎？天既然化
育所有人，供養所有人，怎能說天不喜歡人相愛
相利呢？所以說：「愛人利人的人，天必賜福於
他；相互厭惡和殘害的人，天必降禍於他。」所
以說：「殺害無辜的人，會得到不祥的後果。為
何說人若相互殘殺，天就會降禍呢？這是因為知
道天喜歡人相愛相利，而不希望人相互厭惡和殘
害。」

　　昔日的聖王禹、湯、周文王、周武王，兼愛
天下百姓，帶領百姓崇敬上天，侍奉鬼神。他們
給人們的利益多，所以天就降福給他們，立他們
為天子。天下的諸侯，都恭敬地服侍他們。暴虐
的君王桀、紂、周幽王、周厲王，厭惡天下所有
的百姓，帶領百姓咒罵上天，侮辱鬼神。他們殘

of Heaven, and they were respectably served by the vassal states all around the world. The tyrannical kings Jie, Zhou, You and Li despised the people of the world and taught them to curse heaven and insult the spirits and gods. The harm they brought to people was great, so heaven brought them misfortune and took away their states. After their deaths, they were insulted by all the people of the world and until now have been condemned by their descendants. So those who committed evil deeds and therefore suffered misfortune were Jie, Zhou, You and Li; those who loved and benefited people and were therefore blessed with fortune were Yu, Tang, Wen and Wu. There are many who earn their fortune by loving and benefiting others; there are also many who bring misfortune to themselves by hating and doing harm to others. ("Fa Yi")

Contemporary interpretation:

In the preceding passage, Mozi notes that just as craftsmen need the try square and the compass to make furniture, the ruler needs principles to guide his governance of the state and the world. Yet whose principles should we look up to? We cannot look to our fathers and mothers, the teachers and the rulers because even though there are many fathers and mothers, teachers and rulers around us, the compassionate among them are rare. If one mistook the uncompassionate for a standard, it would cause harm to the state and the world. Therefore, among the "five significant others" — "heaven,

害的人多，所以天降禍給他們，使他們喪失國家，死後遭到天下人羞辱，還被後代子孫責罵，至今不休。所以做壞事而得禍的，桀、紂、周幽王、周厲王即是例證。愛人利人而得福的，禹、湯、周文王、周武王即是例證。因愛人利人而得福的大有人在，因厭惡人殘害人而得禍的也大有人在！

【時析】

在這段話的前面，墨子指出，工匠製作傢具，要有規矩，治國治天下也要有法度。但是以誰為法度呢？父母、老師、君王都不行，因為天下做父母、老師、君王的很多，但是仁愛的卻很少，如果以不仁愛者為法度（標準），就會壞事。這樣，在「天地君親師」這「五大」之中，就只剩下「天地」可「法」，最終只有「天」可「法」（因為「地」也要法「天」）。應該說，墨子看出了君、親、師的局限，指出其非終極性，指出唯有「天」才最終可法，是很了不起的。從中國思想後來的發展來看，由於「天」、「地」很抽象，因此，人們所「法」的，主要還是「君」、「親」、「師」，這導致了一系列的問題，比如常常把君、

earth, ruler, father and mother, and teacher," "heaven and earth" are the only ones whose "principles" we should "adopt." Ultimately, it should be "heaven's principles" that we should assume (since "earth" ought to follow "heaven").

In other words, Mozi was aware of the limitations of rulers, fathers and mothers, as well as teachers, and was certain that none of them could set the ultimate standard for our acts. He argued that only "heaven's principles" can be our ultimate guide. This is indeed remarkable thinking. If we look at the later development of Chinese thought, we can see that most people tended to take "the ruler," "the father and the mother" and "the teacher" as the ones to look up to instead of "heaven" and "earth." This is because these last two were of such a seemingly abstract nature. This has since caused a number of problems. For example, people often look up to their ruler, their father and mother, as well as their teacher as "heaven," thus seeking to substitute "heaven" by these people. In contrast, Mohist philosophy is more like Christianity. Between the late Ming dynasty and the early Qing dynasty, Jesuit missionaries came to China, among whom was Matteo Ricci. Ricci stressed that there is always one "great father-mother" (i.e. God) above our fathers and mothers on earth, who is the one to be worshiped and obeyed. Whenever there are conflicting views between the two, we must always listen to the words of God, our "great father-mother."

親、師當作「天」，用他們替代「天」。墨子的思想更近似於基督教。明末清初耶穌會傳教士來中國的時候，利瑪竇就強調，在人世父母之上還有「大父母」（即上帝）要崇拜和聽從，當二者發生衝突時，首先要聽從「上帝」這個「大父母」的話。

那麼，墨子的「天」是怎樣的呢？墨子對「天」的德性加以描述，天對萬物是兼而有之、兼而食之（容納並供養他們），因此是兼而愛之、兼而利之。天既然是如此，它當然希望作為萬物之靈的人也像它那樣，兼相愛、交相利，不希望人們相惡相賊。這是天的願望（天欲、天意、天志）。既然天是如此，那麼，順從天的願望的，天就降福於他，違逆天的願望的，天就降禍於他，順理成章。可以說，《法儀》是墨子「法天」神學的「導論」，弄清了《法儀》中「法天」的思路，對我們理解墨子整個「政治神學」非常有幫助。墨子「十論」（兼愛、非攻、天志、明鬼等）都是對「法天」神學的詳細展開。

在基督教神學裏，亦有「法神」的思想，這

If this is the case, how do we understand "heaven" from Mozi's point of view? Mozi perceived "heaven" as a virtuous being, who cherishes and nurtures all living things (embraces them all and nourishes them all). As such, it loves them all-embracingly and benefits them all-embracingly. It therefore would like to see human beings — the most intelligent among all living things — to act like it, loving each other all-embracingly, benefiting each other all-embracingly. It does not want people to hate each other and do harm to each other.

These are heaven's wishes (heaven's desire, heaven's intention, heaven's will).

Since heaven is conceived as such, it seems valid to infer that those who fulfill heaven's wishes, will be blessed by heaven with fortune. While those who act against heaven's wishes, will have misfortune brought upon them.

We may say that "Fa Yi" presents "an introduction" to Mozi's theology of "adopting heaven's principles." When the reasoning behind "adopting heaven's principles" is made clear, it greatly helps us to understand the whole idea of Mohist "political theology." The "Ten Arguments" (such as "Jian Ai," "Fei Gong," "Tian Zhi," "Ming Gui," etc.) presented by Mozi are all attempts to elaborate on the theological details of "adopting heaven's principles."

就是「人是上帝的形象」的教理，人應當以上帝為表率，活出上帝的形象，但這說起來還是比較抽象的，因此，在上帝道成了肉身（成為耶穌其人）的情況下，人們應該以耶穌的愛神愛人的言行為榜樣，「效法基督」，這樣才能成為新人，人人都像耶穌一樣，方能成就一個「新天新地」。可以說，這跟墨子希望人們能夠「法天」，兼相愛、交相利，從而建立一個和平、博愛的世界是完全一致的。只不過落實在「現世榜樣」的層次上，墨子「效法」的不是「基督」，而是「聖王」罷了。

二
天下兼相愛則治，交相惡則亂。

【原文】

聖人以治天下為事者也，必知亂之所自起，焉能治之；不知亂之所自起，則不能治。譬之如醫之攻人之疾者然，必知疾之所自起，焉能攻之；不知疾之所自起，則弗能攻。治亂者何獨不然，必知亂之所

In Christian theology, there is a similar idea of "adopting God's principles." This is articulated in the teachings of "man is created by God in his own image," meaning that man should follow the lead of God and live out the image of God. Given that this might sound abstract to people, God is said to have incarnated himself to become a man (Jesus). It follows that man ought to "emulate Jesus" — to take his words and deeds in which he manifests his love of God and his love of man as the model for regenerating our own lives. If everyone can live out the life of Jesus, then the world will become "a new heaven, a new earth."

We can say that such an idea is entirely consistent with Mozi's aspiration to have people "adopting heaven's principles" in their acts of all-embracing mutual love and benefit, through which a peaceful and compassionate world will eventually be created. The only difference rests on the question of who takes the role of "the real-life example." For Mozi, the role model is not "Jesus", but "the sage king."

Two
With an all-embracing mutual love in the world, the world will be in good order; with a pervasive mutual hatred, the world will be disordered.

自起，焉能治之；不知亂之所自起，則弗能治。

聖人以治天下為事者也，不可不察亂之所自起。當察亂何自起？起不相愛。臣子之不孝君父，所謂亂也。子自愛不愛父，故虧父而自利；弟自愛不愛兄，故虧兄而自利；臣自愛不愛君，故虧君而自利，此所謂亂也。雖父之不慈子，兄之不慈弟，君之不慈臣，此亦天下之所謂亂也。父自愛也不愛子，故虧子而自利；兄自愛也不愛弟，故虧弟而自利；君自愛也不愛臣，故虧臣而自利。是何也？皆起不相愛。

雖至天下之為盜賊者亦然，盜愛其室不愛其異室，故竊異室以利其室；賊愛其身不愛人，故賊人以利其身。此何也？皆起不相愛。雖至大夫之相亂家，諸侯之相攻國者亦然。大夫各愛其家，不愛異家，故亂異家以利其家；諸侯各愛其國，不愛異國，故攻異國以利其國，天下之亂物具此而已矣。察此何自起？皆起不相愛。

Translation:

A sage who takes the governance of the world as his vocation should know the cause of any disorder so that he can rectify it. If he does not know the cause of the disorder, he will not be able to rectify it. This is like a doctor treating a patient with an illness: he must know the cause of the illness before he can cure it. If he does not know the cause of the illness, he will not be able to cure it. Much the same applies when it comes to rectifying a disorderly situation: one needs to know the cause of the disorder in order to correct it. If one does not know the cause of the disorder, he will not be able to put it right.

A sage who takes the governance of the world as his vocation must not overlook the cause of any disorder. What then might cause a disorder? Disorders arise from people not loving each other. When an official or a son does not show filial piety to his ruler or his father, we call it a disorder. If a son loves himself but does not love his father, he will hurt his father by his self-interest; if a younger brother loves himself but does not love his elder brother, he will hurt his elder brother by the same self-interest. We call these disorders. In contrast, if a father does not care about his son, if an elder brother does not care about his younger brother, or if a ruler does not care about his officials, we would say the *world* is in disorder. If a father loves himself but does not love his son, he will hurt his son by his self-interest; if an elder brother loves himself but does not

　　若使天下兼相愛，愛人若愛其身，猶有不孝者乎？視父兄與君若其身，惡施不孝？猶有不慈者乎？視弟子與臣若其身，惡施不慈？故不孝不慈亡有。猶有盜賊乎？故視人之室若其室，誰竊？視人身若其身，誰賊？故盜賊亡有。猶有大夫之相亂家、諸侯之相攻國者乎？視人家若其家，誰亂？視人國若其國，誰攻？故大夫之相亂家、諸侯之相攻國者亡有。若使天下兼相愛，國與國不相攻，家與家不相亂，盜賊無有，君臣父子皆能孝慈，若此則天下治。故聖人以治天下為事者，惡得不禁惡而勸愛？故天下兼相愛則治，交相惡則亂。故子墨子曰「不可以不勸愛人者」，此也。（《兼愛上》）

【今譯】

　　聖人是以治理天下為事業的人，必須知道混亂從何而起，才能對它進行治理。不知道混亂從何而起，就不能進行治理。就好像醫生給人治病一樣，必須知道疾病從何而起，才能進行醫治。

love his younger brother, he will hurt his younger brother by his self-interest; if a ruler loves himself but does not love his officials, he will hurt his officials by his self-interest. Why does this happen? The root cause of the problem is the lack of love people show towards one another.

The same applies to robbers and thieves. A robber respects only his home but not that of others, so he breaks into others' homes in order to benefit his own home. A thief loves only himself but not others, so he hurts other people in his own interest. Why does this happen? The root cause is also that thieves do not show love to other people. It is the same when we talk about how ministers bring disorder to the homes of each other, and how vassal state rulers attack each other's states. The ministers love their own families but do not show love to other families, so they upset other families in order to benefit their own; vassal state rulers love their own states but do not show love to other states, so they attack other states in the interest of their own states. These are the disorders in the world. If we examine the root of the cause, it is clear that it is that they do not show love to each other.

If all the people in the world love each other all-embracingly and love others in the same way that we love ourselves, how can there be any unfilial people? If a person treats his father, his elder brother and his ruler in the same way he treats

如果不知道疾病從何而起，就不能醫治。治理混亂何嘗不是如此，必須知道混亂從何而起，才能進行治理。如果不知道混亂從何而起，就不能治理。

聖人是以治理天下為事業的人，不可不考察混亂從何而起。試問混亂從何而起？起於人與人不相愛。臣與子不孝敬君和父，就是所謂混亂。兒子愛自己卻不愛父親，所以會損害父親以自利；弟弟愛自己卻不愛兄長，所以會損害兄長以自利；臣下愛自己卻不愛君上，所以會損害君上以自利，這就是所謂混亂。反過來，父親不慈愛兒子，兄長不慈愛弟弟，君上不慈愛臣下，也是天下所謂混亂。父親愛自己而不愛兒子，所以會損害兒子以自利；兄長愛自己而不愛弟弟，所以會損害弟弟以自利；君上愛自己而不愛臣下，所以會損害臣下以自利。這是為甚麼呢？都是起於不相愛。

至於天下做盜賊的人，也是這樣。盜賊只愛自己的家，不愛別人的家，所以盜竊別人的家以利自己的家；盜賊只愛自身，不愛別人，所以殘

himself, how can he become unfilial? Will there then still be uncaring people? If a person treats his younger brother and officials in the same way he treats himself, how can he become uncaring? So, all the unfilial and the uncaring people will be gone. But will there still be robbers and thieves? If a person regards others' homes as his own, who will break into others' homes? If a person regards others as dearly as himself, who will steal from others? So, robbers and thieves will be gone. Will there then still be ministers who upset other families, or vassal state rulers who attack other states? If a person regards the families of others as his own, who will upset them? If a person regards other states as his own, who will attack them? So, ministers who upset the families of others and vassal state rulers who attack other states will be gone.

If we can bring all-embracing mutual love to all the people of the world, states will not attack each other, families will not upset each other, robbers and thieves will be gone, the rulers and the officials as well as the fathers and the sons will treat each other with filial piety and care. As a result, order will be brought back to the world. Therefore, how can a sage who takes governance as his vocation not discourage hate and encourage love? If there is all-embracing mutual love in the world, the world will be in good order. If there is pervasive mutual hatred, the world will be disordered. This is what Master Mozi meant when he said, "A person should not

害別人以利自己。這是甚麼原因呢？都起於不相愛。至於大夫相互侵擾家族，諸侯相互攻伐分封國，也是這樣。大夫愛自己的家族，不愛別人的家族，所以侵犯別人的家族以利自己的家族；諸侯愛自己的國家，不愛別人的國家，所以攻伐別人的國家以利自己的國家。天下的亂事，全都在這裏。細察它是從哪裏產生的呢？都起於不相愛。

假若天下人都能相親相愛，愛別人就像愛自己，還能有不孝的嗎？看待父親、兄弟和君上像看待自己一樣，還會做出不孝的事情嗎？還會有不慈愛的嗎？看待弟弟、兒子與臣下像看待自己一樣，還會做出不慈的事情嗎？這樣不孝不慈就都沒有了。還有盜賊嗎？如果看待別人的家像看待自己的家一樣，誰還會盜竊呢？如果看待別人就像看待自己一樣，誰還會害人呢？這樣盜賊也就沒有了。還會有大夫相互侵擾家族，諸侯相互攻伐分封國嗎？如果看待別人的家族就像自己的家族，誰還會侵犯呢？如果看待別人的分封國就像自己的分封國，誰還會攻伐呢？所以大夫相互侵犯家族，諸侯相互攻伐分封國，就沒有了。

himself refrain from encouraging others to love people." ("Jian Ai I")

Contemporary interpretation:

When Mozi endeavored to teach people about his "ethics of love" as inspired by the notion of the "kingdom of heaven" (to adopt heaven's principles), he found that the actual world was a place full of chaos. Most people acted like "deviant" Sons of Heaven, stealing and hurting each other, harming others for their own benefits, making it hard for anyone to feel safe or even to survive. In particular, what went on between states was like a slaughterhouse.

Just like Jesus who preached four hundred years later, Mozi promoted his ethics of love, aiming at establishing a "heaven" upon earth. Perhaps the early Christian Church did have a taste of the "kingdom of heaven," perhaps the semi-religious, non-governmental organizations of the Mohists did look like "heavenly organizations" and they were successful in realizing the "kingdom of heaven" to a certain extent. However, if we look at society then as a whole, it was still far from becoming a "Kingdom of Heaven" as later understood by Christians.

Mozi persuaded people to practice an ethics which "adopts heaven's principles," that is, to love indiscriminately like heaven — to love others as well as oneself, to love other

　　假若天下人都相親相愛，國家與國家不相互攻伐，家族與家族不相互侵犯，盜賊沒有了，君臣父子都能孝敬慈愛，如能這樣，天下也就治理了。所以聖人既然是以治理天下為事業的人，又怎麼能不禁止相互仇恨而鼓勵相愛呢？因此天下人若相親相愛就會治理好，相互憎惡就會混亂。所以墨子說「不能不勸人愛別人」，道理就在這裏。

【時析】

　　墨子帶着他的「天國」（法天）的「愛的倫理」來到人世間時，發現人世間一片混亂，因為人們現在都是天的「逆子」，相賊相殘，以鄰為壑，結果人人自危，簡直沒法生存，尤其國際社會跟屠場差不多。像四百多年後的耶穌一樣，墨子宣揚他的愛的倫理，想要在人間建立「天國」。

　　早期的基督教教會，也許部份有一點「天國」的味道，墨家的半宗教化的非政府組織，也許有一點「法天團體」的樣子，提前實現了「天國」的部份指標。但就整個社會來說，離變成「天國」是多麼遙遠啊！

families as well as one's own, to love other states as well as one's own. This sets a standard so high that it would undoubtedly reach heaven high above, but it is an ethics that is too hard to realize in the human world. During his lifetime, Mozi was called "the sage" by people around him. While his ultimate model was "heaven" above, his human model on earth was Yu the Great. Like Yu the Great, who worked day and night "to promote the interest of the world, to save the world from calamities," Mozi ran around the different states trying to persuade their rulers to end their wars. During this time he is said to have shed all the hair on his legs and got so suntanned that he won great respect from the people.

A demanding teacher, Mozi urged all his students to become "super-human." Such a lofty moral standard, however, is hardly an attainable goal for the ordinary person. The average man needs to feed his family, get married and start a career, and it is difficult for him to abandon all his old habits and weaknesses. If we want to teach morality to everyday people, we need to start with their daily lives, offering feasible and step-by-step means for them to follow. Otherwise, the principles will appear too high-sounding and out of reach to achieve. This is the reason why, in the end, the Confucian tradition that asked people to "extend from self to others" survived while Mohism waned. The Mohist "super-human" moral standard, which was insensitive to our common

　　墨子要求人們實行「法天」倫理，像天那樣一視同仁地愛護自己和他人、自己家和他家、自己國和他國，無疑是一種極高的標準，達到了「天」的高度，但卻難以落實在人間。墨子生前就被人稱作「聖人」，他的終極榜樣是「天」，但在人間的榜樣卻是大禹，他像大禹那樣為「興天下之利，除天下之害」而早出晚歸地奔波，為止戰而在各國奔走，飽經滄桑，皮膚曬得黝黑，贏得了人們的尊敬。他對弟子也嚴格要求，要求他們個個都成為「超人」，但這樣的道德標準確實是普通人難以達到的。普通人要養家糊口，成家立業，也難以戒除各種各樣的習氣和毛病，對他們講道德，就要從他們的生活常態出發，提出可操作、可逐步實行的步驟，否則就很容易因陳義過高而落空。因此，後來反而是講求「由己推人」的儒家流傳下來，墨家卻難以為繼，墨家「超人式」的道德標準違背了普通人的人情，無疑是一大因素。

　　倒是持有跟墨家相似的「天國倫理」標準的基督教，由於其教會在歷史上傳承了下來，其「天國倫理」在社會中擴散而深刻影響了整個西方。

humanity and man's imperfection, undoubtedly contributed to its decline.

Nonetheless, the Christian religion, which upheld similar "Kingdom of Heaven" ethics to Mohism, was passed on in Europe; the Christian Church survived, and its "Kingdom of Heaven" ethics was able to spread and eventually have a great impact on the West as a whole.

The Mohist principle of "all-embracing mutual love" is most often seen alongside "mutually beneficial acts"; in fact, we may even say they are interchangeable phrases. Besides, when Mozi talked about all-embracing mutual love and mutually beneficial acts, he always focused on the interests of both parties. Because of this, some people now say that Mozi was the first person who put forward the "win-win" theory. What an accurate description! In a closed society where resources were scarce, where the dominant strategies were "cutthroat competition" and "wars of survival," people constantly fought against each other over what few resources there were and in so doing turned the human world into a living hell. Mozi tried patiently to persuade all the people, families and states to co-exist peacefully and to collaborate for the betterment of their mutual interests with his "win-win" theory grounded in "mutually beneficial acts." His thinking was so brilliantly far ahead of his time.

由於墨家的「兼相愛」總是跟「交相利」連在一起，甚至二者可以互換，而墨子在強調兼相愛、交相利時，總是從雙方的互利出發，因此，今天有人說，墨子是最早提出「雙贏」（win-win）思想的人。誠哉斯言！在封閉社會中，由於資源稀缺，更由於傳統上總是存着一種「不是你死就是我活」的鬥爭思維，常常為了爭奪資源彼此廝殺，把人間弄成地獄一般。墨子以「交相利」的「雙贏」思想，苦口婆心地奉勸各人、各家、各國要看到和平相處與合作帶來的更大好處，確實是非常超前。

三
夫愛人者，人必從而愛之。

【原文】

子墨子曰：「凡天下禍篡怨恨，其所以起者，以不相愛生也，是以仁者非之。」既以非之，何以易之？子墨子言曰：「以兼相愛、交相利之法易之。」然則兼相愛、交相利之法將柰何哉？子墨子言：「視人

Three
If you love others, others will certainly love you in return.

Translation:

Master Mozi said, "All the calamities, rebellions, resentment and hatred are caused by a lack of mutual love. Therefore, benevolent people disapprove of the lack of mutual love."

If there is such a universal disapproval, how can we change the situation?

Master Mozi said, "We can replace it with all-embracing mutual love and mutually beneficial acts."

Then how should we love each other with all-embracing love and mutually beneficial acts?

Master Mozi said, "To regard others' states as our own state, to regard others' clans as our own clan, to regard others' bodies as our own bodies. Hence, if the vassal state rulers love each other, they will not battle with each other; if the heads of clans love each other, they will not rebel against each other; if people love each other, they will not do harm to each other; if the rulers and the officials love each other, they will benefit and

之國若視其國，視人之家若視其家，視人之身若視其身。是故諸侯相愛則不野戰，家主相愛則不相篡，人與人相愛則不相賊，君臣相愛則惠忠，父子相愛則慈孝，兄弟相愛則和調。天下之人皆相愛，強不執弱，眾不劫寡，富不侮貧，貴不敖賤，詐不欺愚。凡天下禍篡怨恨可使毋起者，以相愛生也，是以仁者譽之。……夫愛人者，人必從而愛之；利人者，人必從而利之；惡人者，人必從而惡之；害人者，人必從而害之。此何難之有！特上弗以為政，士不以為行故也。」（《兼愛中》）

【今譯】

舉凡天下的禍患、爭奪、怨憤、仇恨，其產生的原因，都是因為不相愛，所以仁者認為不相愛是不對的。既已認為這是不對的，那用甚麼去改變它呢？墨子說：「用兼相愛、交相利的辦法去改變它。」那麼，兼相愛、交相利的法子，又是怎麼做的呢？墨子說：「視別人的國家如同自己的國家，視別人的家族如同自己的家族，視別人之身如同自己。」如果這樣，諸侯之間相愛，

trust each other; if fathers and sons love each other, they will be caring and filial to each other; if brothers love each other, they will get along well with each other. If all the people of the world love each other, those with power will not oppress the powerless, the majority will not rob the minority, the rich will not insult the poor, the honored will not despise the inferior, and the shrewd will not fool the unintelligent. All the calamities, rebellions, resentment and hatred can be prevented with all-embracing mutual love. Therefore, benevolent people approve of it. If we love others, others will certainly love us in return; if we benefit others, others will certainly benefit us in return; if we hate others, others will certainly hate us in return; if we do harm to others, others will certainly do harm to us in return. Is this so hard to follow? It is only that the rulers do not practice it in their governance, and the officials do not practice it in their service. " ("Jian Ai II")

Contemporary interpretation:

Mozi's thoughts were too far ahead of his time and they lacked feasibility. Let's look at an example of his view on the interstate relationship during late Spring and Autumn period. Although he put forward the idea of regarding others' states as our own states, in concrete terms exactly what did he suggest should be done to achieve this? Apart from maintaining the status quo and doing no harm to each other, he seemed to have nothing else to offer. If he had offered a constructive solution

就不會發生野戰；家族宗主之間相愛，就不會發生爭奪；人與人之間相愛，就不會相互殘害；君臣之間相愛，就會有恩惠和效忠；父子之間相愛，就會有慈愛和孝敬；兄弟之間相愛，就會融洽協調。天下的人都相愛，強者就不會欺負弱者，勢眾者就不會強迫人少者，富足者就不會欺侮貧困者，尊貴者就不會傲視卑賤者，狡詐者就不會欺騙愚笨者。舉凡天下的禍患、爭奪、怨憤、仇恨，都可以不產生，這是因為人們相愛的緣故，所以仁者稱讚它。……愛別人的人，別人也會同樣愛他；有利於別人的人，別人也會同樣有利於他；憎惡別人的人，別人也會同樣憎惡他；損害別人的人，別人也會同樣損害他。這有甚麼難的呢？只不過君上不把它當作政事，士不把它付諸行動罷了。」

【時析】

墨子的思想太超前，又沒有可操作性，比如對春秋末期的國際關係，他雖然提出了視人之國若己之國的觀點，但具體要如何相處呢？除了維持現狀，互不侵犯外，好像沒有別的辦法。如果他能想出類似於今天歐盟這樣的先從經濟合作入

in the same manner as the European Union: to start with economic cooperation, then set up a unified trading market before paving the way towards establishing a political alliance among countries, he might have succeeded in seeking consent from the states. Sadly, he was not able to devise such a plan. Later, China's history went down the path of "annexation" and unification by force and did not fulfill Mozi's wish of maintaining the status quo. Taken from this point of view, what the Mohist warriors did, as depicted in the 2006 movie *A Battle of Wits*, in trying to stop the big states invading the small states, was indeed "against the trends of history"!

Even though Mozi was unable to put forward a feasible solution comparable to the "peaceful alliance" devised by the European Union, his ideas on "ways to love each other all-embracingly and mutually beneficial acts" are very commendable. Later, Confucians like Mencius criticized Mozi's idea of all-embracing love as "having no regard for the ruler and no regard for the father," calling it "a beast's way." Such criticism sounds rather harsh and fails to recognize how great Mozi's thoughts were. As an antagonist to Confucianism, what Mozi opposed was the unequal system of "respecting the parents and honoring the honorable." He therefore asked us to treat others in the same way as we treat ourselves, since we are all equal in the eyes of heaven. Mozi, however, knew that people by nature "prioritize themselves over others," and that

手，建立統一市場，建立政治聯盟的操作步驟，也許當時還真的會有國家贊成，可惜他沒有想出這樣的辦法來。中國後來的歷史還是順着「兼併」和武力統一的路子走了下去，並沒有維持墨子所願意保持的現狀。從這個角度說，像電影《墨攻》裏面所描繪的墨子團體阻止大國侵佔小國，說不定還是「違背歷史潮流」的呢！墨子雖然沒有想出類似歐盟這樣的「和平聯盟」的操作辦法，他的「兼相愛、交相利」之法卻是很偉大的思想。後來的儒家如孟子批評墨子講兼愛是「無君無父，是禽獸也」，未免過於嚴苛，無視墨子思想偉大的一面。墨子作為儒家的反對派，是反對「親親尊尊」那一套的，因此要人們對自己和他人一視同仁，老天面前人人平等。但是，他又知道人們的天性必然是「先己後人」，親疏遠近總是免不了的，因此，如何來說服人們「兼相愛」呢？他從「交相利」這樣的人人關心的利害關係着手，講的就相當於今天的「雙贏」。

墨子在這時像儒家那樣，知道要從「常情」「常理」出發來「講道理」了。墨子說：「愛人者，人必從而愛之；利人者，人必從而利之；惡人者，

it is natural for people to have priorities based upon degrees of intimacy and familiarity. Therefore, how can people be convinced to love each other "all-embracingly"? Mozi's answer is to emphasize "mutually beneficial acts," taking everyone into consideration as the interested party. The idea he came up with has an equivalent in the "win-win" strategy of today.

Mozi later realized that he should follow the Confucians in appealing to "the conventional feelings and reasoning" in his "arguments." Mozi said, "If we love others, others will certainly love us in return; if we benefit others, others will certainly benefit us in return; if we hate others, others will certainly hate us in return; if we do harm to others, others will certainly do harm to us in return." Although Mozi used the word "certainly," reciprocity may well not be a certainty — despite it applying in the majority of cases.

All people share the same feelings, all people share the same thoughts. Isn't this the same in principle as "returning the favor" that we adopt in daily human transactions? If you treat others well, in general others will treat you well. If you treat others badly, others will not treat you much better than you treat them. For example, if you take time in your local community to look after other people's kids, others will gladly come forward to help when you are too busy to take care of your own. On an international level, if you offer help to a poor

人必從而惡之；害人者，人必從而害之。」雖然墨子在這裏用「必」，實際上並不「必」，但也差不太遠。人同此心，心同此理，日常生活中人際交往之「禮尚往來」不就是如此嗎？你對人好，人一般也會對你好；你對人不好，人一般也不會對你好到哪裏去。比如在一個社區裏，你照顧人家的小孩，等你抽不出空來照顧自己的小孩時，人家也會樂意幫你照顧小孩。在國際上，你幫助一個窮國家，人家發達起來後，也會對你有所回報。關係總是相互的，善意和惡意都是互動的。雖然不乏一些人和國家受了人家恩惠卻不回報或恩將仇報的例子，因此並不存在墨子這裏所說的「必」（必定），而是有一定的「博弈」性，但無論如何，這種「以善報善，以惡報惡」的現象一般來說是常態。

「此何難之有！特上弗以為政，士不以為行故也。」這有何難呢？不過上上下下不把這當一回事罷了！相信墨子說的這種「雙贏」的道理，當時的人也是能夠明白的，只是，處在歷史潮流中的人們，被種種歷史積累和現實的利害關係所裹脅，「有心相愛，無力回天」罷了。

country, when that country becomes rich, it will repay your kindness. Relationships are always reciprocal, whether it be with good intentions or bad ones. Of course, there are people and countries that get favors from others but never return them, and there are even examples of repaying kindness with hatred. For this reason, it may not be as "certain" as Mozi thought; invariably, there is often a "game" at play. Yet "to return good with goodness, to return evil with evil" does appear to be the general norm.

"Is this so hard to follow? It is only that the rulers do not practice it in their governance, and the officials do not practice it in their service." How would it be so hard? Just because those in power and those who serve them do not take it seriously!

We believe that the "win-win" strategy put forward by Mozi was well understood by people at the time. The problem is that we are all historical beings who are swept along with the trends of history and become manipulated by historical burdens and realistic calculations. These make us "incapable of returning to heaven even when we love each other with all our heart."

For an example, when a country attempts to invade my country, how can I love everyone all-embracingly and act in

　　比如當別國來侵略我的國家時，我怎麼能跟它兼相愛、交相利呢？跟一個和平的、講道理的國家也許可以討論兩國合作的事，跟一個進行武力侵略的國家就不同了。所以，即使換了墨家信徒，也只好以戰止暴，幫助弱小國家抵禦強國侵略了。

四

說子亦欲殺子，不說子亦欲殺子，是所謂經者口也，殺常之身者也。

【原文】

　　巫馬子謂子墨子曰：「我與子異，我不能兼愛。我愛鄒人於越人，愛魯人於鄒人，愛我鄉人於魯人，愛我家人於鄉人，愛我親於我家人，愛我身於吾親，以為近我也。擊我則疾，擊彼則不疾於我，我何故疾者之不拂，而不疾者之拂？故有我有殺彼以我，無殺我以利。」子墨子曰：「子

mutual interest? It is one thing to discuss collaboration with a peaceful and sensible country, and it is quite another to do so if that country is bent on invasion.

Therefore, even Mohist followers should agree to fight tyranny by war and to help weak countries defend themselves against invasion by those more powerful.

Four
If someone favors your idea, he will want to kill you; if someone disfavors your idea, he will also want to kill you. This is what people say, that an incautious tongue costs you your own life.

Translation:
Wu Mazi spoke to Master Mozi and said, "I am different from you. I cannot love others all-embracingly. I love the people of Zou more than the people of Yue. I love the people of Lu more than the people of Zou. I love the people of my region more than the people of Lu, and I love my kin more than the people of my region. I love my parents more than my kin, and I love myself more than my parents. It all depends on the closeness

之義將匿邪，意將以告人乎？」巫馬子曰：「我何故匿我義？吾將以告人。」子墨子曰：「然則，一人說子，一人欲殺子以利己；十人說子，十人欲殺子以利己；天下說子，天下欲殺子以利己。一人不說子，一人欲殺子，以子為施不祥言者也；十人不說子，十人欲殺子，以子為施不祥言者也；天下不說子，天下欲殺子，以子為施不祥言者也。說子亦欲殺子，不說子亦欲殺子，是所謂經者口也，殺常之身者也。」子墨子曰：「子之言惡利也？若無所利而不言，是蕩口也。」（《耕柱》）

【今譯】

巫馬子對墨子說：「我跟你不同，我不能兼愛。我愛鄒國人超過越國人，愛魯國人超過鄒國人，愛我家鄉的人超過魯國人，愛我家族的人超過家鄉的人，愛我的父母超過我家族的人，愛我自己超過我父母，這是因為更切近自身緣故。打我，我會痛，打別人，不會痛在我身上，我為甚麼不去解除自己的疼痛，卻去解除事不關己的別人的疼痛呢？所以我只會殺他人以利於我，而不

to me. If I am hit, I feel the pain; if another person is hit, I don't feel the pain. How come I do not ease my own pain, but instead ease someone else's pain that I do not feel? That is why I would kill others out of my own interest, yet I would not kill myself out of the interests of others."

Master Mozi said, "Would you keep your reasoning to yourself or make it known to others?"

Wu Mazi said, "Why should I keep my reasoning to myself? I will make it known to others."

Master Mozi said, "In that case, if there is one person who favors your idea, this one person will want to kill you for the sake of his own interests. If there are ten people who favor your idea, these ten people will want to kill you for the sake of their own interests. If the people of the whole world favor your idea, the people of the whole world will want to kill you for the sake of their interests. If, however, there is one person who disfavors your idea, he will want to kill you because he accuses you of being a doomsayer. If there are ten people who disfavor your idea, these ten people will want to kill you because they accuse you of being a doomsayer; if the people of the whole world disfavor your idea, the people of the whole world will want to kill you because they accuse you of being a doomsayer. Thus, if one favors your idea, he will want to kill

會殺自己以利於他人。」墨子問：「你的這種義，是要私下裏藏起來呢，還是要告訴別人？」巫馬子答：「我為甚麼要隱藏自己的義呢？我將告訴別人。」墨子說：「那麼，如果有一個人喜歡你的主張，這一個人就要殺你以利於自己；有十個人喜歡你的主張，這十個人就要殺你以利於自己；天下人都喜歡你的主張，天下人都要殺你以利於自己。反之，有一個人不喜歡你的主張，這個人就要殺你，因為他認為你是散佈不祥之言的人；有十個人不喜歡你的主張，這十個人就要殺你，因為他們認為你是散佈不祥之言的人；天下人都不喜歡你的主張，天下人都要殺你，因為他們也認為你是散佈不祥之言的人。這樣，喜歡你主張的人要殺你，不喜歡你主張的人也要殺你，這就是所說的輕率之言帶來殺身之禍的道理啊。」墨子還說：「你的話有甚麼益處？假如沒有益處卻還要說，就是胡說八道了。」

【時析】

雖然墨家跟儒家都講「愛」，最終目標都是愛及萬物，但一個是兼愛，一個是仁愛，而且「兼愛」就是針對「仁愛」提出的。儒家的「仁愛」

you; if one disfavors your idea, he will also want to kill you. This is what people say: an incautious tongue costs you your own life."

Master Mozi said, "Aren't your words against your own interests? If your words cannot serve any of your interests, they are absurd." ("Geng Zhu")

Contemporary interpretation:
Both Mohism and Confucianism advocate "love." They share the same ultimate goal in spreading our love to all things. Yet one stresses all-embracing love, and the other stresses benevolence. What is more, "all-embracing love" is put forward against "benevolence." For Confucians, "benevolence" is a kind of "differential love" that extends from self to others, starting from cherishing our families and honoring the honorable; there is an order of worth prioritizing the important over the insignificant. For Mohists, however, all should be treated as equal — whether it be us or others, our families or families of others, our country or other countries; we can say that "we are all equal before heaven," and we should love each other equally without any preference or priority.

As Wu Mazi was a Confucian, his ideas were based upon the typical Confucian way of love "extending from self to others."

講的是「差等之愛」，由己推人，親親尊尊，有一個先後輕重的順序；墨家卻認為自己與他人平等，自家與別人家平等，祖國與別國平等，可以說是「上天面前人人平等」，應該平等地去愛，沒有一個先後順序的問題。

巫馬子是一個儒家，他的話前面是典型的儒家「推己及人」的施愛方式，就是以自己為圓心，由自己一層層外推，按照親疏等差依次施愛於親友、近鄰、國人、異國、萬物。他的話最後一句卻把這種「由己推人」的邏輯極端化。如果沒有「自己」，施愛從何談起呢？因此，他在這裏強調施愛的出發點是「己」，只有自己有痛感、有親身感，才能作為基礎去愛別人，換言之，只有保存了自己，才有基礎去做別的事。如果自己的命都保不了，自己的感受都顧不過來，談甚麼去愛別人、照顧別人？那是荒謬的。在巫馬子看來，把這種「等差之愛」的邏輯推到極點，就是當自己與他人發生生死選擇時，我只能保存自己的生命，而犧牲他人的生命。

巫馬子這只是極而言之，其實他不一定明瞭

With the self at the center of the circle, we should first love ourselves and extend our love to others based on ties and differences. We should put families and friends, neighbors, fellow countrymen, foreign countries and all other things in order of priority. As seen from his last sentence in the passage, he had taken the meaning too far of "to extend from self to others." If there exists no "self," how can we love? Therefore, he placed stress on "the self" as the source of love. Only when we have first-hand experience of pain, can we then possess the basis for loving others. In other words, if we can barely preserve our own lives and pay attention to our feelings, it is ridiculously presumptuous of us to say we can love and care about others. For Wu Mazi, the way to magnify the principle of "differential love" to its farthest extent is to always opt to save our own life at the cost of someone else's, if ever we have to choose between the two.

Wu Mazi's words might be extreme, and his understanding of Confucianism may not be thorough. Confucius himself did not cling to his own life as much as Wu Mazi did. Didn't Confucius talk about "sacrificing one's life for benevolence" and "if I heard the Way in the morning, I would not regret dying in the evening"? In later years, was it not Mencius who said, "My life is also what I want; righteousness is also what I want. If I cannot have both, I would sacrifice my life for the sake of righteousness"? We can see from these instances what the true

儒家的真精神。在孔子那裏，對於自己的生命並不像巫馬子這樣愛惜。孔子不是也說過「殺身成仁」、「朝聞道，夕死可矣」的話嗎？後來的孟子不是也說「生，亦我所欲也，義，亦我所欲也，二者不可得兼，捨生而取義者也」嗎？可見在真正的儒家那裏，當「仁」、「義」、「道」這類最高價值向人召喚時，為了實現它們，仁人志士是可以犧牲自己的生命的。真儒家的精神跟墨家的為了「義」而「赴湯蹈火」、「死不旋踵」是一致的。

墨子對巫馬子的反駁，是揭露巫馬子的邏輯必然導致的嚴重後果。按照巫馬子的「等差之愛」的邏輯，個人的價值比親友、鄉鄰、國人、世人都要高，他對自己的愛是最高等級的（其次才是親友、鄉鄰等），因此必須優先保存，當二者發生生死衝突時，他必須犧牲他人以保存自己。墨子接過了巫馬子的這個邏輯，使用歸謬法指出，如果別人也贊同巫馬子，那麼他們在跟巫馬子產生對立時，一定會犧牲巫馬子以保全自己。反之，如果別人不贊同巫馬子，他們也對會巫馬子不客氣，犧牲他以保全自己。總之，巫馬子的觀點沒

Confucian would do. In order to realize the highest ideals of "benevolence," "righteousness" and "the Way," a benevolent and aspiring gentleman will choose to sacrifice his own life. Confucianism is on a par with Mohism in its persistent commitment to "righteousness," for the sake of which one would "risk being burnt," or "not flinch in face of death."

Mozi refuted Wu Mazi's argument by pointing out its unavoidable yet fatal consequence. According to Wu Mazi's perception of "differential love," the worth of one's life is greater than families and friends, neighbors and fellow villagers, countrymen, as well as the people of the world. Love of oneself is ranked highest (next are families and friends, neighbors and fellow villagers, etc.); the preservation of one's life is therefore granted highest priority. Whenever a life-threatening conflict occurs between one person and others, he is obliged to sacrifice others in order to save his own life. Mozi followed this argument and, by reductio ad absurdum, inferred that if others agreed with Wu Mazi, then when they were in conflict with Wu Mazi, they would sacrifice him in order to save themselves. In contrast, if others disagreed with Wu Mazi, then they would be indifferent to him and would sacrifice his life for the sake of their own. Either way, neither conclusion would be beneficial to Wu Mazi. According to the third criterion of "the three appraisals of a text," that is, "to see whether such a view can bring about any real benefit," Wu

有任何好處。按照墨子的「三表法」中的最後一條「看一種觀點能否產生實際利益」，巫馬子的這種「等差之愛」的極端化表達，顯然對社會不會產生任何好處。這樣，墨子就從邏輯上否定了巫馬子所表達的「等差之愛」。

平情而論，墨子的「兼愛」代表了最高的道德理想，代表着道德的超越性，而儒家的「等差之愛」則更順應人情，更適於普通人的心性，而且具有可操作性。假如把「兼愛」和「等差之愛」加以結合，落實在現實生活中，定能收到好的功效。「等差之愛」要求我們切切實實地由近及遠施愛於人，而不是愛抽象的「人」，「兼愛」則給我們一個理想，要求我們即使面對來自他鄉異國的陌生人，也泯除「彼此」、「你我」的界限，予以親人般的待遇，待他人如自己。考慮到儒家的「大同」世界的理想，我們未嘗不可以說，其實，孔墨歸根結底目標一致，都是為了建設一個充滿愛心的世界，只不過在表達與方法上有所不同而已。

Mazi's exaggerated version of "differential love" clearly will not bring about any real benefit to society. Hence, Mozi refuted Wu Mazi's idea of "differential love" on logical grounds.

Honestly speaking, Mozi's idea of "all-embracing love" embodies the highest moral ideal, and it serves as a symbol of moral transcendence. The Confucian idea of "differential love," on the other hand, is more compliant with human nature and thus speaks to the hearts of ordinary people, making the idea more feasible. If we can link "all-embracing love" with "differential love" and put them both into our daily lives, we should be able to accomplish the best effects. "Differential love" asks us to extend our love step by step from our close associates to distant others, and it does not compel us to love an abstract "person." At the same time, "all-embracing love" puts forward an ideal that asks us to overcome the distinction between "others" and "us" as well as between "you" and "me": we are asked to try to treat strangers as if they were our families, and try to treat others as if they were ourselves. If we link this to the Confucian ideal of a "harmonizing" world, we may say that both Confucianism and Mohism share the same goal. That is, to create a world full of compassion.

The difference between the two seems to lie only in their means of expression and their practice of achieving that aim.

戰爭與和平

War and Peace

一

以七患居國，必無社稷；以七患守城，敵至國傾。

【原文】

　　子墨子曰：「國有七患。七患者何？城郭溝池不可守而治宮室，一患也。邊國至境四鄰莫救，二患也。先盡民力無用之功，賞賜無能之人，民力盡於無用，財寶虛於待客，三患也。仕者持祿，遊者愛佼，君脩法討臣，臣懾而不敢拂，四患也。君自以為聖智而不問事，自以為安彊而無守備，四鄰謀之不知戒，五患也。所信不忠，所忠不信，六患也。畜種菽粟不足以食之，大臣不足以事之，賞賜不能喜，誅罰不能威，七患也。以七患居國，必無社稷；以七患守城，敵至國傾。七患之所當，國必有殃。」（《七患》）

【今譯】

　　墨子說：「國家有七種禍患。哪七種禍患？內城、外城和壕溝不足以防守，卻去修造宮室，

One

A ruler governing a state has seven causes for worry. If they are ignored, he is doomed to lose the state. If a city defends itself while these seven causes for worry remain, the state is doomed to fall when the enemy arrives.

Translation:

Master Mozi said, "A state has seven causes for worry. What are these seven worries? If the inner walls, outer walls, trenches and moats are not made defensible, while the palaces and courts are being renovated, this is the first worry. When enemies approach and the neighboring states refuse to offer help, this is the second worry. Wasting people's efforts on worthless matters, rewarding the incompetent, draining people's energy in pointless tasks and emptying the treasury to entertain guests — these are the third worry. The officials care only about their salaries; the traveling scholars like to form cliques; the ruler revises the state's laws in order to punish his officials; and the officials never go against the ruler's will out of fear — these are the fourth worry. The ruler considers himself wise and sage yet never gets involved in governance; he deems the territory safe and strong yet never prepares adequate defense, and he is not wary of neighboring

這是第一種。敵兵壓境，四面鄰國都不願來救援，這是第二種。浪費民力做無用之事，賞賜無能之人，搞得民力在無效之功中耗盡，財寶在款待賓客中用空，這是第三種禍患。做官的人只求保住俸祿，遊學未仕的人只顧結交朋黨，國君修訂法律來懲治臣下，臣下因畏懼而不敢違逆君意，這是第四種。國君自以為神聖而聰明，不過問國事，自以為安穩而強盛，不作防禦準備，四面鄰國在圖謀攻打他，他卻尚不知戒備，這是第五種。所信任的人並不忠心，忠心的人卻不被信任，這是第六種禍患。貯存和種植的糧食不夠吃，大臣不能勝任國事，賞賜不能使人歡喜，責罰不能使人畏懼，這是第七種。若是帶着這七患治國，必定喪失政權；帶着這七患守城，敵軍一到，國家就會完蛋。哪個國家有七患，哪個國家就必定遭殃。」

【時析】

墨子時代，國際關係緊張，動不動就有仗打，那些弱小國家不能有絲毫的鬆懈，否則就被人欺負或兼併了。墨子這裏的「七患」警告，主要是針對這些小國家的國君說的。這些「患」，不外

states planning to invade his state — this is the fifth worry. Trusting those who are disloyal while mistrusting those who are loyal — this is the sixth worry. When there are not enough livestock or crops to feed the people, when the ministers are not competent at serving the state, when rewards cannot please people, and when punishments cannot deter people, this is the seventh worry.

A ruler governing a state has seven causes for worry. If they are ignored, he is doomed to lose the state. If a city defends itself while these seven causes for worry remain, the state is doomed to fall when the enemy arrives. When these seven worries prevail in a state, the state is doomed to perish." ("Qi Huan")

Contemporary interpretation:

During Mozi's time, interstate relationships were rather tense, and wars broke out all too easily. Weak states had to remain on high alert in order not to be harassed or annexed.

The warning Mozi gives here about the "seven worries" is mainly targeted at the rulers of these smaller states. The worries all center around domestic and foreign threats and involve national defense, military arms, domestic affairs, diplomatic relationships and intelligence. All of which we can of course pretty much observe in the contemporary

是內憂外患，涉及國防、軍備、內政、外交、情報系統，跟現代國際社會無異。晚清和民國時期，中國雖是大國，卻是弱國，屢遭帝國主義列強欺負。孫中山先生曾經說過，國家要強大，就要文官不貪錢，武官不怕死，這跟墨子所說的七患之內患有些相似。

墨子「非攻」，反對一國攻打另一國，但墨子並非和平主義和不抵抗主義，他主張當一切和平手段用盡後，弱小國家是可以進行「正義戰爭」的，在他那裏，「正義戰爭」就是正當防衛，保家衛國，而且作為一個半軍事性非政府組織的首領，墨子還會派出「國際縱隊」扶弱鋤強，幫助弱小國家不被大國欺負，這又有了一點點「人道主義干涉」的味道。所以在後世，墨家又被稱為「俠客」的先驅。

在當今世界，即使像瑞士這樣的「中立國」，也仍舊會備有民兵，以防萬一。這也符合墨子「七患」所提到的情況，也正是一句中國諺語所表達的觀點：「害人之心不可有，防人之心不可無。」

international arena. China's power during the late Qing dynasty and the early years of the Republic was, despite its size, weak. It was repeatedly harassed by imperial forces.

Dr Sun Yat-sen once said, "If a country wants to become a big power, its civilian officials must be incorruptible, and its military officials must not fear sacrificing their lives." This view has similarities with Mozi's on how the seven worries have a bearing on the domestic life of states. Mozi advocated an "anti-aggression" policy and opposed the idea of any state attacking another state. Nevertheless, Mozi was not a true pacifist nor a believer in non-resistance. He claims that when all peaceful means are exhausted, the weak state under attack is justified in waging a "just war." Mozi believes that a "just war" is a righteous way to defend and safeguard one's state; it is a means by which weak states can protect themselves from being harassed by big states. What is more, as the leader of a paramilitary non-government organization, Mozi is willing to send "international allied troops" to help the weak defend themselves against a powerful enemy so that they will not be harassed by the big states. Here we may sense a suggestion of "humanitarian interference" in his ideas. For this reason, Mohists in later generations were called the pioneers of "the knight errant."

In the contemporary world, even a "neutral country" like

二

故備者，國之重也。食者，國之
寶也；兵者，國之爪也。

【原文】

　　子墨子曰：「今有負其子而汲者，隊
其子於井中，其母必從而道之。今歲凶，
民饑道餓，重其子此疚於隊，其可無察
邪？故時年歲善，則民仁且良；時年歲凶，
則民吝且惡。夫民何常此之有？為者疾，
食者眾，則歲無豐。故曰：『財不足則反
之時，食不足則反之用。』故先民以時生
財，固本而用財，則財足。

　　「故雖上世之聖王，豈能使五穀常
收而旱水不至哉？然而無凍餓之民者，何
也？其力時急而自養儉也。故《夏書》曰：
『禹七年水。』《殷書》曰：『湯五年旱。』
此其離凶餓甚矣。然而民不凍餓者，何也？
其生財密，其用之節也。故倉無備粟，不
可以待凶饑；庫無備兵，雖有義不能征無

Switzerland has its own militia in case it should ever come under military attack. This sort of measure tallies with the "seven worries" that Mozi talked about, and is clearly expressed in the well-known Chinese proverb: "While you should not deliberately hurt others, you should also not stop being vigilant about others hurting you."

Two
Vigilance is an imperative for a state: a food supply is a state's treasury; and weaponry represents the claws of a state.

Translation:

Master Mozi said, "Suppose a mother is carrying her child on her back while drawing water from a well. If the child falls into the well, she will surely hasten to pull him out. Now suppose it is a year of famine. People are starving to death by the roadside causing dismay far greater than a child falling into a well. How can one ignore it? When it is a year of good harvest, people are benevolent and kind; when it is a year of famine, people become mean and cruel. Yet, is it true that people always act like this? If there are only a few people who work but many people to feed, then it cannot be a plentiful

義；城郭不備全，不可以自守；心無備慮，不可以應卒。是若慶忌無去之心，不能輕出。夫桀無待湯之備，故放；紂無待武王之備，故殺。桀、紂貴為天子，富有天下，然而皆滅亡於百里之君者，何也？有富貴而不為備也。故備者，國之重也。食者，國之寶也；兵者，國之爪也。城者所以自守也。此三者國之具也。」（《七患》）

【今譯】

墨子說：「現有背着孩子到井邊汲水的，孩子掉到了井裏，他母親必定趕緊把他拉上來。現在遇到饑年，路上有餓死的人，其慘痛比孩子掉入井中更為嚴重，怎麼能忽視呢？收成好的時候，百姓就仁義善良；遇到凶災，百姓就吝嗇凶惡。民眾的性情，哪有一定的呢？幹活的少，吃飯的多，就不可能有豐年。所以說：『財用不足就要注重農時，糧食不足就要注意節約。』因此，古人按照農時生產財富，鞏固本業，節省開支，財用自然就充足。

「前世的聖王豈能使五穀永遠豐收，水旱之

year. Therefore, it is said, 'When there is not enough wealth, one must be mindful of the planting seasons; when there is not enough food, one must be mindful of what is eaten.' Hence, people in the past created wealth by planting in the right seasons, consolidating their possessions and being prudent. In this way, their wealth grew.

"Even for the sage kings of the past, would it not be impossible for them to ensure forever a good harvest of the five grains and to prevent droughts from happening? Yet why was there no one who ever suffered cold or hunger? It was because they worked hard during the planting seasons and were frugal in the way they lived. The *Books of Xia* said, 'The deluge lasted for seven years during the time of Yu.' The *Books of Yin* said, 'The drought lasted for five years during the time of Tang.' Those were severe times of calamity and hunger. Yet why didn't people suffer cold or hunger? It was because they produced a lot and ate sparingly. Hence, if there is no grain reserve in the granaries, years of famine and hunger cannot be endured. If there is no military reserve in the army, even when there is a righteous cause, the army will not be able to fight against injustice. If the outer city walls are not well built, the city cannot defend itself. And if a man is not vigilant of mind, he cannot cope with emergencies.

"For the same reason, if Qing Ji was unprepared for leaving

災永遠不至？但從無受凍挨餓之民，卻是為何？
這是因為他們努力耕作，農時抓得緊，而自己花
錢又很節儉。《夏書》說『禹時有七年水災』，
《殷書》說『湯時有五年旱災』。遭受的饑荒
夠嚴重的了，老百姓卻沒有受凍挨餓，這是何故
呢？因為他們生產的財富很多，花起來卻很節
儉。所以，糧倉中沒有儲備，就不能防凶年饑荒；
兵庫中沒有武器，即使自己有義也不能去討伐無
義；內外城池若不完備，就不可以自衛；心中沒
有戒備，就不能應付突發事件。就像慶忌沒有離
開衛國的思想準備，就不應該輕易出走。夏桀沒
有防禦商湯的準備，因此被商湯放逐。商紂沒有
防禦周武王的準備，因此被殺。夏桀和商紂雖貴
為天子，富有天下，卻都被方圓百里的小國之君
所滅，這是為何？只因為他們雖然富貴，卻沒有
做好防備。所以，防備是國家最重要的事情。糧
食是國家的寶物，兵器是國家的爪牙，城郭是用
來自我防禦的：這三者是維持國家的工具。」

【時析】

在這裏，墨子提到夏桀、商紂亡國時，說他
們亡國的原因在於「不為備」，而未像他在《天

Wei, he should not have left so hastily. Jie of Xia had no defense against the attack by Tang, and he was therefore exiled. Zhou of Shang was unprepared for the attack of the King of Wu, and he was therefore killed. Jie and Zhou were honorable Sons of Heaven who possessed the wealth of the whole world, yet they were eliminated by the rulers of states with only a hundred *li* of territory. How come? It was because even though they were rich and wealthy, they were unprotected. So, vigilance is an imperative for a state: a food supply is a state's treasury; weaponry represents the claws of a state; and city walls are essential for self-defense. These three are the instruments of a state." ("Qi Huan")

Contemporary interpretation:

In this passage, when Mozi talks about the annihilation of Jie of Xia and Zhou of Shang, he takes the cause to be "the unpreparedness" instead of not respecting heaven and the spirits as he said in "Tian Zhi" and "Ming Gui." Was Mozi contradicting himself?

Some people think that "Qi Huan" is one of Mozi's early works, written at a time when his thoughts were still deeply influenced by Confucianism and the concept of heaven and spirits; therefore, they were not seen as important as his thoughts in his maturity. This view needs discussion because, as seen in another early work, "Fa Yi," Mozi did talk about

志》、《明鬼》中說是因為不尊天鬼，這是否意味着墨子自相矛盾呢？

有人認為，《七患》是墨子早期的作品，那時他受儒家的影響較深，故對天鬼尚不如成熟時期重視。這種看法是可以商榷的。因為，在同樣是早期作品的《法儀》中，墨子已經提到天對順天者、逆天者有不同的處理結果，順天者得賞，逆天者受罰，並同樣舉了夏桀、商紂亡國的例子。那麼，問題就來了，到底他們亡國，是因為人事（如不做準備），還是因為老天的懲罰呢？是否如墨子在回答跌鼻時所說，不是因為天的懲罰而是因為其他的原因？

其實，夏桀、商紂為何亡國，並不像「好人為何受苦」那樣難以回答。墨子可以回答說，夏桀、商紂亡國，是因為他們不順從天志，而天志的內容之一，就是希望國君保護好人民，具體到內容上，就包括了防備。夏桀、商紂內政不修，外交不整，讓人民受苦，當然違逆天意，因此上天懲罰他們，令其亡國，也就順理成章。這樣，墨子就可以將《七患》之重人事與《天志》、《明

the different consequences for those who obey heaven and for those who don't: those who obey heaven will be rewarded while those who disobey heaven will be punished. It can be seen then that Mozi also took the annihilation of Jie of Xia and Zhou of Shang as examples of punishment. This then raises the question of whether they lost their states at their own hands (being unprepared for an attack), or was it a punishment from heaven? Would this then be like the reply Mozi gave Die Bi that it was not a punishment by heaven but by something else instead?

In fact, it should not be difficult to explain why Jie of Xia and Zhou of Shang lost their states (essentially, they were bad), but it doesn't explain "why good people suffer." Mozi could have replied that Jie of Xia and Zhou of Shang lost their states because they did not obey the will of heaven, since the will of heaven requires the ruler of a state to protect his people, and this specifically includes national defense. Jie of Xia and Zhou of Shang failed in both internal governance and foreign policies, thus causing their people to suffer. This is obviously a betrayal of the will of heaven. As a result, heaven punished them by annihilating their states. This sounds like a good argument.

In this way, it is possible for Mozi to consolidate his arguments in favor of human factors as seen in "Qi Huan" and his

鬼》之重鬼神統一起來了。如果說墨子有甚麼邏輯問題，就是出在經驗證據上。因為，在當時的春秋末年，人們已經看到不少國家的國君，也算不上多好，甚至很壞，但卻國力強大，而一些好國君，只因為國家小，就被別國兼併。這就打破了墨子所說的「現世報」規律，令其神學不那麼令人信服。

三

少嘗苦曰苦，多嘗苦曰甘，則必以此人為不知甘苦之辯矣。

【原文】

今有一人，入人園圃，竊其桃李，眾聞則非之，上為政者得則罰之。此何也？以虧人自利也。至攘人犬豕雞豚者，其不義又甚入人園圃竊桃李。是何故也？以虧人愈多，其不仁茲甚，罪益厚。至入人欄廄，取人馬牛者，其不仁義又甚攘人犬豕雞豚。此何故也？以其虧人愈多。苟虧人

arguments in favor of heaven and the spirits as seen in "Tian Zhi" and "Ming Gui." If one wants to suggest any weakness in his argument, it would be the lack of empirical evidence of the time. During those final years of the Spring and Autumn period, people witnessed many not-so-good or even really bad rulers creating powerful states, while some good rulers had their states annexed just because they were small. These cases serve to repudiate Mozi's idea of the law of "retribution during one's lifetime," and result in it being less than convincing.

Three
If a person tastes a little bitterness and says something is bitter, yet when he tastes a lot of bitterness he says it is sweet, then we shall take this man as not being able to distinguish bitter from sweet.

Translation:
A man enters someone else's orchard and steals peaches and plums from it. When people learn what he has done, they will condemn his act; when the authorities catch him, they will punish him. Why? Because he seeks to do harm to others for his own benefit. And those who seize the dogs,

愈多，其不仁茲甚，罪益厚。至殺不辜人也，扡其衣裘，取戈劍者，其不義又甚入人欄廄取人馬牛。此何故也？以其虧人愈多。苟虧人愈多，其不仁茲甚矣，罪益厚。當此，天下之君子皆知而非之，謂之不義。今至大為攻國，則弗知非，從而譽之，謂之義。此可謂知義與不義之別乎？

殺一人謂之不義，必有一死罪矣，若以此說往，殺十人十重不義，必有十死罪矣；殺百人百重不義，必有百死罪矣。當此，天下之君子皆知而非之，謂之不義。今至大為不義攻國，則弗知非，從而譽之，謂之義，情不知其不義也，故書其言以遺後世。若知其不義也，夫奚說書其不義以遺後世哉？

今有人於此，少見黑曰黑，多見黑曰白，則以此人不知白黑之辯矣；少嘗苦曰苦，多嘗苦曰甘，則必以此人為不知甘苦之辯矣。今小為非，則知而非之。大為非攻國，則不知非，從而譽之，謂之義。此

pigs, chickens and suckling pigs of others, what they do is even more unrighteous than those who enter the orchards of others to steal their peaches and plums. Why? Because the more harm a person does to others, the more malevolent he is, and the greater his crime becomes. And those who enter the stalls and stables belonging to others and take their horses and oxen, what they do is more unrighteous than those who seize the dogs, pigs, chickens and suckling pigs belonging to others. Why? Because they are doing even more harm. For the more harm a person does to others, the more malevolent he is, and the greater his crime becomes. And as for those who kill innocent people, stripping them of their clothes and taking away their swords, what they do is more unrighteous than those who enter the stalls and stables belonging to others and take their horses and oxen. Why? Because they do even more harm. For the more harm one does to others, the more malevolent he is, and the greater his crime becomes.

All the gentlemen of the world know these crimes as offences and condemn them, calling them unrighteous. But when a state launches a big attack, people do not condemn it. Instead they praise it, calling it righteous. Can we say people know how to distinguish righteousness from unrighteousness?

Killing a man is considered unrighteous and can result in the death penalty. The inference from this is that killing ten

可謂知義與不義之辯乎？是以知天下之君
子也，辯義與不義之亂也。（《非攻上》）

【今譯】

　　現今有一人，跑進人家的園圃，偷竊裏面的
桃子和李子，人們聽說後就會指責他，上邊管事
的人抓到就會處罰他。這是為甚麼呢？因為他損
人利己。至於盜竊別人的雞、狗、豬，他的不義
又超過了跑到人家園圃裏偷桃子、李子。這是為
甚麼？因為他損人更大，他的不仁更突出，罪也
更重。至於跑進別人的牛欄、馬廄內偷盜牛馬，
他的不仁不義，又超過盜竊別人家的雞、狗、豬。
這是為甚麼呢？因為他損人更大。如果損人更
大，他的不仁就更突出，罪也就更重。至於妄殺
無辜之人，奪取他的衣裘，搶走他的戈劍，則不
義又甚於跑進別人家的牛欄、馬廄偷盜牛馬。這
是為甚麼呢？因為他損人更大。一旦損人更大，
他的不仁就更突出，罪也更重。對此，天下的君
子都知道指責他，稱他為不義。現在，有人大行
不義，攻打別人的國家，人們卻不知道指責其錯
誤，反而跟着加以讚美，稱之為義。這能算是明
白義與不義的區別嗎？

men is ten times as unrighteous and is subject to ten times the death penalty; killing a hundred men is a hundred times as unrighteous and is subject to a hundred times the death penalty.

All the gentlemen of the world know these crimes as offences and condemn them, calling them unrighteous. But when an unrighteous state launches a big attack, people do not condemn it. Instead they praise it, calling it righteous. The fact is they do not recognize just how unrighteous this is, and they even document the words of the state's ruler so that they can be passed on to future generations. If they had understood the unrighteousness of his deeds, they would instead have written about his unjust actions and passed this on to future generations.

If there is a man who when he sees a little bit of black, says it is black, and yet when he sees a lot of black he says it is white, we will take this man as not being able to distinguish black from white. If a man tastes a slight bitterness and says it is bitter, and yet when he tastes a lot of bitterness he says it is sweet, then we shall take this man as not being able to distinguish bitter from sweet. Now, for the little wrongdoings a person knows to be wrong and condemns, when it comes to the big wrongdoing and he does not recognize a state in attacking other states is at fault and instead praises it, calling

　　殺死一個人，叫做不義，必定構成一條死罪，假如依照這種道理類推下去，殺死十個人，就有十倍的不義，則必然構成十重的死罪；殺死一百個人，就有百倍的不義，則必然構成百重的死罪。

　　對此，天下的君子都知道指責他，稱他不義。如今有人行大不義，攻打別人的國家，他們卻不知道非難他，反而跟着稱讚他，說是義舉，他們確實不明白他的不義，還要記載他的話，傳給後代。倘若他們知道那是不義的，怎麼還會記下這些不義之事，傳給後代呢？

　　假如現在有一個人，看見少許黑色說是黑的，看見很多黑色卻說是白的，那麼人們就會認為他黑白不分；嘗一點小苦就說是苦的，多嘗一些苦卻說是甜的，那麼人們就會認為這個人甘苦不辨。現在，有人犯了小錯，人們都知道並指責他；有人犯了大罪，攻打別人的國家，人們卻不知道指責其錯誤，反而跟着稱讚他，說他為義。這能算是懂得義與不義的區別嗎？我由此知道天下的君子，把義與不義的區別弄得很混亂了。

it a righteous deed, can we then say a person knows how to distinguish righteousness from unrighteousness? This explains how all the gentlemen of the world are confused about how to distinguish righteousness from unrighteousness. ("Fei Gong I")

Contemporary interpretation:
This passage from Mozi is well reasoned using deductive arguments and therefore very convincing.

The biggest problem of the Spring and Autumn and Warring States periods was interstate warfare. If the ruler of a state sought only his own pleasure and his officials were corrupt, then it was the people of the state alone who suffered poverty. If, however, a war broke out between states, it might at its best cause hundreds or thousands of casualties, and at its worst tens of thousands. An example of this is the Battle of Changping between Qin and Zhao during the Warring States period. In this calamitous event, General Bai Qi of Qin buried alive four hundred thousand soldiers of Zhao who had surrendered. Coupled with the considerable collateral casualties of common people in both states as well as the material and spiritual damage, the war deserves to be named "the most horrific ever seen." In view of the relatively small population of the whole Central Plains region at that time, it is truly "appalling" to imagine how significantly the population would be reduced by such wars.

【時析】

墨子這篇文章，邏輯分明，層層推進，頗具說服力。

春秋戰國的最大問題，就是國與國之間的戰爭。如果說一國之內的國君貪圖享樂，官吏貪污，尚只是使一國人民貧窮，那麼國與國之間的戰爭，輕則死傷千百人，重則數以萬計，像戰國時期秦趙之間的長平之戰，秦將白起一次就坑殺了趙國四十萬降卒，加上雙方老百姓的傷亡人數，以及物質和精神的損傷，用「慘絕人寰」來形容也不為過。那時整個中國的人口也不會很多，因戰爭帶來的人口減少真可謂「觸目驚心」。

墨子所處的春秋晚期，周天子已沒有權威，是一個「虛君」，指揮不動各國諸侯。周初時所封的諸多國家，經過幾輪廝殺和兼併後，只剩下了晉、楚、秦、齊、吳、越這些大國，歷史正朝着「武力統一」的道路邁進。如果說孔子是夢想通過「克己復禮」，通過請諸侯克制自己的私欲以遵守「親親尊尊」這套禮樂制度來恢復周初的秩序，「開歷史倒車」，「回到當初的光榮」，

During the late Spring and Autumn period, when Mozi lived, the king of the Zhou dynasty was no longer seen as an authoritative figure, he was considered instead a "pseudo-king" to whom no states submitted. The many states that had been established since the early Zhou underwent a series of mutual assaults and annexations, and only the most powerful like Jin, Chu, Qin, Qi, Wu and Yue survived. At that time, history was striding along the path of "unification by force."

We may say that Confucius dreamed of restoring the order of the early Zhou through "disciplining oneself to complete tasks according to the protocol," that is, to ask vassal state rulers to restrain their personal desires and follow the system of rituals and music that "respects the family and honors the honorable" — in other words, "trying to turn the clock back," or "returning to the glory of the past."

In contrast, Mozi's dream was to return to the Xia dynasty where he envisaged an all-embracing love reigning over the entire world: the rule was virtuous, the good people were functioning well, the people loved each other, the Son of Heaven followed heaven's will and united people's opinions. As a consequence, those in positions of power governed well and those they governed did as they were asked, all contributing to an effective governance that served the interests of everyone with all-embracing love. However, Mozi

那麼墨子就是夢想回到他所想像的夏朝時代的「兼愛」的天下，國君尚賢，賢良盡得其用，人民尚同，由順從天意的天子統一人民的意見，上行下效，雷厲風行，實行兼相愛、交相利的政策。但是，墨子沒有給出「路線圖」，沒有給出如何達到一統天下的方法和步驟（比如像歐盟這樣的「和平統一」的方法），而只是要求諸侯不要「兼相攻，交相害」，不要搞侵略戰爭，要維持現狀。而墨子之後的法家，遵循現實主義的原則，贊成用武力（暴力）的方法統一天下，他們在秦獲得大力支持，理論得到應用，並最終獲得成功。

墨子已經看出，一國的「正義」有可能是非常「不義」，是一種集體自私自利。用基督教現實主義神學家尼布林的話來說，就是「集體的罪」。歷史上經常可以看到，一些所謂「民族英雄」、「國家偉人」，實際上不過是大屠夫，他們的功名建立在殺戮無數人的基礎之上，真是「一將功成萬骨枯」。墨子所說的奉大規模殺人犯為義人並歌功頌德的現象，在近代民族主義興起後，亦是普遍現象。法國人以拿破崙為驕傲，其實他對於西班牙人、德國人和俄國人來說，只

did not offer a "road map" to this ideal world — he did not point out the way and the steps needed (such as the "peaceful unification" proposal offered by the European Union) to show how the world could be unified. All he did was to ask the vassal states rulers not to "attack and do harm to each other," not to invade other states by means of war, and to maintain the status quo. The later Legalist school, which, instead, followed realist principles and supported unifying the world by force (violence), was well-received and adopted by the Qin — eventually succeeding.

Mozi was able to identify the "unrighteousness" implied in the "righteousness" proclaimed by a state, which is in fact a kind of collective of self-interests. In the words of Christian-Realism theologian Reinhold Niebuhr, it is a "collective sin."

As often seen in history, many who were named "heroes of the nation" or "great people of the state" were actually murderers who built their success upon countless killings, as expressed in the poetic phrase, "a general triumphs at the expense of tens of thousands of lives." The phenomenon Mozi referred to: admiring and applauding those who committed large-scale massacres as the righteous, has not been uncommon following the rise of modern nationalism.

The French take pride in their Napoleon, despite his being

不過是侵略者而已。幸虧希特勒沒有成功，否則可能今天的歷史書，會說他是如何拯救世界的偉人呢！「名」與「實」差距如此之大，不能不令我們反思和深思從小接受的一些習以為常的觀念。

四
不知日月安不足乎，其有竊疾乎？

【原文】

　　子墨子謂魯陽文君曰：「今有一人於此，羊牛犓豢，饔人但割而和之，食之不可勝食也。見人之作餅，則還然竊之，曰：『舍余食。』不知日月安不足乎，其有竊疾乎？」魯陽文君曰：「有竊疾也。」子墨子曰：「楚四竟之田，曠蕪而不可勝辟，呼虛數千，不可勝，見宋、鄭之閒邑，則還然竊之，此與彼異乎？」魯陽文君曰：「是猶彼也，實有竊疾也。」（《耕柱》）

viewed as a plain invader in the eyes of the Spanish, Germans and Russians. Fortunately, Hitler failed. Had he not, he might be celebrated now by some historians as a great person who saved the world. In the face of the huge discrepancy between "the appearance" and "the reality," it is our obligation to reflect on many of the beliefs we have taken for granted since childhood.

Four
I wonder if he has a big appetite, or whether he is a pathological thief?

Translation:
Master Mozi spoke to Prince Wen of Lu Yang, "Now, there is a man who has so many sheep, oxen and livestock; but no matter how many of them his cook slaughters and prepares, he will never ever not have enough to eat. Yet when he sees others making cakes, he is amazed and tries stealing them. 'I want to eat them!' he says. I wonder if he has a big appetite, or if he is a pathological thief?"

Prince Wen of Lu Yang said, "He is a pathological thief."

Mozi said, "There are countless uncultivated fields scattered around the territory of Chu that are waiting to be ploughed.

【今譯】

墨子對魯陽文君說：「如今這裏有一個人，他的牛羊牲畜任由廚師宰割烹調，吃都吃不完，但他看見人家做餅，就驚訝了，並去偷竊，說：『給我吃！』不知道這是他的美味食物不夠多呢，還是他有偷竊癖？」魯陽文君說：「這是有偷竊癖了。」墨子說：「楚國四面邊境之內的田地，空曠荒蕪，開墾不完，掌管川澤山林的官吏就有數千人以上，數都數不過來，見到宋、鄭的空城，還驚訝了，就去竊取，這與那個偷人家餅的人有甚麼不同呢？」魯陽文君說：「這跟那個人一樣，確實是有偷竊癖了。」

【時析】

魯陽文君是當時南方大國楚國北部的一個大領主，他有實力去攻打北面的宋和鄭這兩個走下坡路的國家。墨子大概是從他的弟子那裏聽說魯陽文君對宋鄭兩國有興趣，準備有所行動，所以才去見魯陽文君，使他打消攻宋鄭兩國的念頭。墨子批評魯陽文君發動不義戰爭，當然批得很有道理。他罵魯陽文君「有病」（有竊疾），真是解氣啊！孫子兵法說，不戰而屈人之兵，乃是上

There are so many that no matter how many people are called upon to work on them, they will never ever finish working all the fields. Yet when someone sees the unoccupied towns of Song and Zheng, he is amazed and tries to steal them. How is he different from the other man?"

Prince Wen of Lu Yang said, "They are the same. They are both pathological thieves." ("Geng Zhu")

Contemporary interpretation:

Prince Wen of Lu Yang was at that time a big landowner in the northern part of the large southern state of Chu. He was powerful enough to attack Song and Zheng in the north since both states were in decline. Probably Mozi heard from his disciples that Prince Wen of Lu Yang was interested in taking the territories of Song and Zheng and was about to act.

He therefore went to see Prince Wen of Lu Yang and tried to dissuade him from attacking Song and Zheng. Mozi's disapproval of Prince Wen of Lu Yang in waging an unrighteous war was well grounded. He reprimanded Prince Wen of Lu Yang as "pathological" (a pathological thief) — how satisfying this was to people's ears! *The Art of War* states that the best strategy is to subdue the enemy without fighting. It seems that Mozi's uses of a "mental war" and "debate" are examples of "subduing the enemy without fighting."

策。看來墨子的「心戰」和「辯論」，就是「不戰而屈人之兵」啊！

五
說忠行義，取天下。

【原文】

　　魯君謂子墨子曰：「吾恐齊之攻我也，可救乎？」子墨子曰：「可。昔者，三代之聖王禹湯文武，百里之諸侯也，說忠行義，取天下。三代之暴王桀紂幽厲，讎怨行暴，失天下。吾願主君，之上者尊天事鬼，下者愛利百姓，厚為皮幣，卑辭令，亟遍禮四鄰諸侯，毆國而以事齊，患可救也，非此，顧無可為者。」（《魯問》）

【今譯】

　　魯國國君對墨子說：「我害怕齊國攻打我國，可以解救嗎？」墨子說：「可以。從前三代的聖王禹、湯、文、武，只不過是百里見方土地的首領，他們喜愛忠誠，實行仁義，終於取得了天下。

Five

They upheld loyalty and practiced righteousness, and they gained the world.

Translation:

The ruler of Lu said to Master Mozi, "I fear that Qi will attack my state. Is there any solution?"

Mozi said, "Yes. In the past, the sage kings of the Three Dynasties, Yu, Tang, Wen and Wu, were vassal state rulers of just a hundred *li* of land; they upheld loyalty and practiced righteousness, and they gained the world. The tyrants of the Three Dynasties, Jie, Zhou, You and Li, provoked hostility and ruled by cruelty, and they lost the world. I wish that your Majesty would honor heaven and serve the spirits above you, love and serve the interests of the people under you, stock up on fur and money, humble your words, swiftly befriend the rulers of all your neighboring states, and summon the people of your own state to serve Qi, then the problem will be solved. Otherwise, there will be no way out. ("Lu Wen")

Contemporary interpretation:

The state of Lu was granted to Bo Qin, the eldest son of the Duke of Zhou, and the state of Qi was given to the descendants of Jiang Ziya — the renowned minister of the Zhou dynasty.

三代的暴王桀、紂、幽、厲，上下相怨，實行暴
政，最終失去了天下。我希望君主您對上尊重上
天、敬事鬼神，對下愛護並造福百姓，請準備豐
厚的皮毛、錢幣，辭令謙恭，趕快禮交四鄰諸侯，
率領全國人民侍奉齊國，禍患就可以解救，不這
樣做，就沒有其他辦法了。」

【時析】

　　魯國本是周公的大兒子伯禽的封國，齊國本
是周朝著名謀臣姜子牙子孫的封國，一開始兩個
國家差距倒也不大，但後來齊國出了個管仲，幫
助齊桓公稱霸，齊國頓時興盛。齊國在山東東部
沿海地區，海產品豐富，鹽業發達，工商業興旺，
在吞併東部沿海的萊人氏族後，齊國的版圖與國
力更是大增。相比之下，魯國處在山東東南內陸，
除完整地保持了「周禮」這一「軟文化」外，其
他就沒甚麼特色。

　　在孔子的時代，魯國國君就被下面的三大家
族幾乎架空了權力，到墨子的時代，國家不少城
市和領土還被齊國一口口吞掉了。更可怕的是，
魯國除了北面有不懷好意的齊國外，南面還有大

To begin with, there was not much difference between the two states. Then a man in Qi called Guang Zhong assisted Duke Huan of Qi to rise to power, enabling the state of Qi to become instantly prosperous. The state of Qi was in the coastal region of eastern Shandong and was blessed with abundant seafood, a well-developed salt industry, and thriving business and commerce. After having annexed the eastern coastal lands of the House of Lai Ren, its territory and power grew tremendously. In contrast, the state of Lu was in the south-eastern inland area of Shandong, and apart from its "soft power" inherited from "the rituals of Zhou," it had little else to offer. During the time of Confucius, the ruler of Lu had almost all his powers usurped by the three big houses who were his subordinates. By Mozi's time, the situation had not improved and many of the cities and lands of Lu had fallen into the hands of Qi. What made it even worse was the fact that Lu was not only intimidated by the malevolent Qi in the north but also the large states of Wu, Yue and Chu from the south. All these states were sizing up the weakness of the state of Lu as they might prey, so it is of little wonder the ruler of Lu was having a bad time!

Lu's ruler asked Mozi how he could save his state from the powerful Qi. Mozi's answer was to a certain extent a textbook example of the Mohist "political theology": that the ruler should "serve the three interests" (serve the interests of heaven

國吳、越和楚，它們都對弱國魯國虎視眈眈，想來魯國國君的日子很不好過呀！

魯國國君問墨子如何面對強齊救國時，墨子的回答比較全面地體現了墨家的「政治神學」，那就是國君應做到「三利」（上利天，中利鬼神，下利百姓），這三利是統一的（天與鬼神都要求國君造福百姓），具體體現在政治上就是明修內政，對國內實行仁政，做好準備，團結百姓一致抗敵，在外交上交好其他鄰國，爭取外援，使齊國攻擊魯國時能進行國際干涉，這樣齊國就不敢貿然攻魯了。（在《七患》中墨子說得更詳細。）

墨子所說的昔者三代聖王禹、湯、文、武以百里之地取得天下，也為後來的孟子經常引用，證明「仁政」是使天下歸心的必要途徑。墨子這裏所說的能夠「取天下」的「忠義」，實際上跟孟子所說的「仁政」相類似，效果都是使「近者悅，遠者來」。墨子所建議的交好鄰國，利用國際各方勢力的影響來救國，也為後來縱橫家所效法。可以說，墨子對後來諸子的影響是很廣泛的。

above, serve the interests of the spirits and gods in the middle, and serve the interests of the people below). These are unified interests (in the sense that heaven as well as the spirits and the gods command the ruler to look after his people). With respect to domestic policies, the ruler should govern benevolently, and be well prepared and unite the people to fight against any enemies. In regard to foreign policies, the ruler should befriend other neighboring states in order to gain their support in keeping Qi's ambitions in check so that the state would think twice about rashly attacking Lu. (Mozi discusses this more thoroughly in "Qi Huan.")

Mozi's story about how in the past the sage kings (Yu, Tang, Wen and Wu) of the Three Dynasties gained the world with just a hundred *li* of land to begin with was later often quoted by Mencius in his attempt to prove that "benevolent governance" was the essential path for gaining the hearts of the world's people. The "loyalty and righteousness" that can help a ruler "gain the world" as described by Mozi is actually similar to Mencius's "benevolent governance." Both are supposed to make "those who are close to you be pleased, and those who are far away come." At the same time, Mozi suggested befriending neighboring states so that their influence could be called upon to save one's own state. This advice later inspired the School of Diplomacy. Mozi clearly had a very broad influence upon the later schools of thought.

六

大國之攻小國也，是交相賊也，過必反於國。

【原文】

　　齊將伐魯，子墨子謂項子牛曰：「伐魯，齊之大過也。昔者，吳王東伐越，棲諸會稽，西伐楚，葆昭王於隨。北伐齊，取國子以歸於吳。諸侯報其讎，百姓苦其勞，而弗為用，是以國為虛戾，身為刑戮也。昔者，智伯伐范氏與中行氏，兼三晉之地，諸侯報其讎，百姓苦其勞，而弗為用，是以國為虛戾，身為刑戮用是也。故大國之攻小國也，是交相賊也，過必反於國。」（《魯問》）

【今譯】

　　齊國將要攻打魯國，墨子對項子牛說：「攻伐魯國，是齊國的大錯。從前吳王夫差向東攻打越國，迫使越王勾踐困居在會稽；向西攻打楚國，迫使楚國人在隨地保衛楚昭王；向北攻打齊國，將齊將國子俘虜了押回吳國。後來諸侯來報仇，

Six

If a large state attacks a small state, it will harm both, and ultimately it will suffer from its own mistake.

Translation:

Qi was about to attack Lu. Master Mozi said to Xiang Ziniu, "To attack Lu would be a big mistake for Qi. In the past, the King of Wu attacked Yue in the east, forcing him [King of Yue] to take refuge in Guiji. He attacked Chu in the west, making people hold fast for King Zhao at Sui. He attacked Qi in the north and took Qi's General Guozi back to Wu. Later, the rulers of the vassal states took revenge. The people suffered great hardships and were too weary to serve him [King of Wu] anymore. As a result, the state fell into ruin, and he [King of Wu] himself was executed. In the past, Zhi Bo attacked the house of Fan and the house of Zhongxing, and then invaded the territories of the Three Jins. Later, the rulers of the vassal states took revenge. The people suffered great hardships and were too weary to serve him anymore. As a result, the state fell into ruin, and Zhi Bo was executed.

Thus, if a large state attacks a small state, it will harm both, and ultimately it will suffer from its own mistake." ("Lu Wen")

百姓苦於疲憊，不肯為他（吳王）效力，因此國家滅亡，吳王自己也被殺死。從前智伯攻伐范氏與中行氏的封地，兼併了晉國三家的土地，結果諸侯來報仇，百姓苦於疲憊，不肯為他效力，搞得國家滅亡，他自己也被殺死。由此可見，大國攻打小國，是互相殘害，災禍必定反及於本國。」

【時析】

項子牛是齊國將領，墨子的一個叫作勝綽的弟子跟着他做事，當他的侍從。墨子大概是從勝綽那裏聽到項子牛要攻魯的事，所以跑去跟項子牛辯論一番，想「舌戰項子牛，不戰而止戰」。墨子是從「反作用力」（報復、報應）來談齊國伐魯的可怕後果，主要論證是舉前車之鑒。他這裏舉了吳國和智伯的例子。這兩個「兼相恨，交相賊」的例子，在墨子看來，完全是違逆天意，對天、鬼神和百姓都是禍害（三不利），因此結果大為不妙。

可是墨子的這些論證，只是「不完全歸納法」，並不能證明「攻打他國一定會導致自己滅亡」，因此，一些強國仍舊仗着自己勢大欺人，

Contemporary interpretation:

Xiang Ziniu was a general of the state of Qi. One of Mozi's disciples, Sheng Zhuo, worked under him. It is probable that Mozi heard from Sheng Zhuo that Xiang Ziniu was about to attack Lu, so he came to confront him with his own advice, hoping that he could "defeat Xiang Ziniu with arguments so that he would stop the war before it started." Mozi illustrated the terrible tolls of Qi's attack on Lu with "counter force" (revenge, retribution), and his main argument draws on the lessons one should learn from past mistakes. In this passage, he took the examples of the state of Wu and Zhi Bo. In Mozi's eyes, these both demonstrated that "provoking mutual hatred, causing harm to each other" represent the utmost betrayal of heaven's will — they cause harm to heaven, the spirits and gods, as well as to people and are therefore anything but good.

However, Mozi's arguments are only "incomplete inferences" which cannot justify the claim that "attacking other states will lead to one's own extinction." Therefore, some big states which kept on harassing others with their power became bigger and bigger, in the same way a small fish grows into a "big fish" through eating shrimps. They thought they could avoid retribution, with a degree of luck, and in the end unify the whole world. The state of Qi is one such example. After Mozi's death and during the time of Mencius, the state of Qi invaded the state of Yan in the north and caused great damage

像小魚吃蝦米一樣吃胖吃大，吃成「大魚」，且存在着僥倖心理，以為並無「報應」，自己可以一統天下。齊國就是如此。在墨子之後，在孟子的時代，齊國一舉攻下北方的燕國，搞得人家國破家亡，燕國上下都痛恨齊國。沒過幾年，燕國名將樂毅就率領燕人一雪國恥，反攻齊國，齊國幾乎被滅，後來雖然僥倖保存，卻從此奄奄一息，再也不是數一數二的強國了。可見墨子的「兼相恨，交相賊」必然導致「報應」的理論，還是頗有道理的。在墨子和項子牛的時代，尚看不到齊國侵略他國的後果。正是由於尚不能看到現世報應，因此項子牛存在着僥倖心理，後來還是侵略了魯國，而墨子的學生勝綽本來是墨子派到項子牛那裏去宣揚「兼相愛、交相利」的，結果他卻跟着項子牛攻魯，弄得墨子老師特別生氣，只好把這位勝同學調回來，不讓他在齊國當官了。可見，墨家是有一套嚴密的組織紀律的。

伊拉克前總統薩達姆當初在美國支持下跟伊朗打了八年的戰爭，把一個好端端富裕的伊拉克弄得十分貧困。兩伊戰爭打完後，他又侵略鄰近的小國科威特，想把人家兼併了，結果反被美國

to it. The people of Yan inevitably developed a deep hatred of Qi. Some few years later, Yan was blessed with an outstanding general, Le Yi, who led the people of Yan in revenge and launched a successful counter-attack against Qi. Qi survived but was left on the edge of collapse. Its power waned and was never regained. Mozi may therefore have good reason to claim that "provoking mutual hatred, causing harm to each other" will absolutely lead to retribution. Mozi and Xiang Ziniu could not observe the consequences that Qi had to bear from its attack on other states. For the same reason — the lack of "retribution during one's lifetime" — Xiang Ziniu attacked Lu hoping luck would be on his side. On the other hand, Sheng Zhuo, whom Mozi sent to Xiang Ziniu in an attempt to promote "all embracing love and mutual interests," served Xiang Ziniu in his attack on Lu instead. Master Mozi was outraged and ordered him to retire from his position in Qi. This case clearly demonstrates that the Mohist school enforced rigorous discipline on its members.

Saddam Hussein, the former president of Iraq, fought a war against Iran for eight years with the support of the United States, dragging the initially wealthy Iraq into poverty and considerable difficulties. After the war against Iran, he attacked and attempted to annex Kuwait, a small country on Iran's southern border, and was counter-attacked by the United States. Year after year of continuing war left Iraq's

攻打。連年戰爭弄得國內人民疲憊不堪。911 事件之後，美國假借「大規模殺傷性武器」的藉口以及「先發制人」的理論攻打伊拉克，伊拉克的大多數老百姓因為薩達姆的多年獨裁和窮兵黷武而不支持他，把美伊戰爭視為「薩達姆和小布希兩個人的戰爭」，連薩達姆最親信的近衛軍也在關鍵時刻背叛了他，結果薩達姆也是死得很慘。這也可以算作證明墨子的「交相賊」必有報應的理論的一個例子吧。

七
並國覆軍，賊殺百姓，孰將受其不祥？

【原文】

　　子墨子見齊大王曰：「今有刀於此，試之人頭，倅然斷之，可謂利乎？」大王曰：「利。」子墨子曰：「多試之人頭，倅然斷之，可謂利乎？」大王曰：「利。」子墨子曰：「刀則利矣，孰將受其不祥？」

people in misery and hardship. Following the atrocity of 9/11, the United States attacked Iraq claiming that Iraq possessed "weapons of mass destruction" and the US needed to adopt a "pre-emptive" policy. Most of the Iraqi people by then no longer supported Saddam Hussein; they had suffered too long from his years of dictatorship and aggressive militarism. They therefore saw the US-Iraqi War as "a war between Saddam Hussein and George W. Bush." In the end, even Saddam Hussein's most trusted personal guard chose to betray him at a critical moment, resulting in a gruesome end to his life.

This is perhaps a 21st-century example which supports Mozi's theory of the certainty of retribution that follows "causing harm to each other" in attacking neighboring states.

Seven
Annexing other states, wiping out their armies, and injuring and killing their people, who should be responsible for these wrongs?

Translation:
Master Mozi went to see the great King of Qi and said, "Now, there is a sword which when used on a man's neck, swiftly

大王曰：「刀受其利，試者受其不祥。」
子墨子曰：「並國覆軍，賊殺百姓，孰將
受其不祥？」大王俯仰而思之曰：「我受
其不祥。」（《魯問》）

【今譯】

　　墨子對齊太公說：「現在這裏有一把刀，用
它來試砍人頭，一下子就砍斷了，可以說是鋒利
吧？」太公說：「鋒利。」墨子又說：「用好多
人頭來試它，都一下子就砍斷了，可以說是鋒利
吧？」太公說：「鋒利。」墨子說：「刀確實鋒利，
但是誰應該承受殺人的惡果呢？」太公說：「刀
受鋒利之名，試刀砍人的人負擔殺人的惡果。」
墨子說：「兼併別國領土，覆滅其軍隊，殘殺其
百姓，誰要承擔這無道不義的責任呢？」太公一
會兒低頭，一會兒抬頭，想了好久，不得不說：
「我應該承受惡果。」

【時析】

　　大概墨子看到齊將項子牛沒有悔改之意，就
直接找項子牛的頂頭上司 —— 齊國國君齊太公田
和去了（齊國國君本來姓姜，後來由田氏家族篡

beheads him. Should we say it is sharp?" The great King said, "It is sharp." Master Mozi said, "When it is used on many men's necks, it still swiftly beheads them. Should we say it is sharp?" The great King said, "It is sharp." Master Mozi said, "Yes, the sword is really sharp, but who should be responsible for its wrong?" The great King said, "The sword is said to be sharp, the one who uses it should be responsible for its wrong." Master Mozi said, "Annexing other states, wiping out their armies, injuring and killing their people, who should be responsible for these wrongs?" The great King lowered his head and looked up, pondered for a while, then said, "I should be responsible for these wrongs." ("Lu Wen")

Contemporary interpretation:

Mozi was probably certain that Xiang Ziniu was irredeemably cruel, so he went to talk to his immediate superior, Tian He, the Grand Duke of Qi. (The former ruler of Qi was surnamed Jiang, but his throne had been seized by the House of Tian and his surname was later changed.)

This passage shows how Mozi reprimanded Tian He and urged him to have "a sense of commitment," and be aware of how any order he gave or an idea he promoted could lead to dire consequences and the sacrifice of countless human lives. Mozi wanted him to experience regret and thus abandon his idea of attacking the state of Lu.

位，國君就易姓了）。這段話就是墨子用「責任意識」來責備田和，使他認識到自己的一個命令、一個念頭就會令千萬人頭落地的嚴重後果，試圖使他反悔，收回攻打魯國的主意。

人類文明的演化其實一直跟「野蠻」脫不了干係。有人統計過，現在我們得享其利的大部份發明，如飛機、冰箱、電腦、核電一類，最初大多是出於軍事目的造出來的。武器的進化一日千里，從拋石和弓箭進化到了中子彈和鐳射武器，甚至文化的演化也跟殖民主義和帝國主義的侵略緊密相連，比如，類似於《菊花與刀》這樣的人類學著作，也是因為美軍要瞭解作為敵人的日本人的社會心理而寫出來的。可見，雖然科技和文化一日千里，人類原始而野蠻的自相殘殺的習性卻一直根深蒂固，絲毫不變。在冷兵器的時代，弓弩機發射一次，可能只殺一兩個人，在核彈時代，一顆原子彈落地，消逝的卻可能是整個國家。任何掌握着「核按鈕」的國家領導人，確實都應該像墨子所教導的齊太公那樣，意識到自己的一個微小的念頭、一個簡短的命令可能帶來的毀滅性後果。

The evolution of human civilization has, in fact, never been free from "barbarism." It is recognized that many of the inventions we enjoy today, such as airplanes, refrigerators, computers and nuclear energy, were developed from prototypes created for military purposes. The advancement of weaponry has been surprisingly rapid, from stones and bows and arrows to bullets and laser weapons. Even some cultural evolution can be viewed as connected to colonialism and imperialism through invasion. For example, the anthropological work *The Chrysanthemum and the Sword* was published out of a need for the US military to understand the sociopsychology of the Japanese as their enemy. We can see that even though we have made rapid advancements in science, technology and culture, the inherent primitive and barbaric human instincts of killing "others" are deep-rooted and difficult to efface. When cold weapons were in use, every shot of the crossbow or strike of the sword was able to kill only one or two persons; now, with the advent of nuclear weapons, the dropping of one atomic bomb can destroy a whole country. Every world leader who is in control of a "nuclear button" should be aware of what Mozi told the great King of Qi, that no matter how small the thought he had on his mind, if it was morally wrong, a simple order could lead to devastating consequences.

In today's world, a regular soldier should understand how his actions can cause casualties, and he should hold dear the value

　　同時，即使是普通的現代士兵，也要意識到自己的任何一個行為，都可能帶來傷亡，意識到同情心的重要性。在美伊戰爭、北約和南斯拉夫戰爭中，掌握了現代高科技的一方，已經可以讓坐在電腦螢幕前的士兵像玩遊戲機一樣，輕輕操縱一下滑鼠或拉杆就能發射炮火、導彈，令敵人死傷無數。在傳統的戰場上，士兵還能耳聞目睹戰爭的血與火，親身體驗戰爭的殘酷，在現代高科技戰爭中，掌握了高科技的士兵卻完全可以做到「戰爭遊戲化」、「戰爭娛樂化」。這時，如果不對士兵進行人道主義教育，不讓他們體驗生命之可貴與自己責任之重大，就不是「正義之師」。這讓我們看到，即使在這個時代，二千五百年前墨子的智慧仍舊是有啟發意義的。

八
天下之所謂可者，未必然也。

【原文】

　　子墨子謂魯陽文君曰：「攻其鄰國，殺其民人，取其牛馬、粟米、貨財，則書

of compassion. In the US-Iraqi war and the NATO-Yugoslavia war, those equipped with advanced technology were able to have soldiers sit before a computer screen and control a mouse or a lever, as if they were playing a computer game. In fact, they were actually launching bombs and missiles to cause countless casualties among the enemy. On the traditional battlefield, soldiers witness the blood and fire of war and have a first-hand experience of its cruelty. Modern technological warfare, however, enables those with advanced technology to distance themselves from the consequences. Soldiers should be taught humanitarian thinking so that they can truly appreciate the supreme value of life and understand their solemn responsibility. Without this, they can hardly serve as members of an "army of just war." Mozi's wisdom from two thousand five hundred years ago remains relevant in our time.

Eight
What the people of the whole world deem alright may turn out to be not necessarily so.

Translation:

Master Mozi said to Prince Wen of Lu Yang, "Attacking his neighboring state, killing its people, seizing its oxen and horses, grains and rice, goods and valuables, a man writes

之於竹帛，鏤之於金石，以為銘於鐘鼎，傳遺後世子孫曰：『莫若我多。』今賤人也，亦攻其鄰家，殺其人民，取其狗豕食糧衣裘，亦書之竹帛，以為銘於席豆，以遺後世子孫曰：『莫若我多。』亓可乎？」魯陽文君曰「然。吾以子之言觀之，則天下之所謂可者，未必然也』。（《魯問》）

【今譯】

墨子對魯陽文君說：「攻打鄰國，殺害它的人民，掠取它的牛馬、粟米、貨財，把事跡書寫在竹帛上，鏤刻在金石上，銘記在鐘鼎上，傳給後世子孫說：『戰果沒有人比我多！』現在那些下賤人，也攻擊他的鄰家，殺害鄰家的人口，掠取鄰家的狗、豬、食、糧、衣服、被子，也書寫在竹帛上，銘記在席子和食器上，傳給後世子孫，說『戰果沒有人比我多！』難道可以嗎？」魯陽文君說：「對。我從您的觀點來看，天下人所說可以的事，就不一定正確了。」

【時析】

在人類歷史上，對於戰爭，在參與的各方（尤

his deeds on bamboo slips, engraves them on metals and stones, carves them on bells and *dings* [cauldrons], passing the message to his descendants: 'No one has ever possessed more than I do.' Now, there is a despicable man, who also attacks his neighbors, kills other people, seizes others' dogs and pigs, food and clothes, and then writes his deeds on bamboo slips, engraves them on furniture and bowls, passing the message to his descendants: 'No one has ever possessed more than I do.' Does this sound right?"

Prince Wen of Lu Yang said, "Indeed, if I take your words and see things from your viewpoint, what the people of the whole world deem alright may turn out to be not necessarily so." ("Lu Wen")

Contemporary interpretation:

In many wars throughout human history, participating parties (especially the adversaries) have written very differently about the facts as well as the war's evaluation. This has given rise to the "Rashomon effect" — the unreliable eyewitness — in history writing. During the difficult time of the Spring and Autumn period in which Mozi lived, the vassal states frequently attacked each other; however, huge variations exist in different states' historical records of each of these wars. Mozi was a diligent and knowledgeable man, and his breadth of knowledge was no less than that of Confucius. However,

其敵對方）書寫的歷史記載中，從事實到評價，往往會有天壤之別，形成「歷史書寫的羅生門」。墨子身處春秋亂世，各國互相攻伐，關於每次戰爭，各國的書寫自然差異很大。墨子是一個勤於讀書的人，知識淵博，不亞於孔子。在歷史書方面，孔子主要是讀過《魯春秋》，墨子卻讀過《百國春秋》，即當時各國的歷史書，因此能夠看出各國歷史書寫在立場、角度、價值上的局限性和問題，這使他能夠成為一個突破國家主義、地方主義等各種偏見和偏執的人，能夠從「上帝之眼」（天志）的高度來俯視各種集團「集體的罪」的偉大思想家。之後的莊子，通過「盜亦有道」的故事，嘲諷竊國者的「仁義禮智」道德倫理，其實是強盜邏輯，成為他們搶劫別人的利器。

在西方，對國家民族之類「集體的罪」的表達，要到奧古斯丁（354-430）那裏才達到最清晰的程度。奧古斯丁認為，皇帝不過是像海盜頭子一樣而已，哪裏有道德可言呢！皇帝所帶領下的全國人民，由於他們所愛的不過是金錢、權力、虛榮這類世俗目標，因此，整個國家也不過是一群俗物，跟上帝所要求的絕對的愛的命令（愛神

Confucius mainly read his history from *Lu's Spring and Autumn Annals*, the official chronicle of the State of Lu, while Mozi read the more comprehensive *Spring and Autumn of a Hundred States*, that is, a history compendium from different states at the time. Mozi was therefore able to recognize the limitations and issues that arose from different states' stances, perspectives and values. This enabled him to become a great thinker who transcended the bias and prejudice of statism and localism, etc. and could identify the "collective sin" of different groups from "the viewpoint of God" (heaven's will) above.

Another Chinese thinker Zhuangzi, by telling the story of "The Way is there among thieves," ridiculed those who stole the country over their ethics of "benevolence, righteousness, propriety and wisdom." He asserted that the ethics are actually handy weapons to rob others.

In the West, the "collective sin" of a state or a nation was given the most assertive statement only when it came to St Augustine (354-430), who regards the king as the wicked pirate chief and devoid of any morality! In turn, the people that the king leads are only driven by secular desires like money, power and vanity. Therefore, the whole country is merely a herd of vulgar people, who can never come any closer to fulfilling the absolute Command of Love (to love God and love people) as mandated by God.

愛人）相差太遠。

　　墨子根據他自己的閱讀和閱歷，早已領悟到歷史書寫的不可靠性，他更從「天志」的高度，看出在一時一地的一國，即使其全體人民有所謂「共識」（如歷史共識），這個「共識」也可能是違背天意的。從墨子的這個思想，我們可以看到，墨子不太可能像孟子那樣，以「天視自我民視，天聽自我民聽」說「民本論」，因為在墨子看來，天不會出錯，而人民卻會出錯，天是天，民是民，天雖然會關心人民的終極利益，人民卻並不總是能跟天一致的。墨子的「尊天」，就是首先尊重「天」的獨立性和客觀性，而不把「天」化約為「民」。這使他能夠站在「天志」的高度上來衡量人類歷史的得失，他的目光確實是非常長遠的。

Grounded in his extensive reading and experience, Mozi was doubtful about the authenticity of history books. Furthermore, he saw from the lofty perspective of "heaven's will" and recognized that even if all of the people could come to a "consensus" (like a historical consensus), given the particularity in time, region or state, such a "consensus" might still be against "heaven's will." With Mozi's view on this in mind, we can see that it would be impossible for Mozi (unlike Mencius) to come to any kind of "people-oriented philosophy" that claims, "Heaven sees through my people's sight, heaven hears through my people's ears." Because for Mozi, heaven never makes mistakes, whereas people often do. Heaven is heaven and people are people, and even though heaven does care about the ultimate interests of people, people do not always share heaven's view.

Mozi placed emphasis on the "respect for heaven" because he saw heaven as having an independent and objective existence, and therefore did not equate "heaven" with "people." This enabled him to take the lofty perspective of "heaven's will" from which the gains and losses in human history can be evaluated. He was really a man of foresight.

民主集中 Democratic Centralization

一

歸國寶，不若獻賢而進士。

【原文】

入國而不存其士，則亡國矣。見賢而不急，則緩其君矣。非賢無急，非士無與慮國，緩賢忘士而能以其國存者，未曾有也。

臣下重其爵位而不言，近臣則喑，遠臣則喑，怨結於民心，諂諛在側，善議障塞，則國危矣。桀紂不以其無天下之士邪？殺其身而喪天下。故曰：「歸國寶，不若獻賢而進士。」（《親士》）

【今譯】

治國而不優待賢士，國家就會滅亡。見到賢士而不急於任用，就是對國君的怠慢。沒有比用賢士更急迫的了，若沒有賢士，就沒有人和自己謀劃國事。怠慢賢士，忽視人才，而能使國家長治久安的，還不曾有過。

如果臣下只以爵祿為重，不對國事發表意

One

Instead of offering state treasures, it would be better to recommend the capable and promote the knowledgeable.

Translation:

If a man governs a state but does not value those who are knowledgeable, he will ruin his state. If a man knows a person to be capable but does not speedily recruit him, he will be ignoring his ruler. Nothing is more urgent than having capable people in government. Without knowledgeable people in a man's midst, there will be no one with whom he can discuss matters of the state. There has never been any state that can govern well if it disregards those who are capable and ignores the knowledgeable.

If ministers and their subordinates only care about their rank and position and do not speak up, then those close at hand will remain silent, while those far away will simply sigh. When grievances accumulate in people's hearts, sycophants gather around and good advice is suppressed; then the state will be in danger. Was it not the case that Jie and Zhou failed to get knowledgeable people from the wider world to work for them? As a consequence, they were killed and lost the

見，近臣緘默不言，遠臣閉口暗歎，怨氣就會
鬱結於民心。阿諛奉承之人圍在身邊，好的建
議被阻塞，那國家就危險了。桀、紂不正是因
為沒有天下賢士嗎？結果遭到殺身之禍，失去
天下。所以說：贈送國寶，不如舉薦賢士，提
拔人才。

【時析】

　　墨子呼籲重視人才，不僅對春秋時期處於競
爭與戰爭狀態的各諸侯國有着生死攸關的重要意
義，即使對今天的人們來說也是一個重要的提
醒。二十一世紀的國與國之間、公司與公司之間
的競爭，說到底就是人才資源的競爭。但是如何
招攬人才、用好人才、讓人才能夠盡呈其才，裏
面卻大有學問。

　　「蘋果」創始人喬布斯去世後，關於他的傳
記、回憶、言說一時紛紜而至。一些地方的領
袖也表示要培養喬布斯式的「創新型人才」，
這大概跟「蘋果」創新所帶動的整個龐大的產
業有關，它給美國帶來了巨大的利潤和利益。
要打造喬布斯式的創造性人才，需要必要的「軟

world. Hence it is said, "Instead of offering state treasures, it would be better to recommend the capable and promote the knowledgeable." ("Qin Shi")

Contemporary interpretation:

Mozi made a call to value talented people. This advice was not only important for the survival of the vassal states during the Spring and Autumn period when they were constantly competing with each other and fighting wars, it remains good advice for the present day. In the twenty-first century, the competition between countries and corporations is in the end a competition for people of talent. However, it is not an easy task to attract people of talent, to enable them to use their talents well and to allow them to excel.

Since the passing away of Steve Jobs, the founder of Apple, many biographies and memoirs about him and much hearsay continue to circulate. Leaders of some regions in the world express their wish to nurture "Jobsian" innovative talents. This may be the result of the enormous impetus that Apple provided to drive a vast tech industry. Indeed, it has brought huge profit and commercial interests to the United States. In order to nurture Jobsian innovative talents, there has first to be a "soft environment"; such talents cannot be produced overnight by command of the government, not even with a massive investment. An approach of this sort will only be

環境」，而不是政府一聲令下，投入鉅資就能成批造成的，那樣做往往只是造成金錢的巨大浪費，是傳統的「計劃經濟」、「計劃學術」這類「官僚行為」的延伸。倘保留着十九世紀俄國、德國式的「書報檢查制」，如果人人寫文章之前先得來一個自我審查，小心謹慎，生怕哪一句話「犯忌」惹禍，這種「軟環境」叫人怎麼能成為「人才」呢？給人們言論自由，綻放他們的才能與熱情，那才是真正的「盡其才」，發揮其創造性呢。

二

天地不昭昭，大水不潦潦，大火不燎燎，王德不堯堯者，乃千人之長也。

【原文】

故雖有賢君，不愛無功之臣；雖有慈父，不愛無益之子。是故不勝其任而處其位，非此位之人也；不勝其爵而處其祿，

a substantial waste of money, repeating the same mistakes made in the past by "bureaucratic behaviors" — as seen in the "planned economy" and "planned scholarship." If we continue to use the same "system of publication inspection" as the Russians and Germans adopted in the nineteenth century, everyone will be on his guard. Then whenever someone wants to write something, he will self-censor his words, fearing that they might "violate the taboo" and thus create trouble for himself. How can this sort of "soft environment" enable one to excel as "man of talent"? People should be given freedom of speech so that they can freely exercise their talents and passions. This is the proper way to allow them to "excel in their talents" and make good use of their creativity.

Two

Heaven and earth may not shine, the water of the great river may not be abundant, the flames of the great fire may not be blazing, the virtue of the king may not be so outstanding even when he is made the leader of thousands of people.

Translation:
Even a good ruler will not love a minister who makes no

非此祿之主也。良弓難張，然可以及高入深；良馬難乘，然可以任重致遠；良才難令，然可以致君見尊。是故江河不惡小谷之滿己也，故能大。聖人者，事無辭也，物無違也，故能為天下器。是故江河之水，非一源之水也。千鎰之裘，非一狐之白也。夫惡有同方取不取同而已者乎？蓋非兼王之道也。是故天地不昭昭，大水不潦潦，大火不燎燎，王德不堯堯者，乃千人之長也。其直如矢，其平如砥，不足以覆萬物，是故溪陝者速涸，逝淺者速竭，墝埆者其地不育。王者淳澤不出宮中，則不能流國矣。（《親士》）

【今譯】

即使有賢君，也不會愛無功之臣；即使有慈父，也不會愛無益之子。所以，凡是不能勝任其事而佔據這一位置的，就不應居於此位；凡是不勝任其爵而享受這一俸祿的，就不當享有此祿。良弓不容易張開，但能射得高沒得深；良馬難以駕馭，但能載得重行得遠；好的人才難以支使，但可以使國君受人尊重。

contribution. Even a caring father will not love a son who does no good. Hence, if one is not capable of doing the job required of the position he occupies, he should not take up that position; if one does not deserve the honor granted to the salary he receives, he should not accept the salary. A good bow is hard to draw, yet it can shoot high and penetrate deep. A good horse is hard to ride, yet it can carry heavy burdens and go far. A talented person is hard to command, yet he can make a ruler a well-respected one. In the same way, rivers do not mind having little streams flow into them so they can become great. The sage is one who never refuses a task, never acts against the way things are, and so he becomes an instrument for the world. Similarly, the water in a river does not come from just one source; the fur used for a priceless coat does not come from just one fox pelt. Who [a sage] would ignore those who share the same principles with him and listen only to those who always favor his views? This is not the way a king would take if he wished to unify the world. Therefore, heaven and earth may not shine, the water of the great river may not be abundant, the flames of the great fire may not be blazing, the virtue of the king may not be so outstanding, even when he is made the leader of thousands of people. If one is straight like an arrow, flat like a whetstone, then he cannot embrace all the things of the world. As a result, the little streams will quickly dry up, the shallow channels will soon be drained, and plants will not grow on the hard and barren land. If the king's

　　所以，江河不嫌小溪的水注入自己，才能成
其大。聖人遇事不推辭，處理事情不違背常理，
所以能成為治理天下的英才。所以江河的水，並
非一個源頭所能匯成；價值千金的狐白裘皮衣，
並非一隻狐狸腋下的白毛皮所能做成。哪裏有將
同道的人拋開不用，只用苟同於自己的人的道理
呢？這不是統一天下的君王的原則。所以大地未
必經常光明，大水並不永遠清澈，大火並不長燃
不熄，君王的德行並非高不可攀，才能做千萬人
的首領。如果只是像箭一樣直，像磨刀石一樣平，
那就不能覆蓋萬物了。所以狹窄的小溪乾得快，
平淺的水流枯得早，堅硬貧瘠的土地不長五穀。
君王的深恩厚澤如果不出宮中，就不能流遍全
國。

【時析】
　　墨子已經注意到，優異的人才往往自信，有
個性，甚至有些「怪癖」，不好相處，這時做「老
闆」的，從集體的利益出發，就一定要能「忍」，
除了忍受他們的個性外，還要忍受他們的批評，
合理的批評就接受，有缺點就改正，「有容乃
大」，如此才能把事業做大。「老闆」自己倒不

kindness and blessings do not issue from his palace, they cannot flow through the whole state. ("Qin Shi")

Contemporary interpretation:

Mozi was aware that talented people were often self-assured, of strong personality and even sometimes "eccentric." They were not easy to get along with, so whoever became their "boss" needed to prioritize the collective interest and be "tolerant" of them. He had to put up with not just their strong personalities but also their criticisms and to accept sensible criticism and rectify his own shortcomings. It is important to be "tolerant and open" in order to foster the development of any collective enterprise. Yet it is not necessary for "the boss" himself to be outstanding in his profession. He needs, instead, to be tolerant and open to different opinions, and be capable of making the right decisions. Any specific tasks outside his expertise he should entrust to specialists.

The ancient Chinese gained much experience and wisdom on matters of human resource management. Liu Bei was not as accomplished as Guan Yu and Zhang Fei in fighting battles, neither was he more sophisticated than Zhuge Liang and Pang Tong in reasoning. Liu Bei, however, was virtuous, tolerant and showed respect for capable and knowledgeable people. Because of this he was able to win people over with his virtues and gain support from them all. This enabled him

一定要在專業上拔尖，他只要在管理上相容並蓄，聽取不同的意見，做出正確的決策就可以，具體的事讓各個專才去做就行了。

關於管理人才，中國古代的經驗和智慧倒是不少。劉備的武功比不上關羽、張飛，文才比不上諸葛亮、龐統，但是劉備有德，能寬容，能禮賢下士，以德服人，得到大家擁戴，因此才能創立蜀國。《水滸傳》中的造反派頭領宋江，自己沒甚麼本事，手下個個武藝都比他厲害，也各有個性，但他能夠領導他們，這是因為他是「及時雨」，總是在英雄們落難時伸出援手幫助他們，享有聲望，並能協調他們之間的關係。

唐太宗統治時的唐朝，是中國不可多得的「盛世」，一個重要原因，就是因為唐太宗用好的人才，讓天下英雄，都進入了他的彀中。無論漢人還是胡人，唐太宗都能一視同仁，有才能者委以重任。他還能虛心納諫，以人為鏡，魏徵、房玄齡也都積極進諫，有時即使令唐太宗很生氣，也直言相諫。這樣，唐太宗做到了「兼聽則明」，消除了「偏聽則暗」，正反意見都能聽取，

to establish the state of Shu. In *Shui Hu Zhuan*, Sung Jiang, the leader of the rebels, was not particularly good at anything and his subordinates were all more skilled in martial arts and had strong personalities, yet he was able to become their leader because he was the "timely rain" to everyone, always giving a hand to the heroes whenever they got into trouble. He therefore earned his reputation and became a mediator between them. The Tang dynasty under the governance of Emperor Taizhong was a "prosperous era" rarely seen in the history of China; one important reason for this is that Emperor Taizhong made best use of talented people, so that all the heroes of the world were recruited into his camp. Whether a man was a true Han or from non-Han northern tribes, Emperor Taizhong treated them alike; he would entrust whoever was capable with important jobs. He was also modest and receptive to criticism, taking others' views as a mirror for himself. Officials such as Wei Zheng and Fang Xuanling were earnest and honest critics at the time, pushing home their points, despite there being times when Emperor Taizhong was upset by their criticisms. In this way, Emperor Taizhong was capable of being "attentive to different opinions and being enlightened." He avoided becoming "attentive to biased opinions and having his mind obscured." In other words, he was prepared to listen to positive and negative comments and make his decisions based upon a comprehensive understanding of a situation.

在全面瞭解實情的基礎上做出正確的決策。

墨子對於治理者的要求，是要有「治德」，即治理才能，即政治公德。他沒有說治理者要在個人道德上多麼完善（像後來的儒家那樣），要在專業技術上多麼高超，他理想中的治理者是能夠相容並包、「和而不同」的人，具備「寬容心」的「自由主義」的味道。

三
夫尚賢者，政之本也。

【原文】

　　子墨子言曰：「今者王公大人為政於國家者，皆欲國家之富，人民之眾，刑政之治，然而不得富而得貧，不得眾而得寡，不得治而得亂，則是本失其所欲，得其所惡，是其故何也？」子墨子言曰：「是在王公大人為政於國家者，不能以尚賢事能為政也。是故國有賢良之士眾，則國家之治厚，賢良之士寡，則國家之治薄。故大

Mozi considered it obligatory for a state governor to possess a "governing virtue," meaning a competence to govern, or political virtue. He did not talk about how morally good a governor had to be (like the later Confucians), nor did he ask him to be exceptionally skillful and professional. In his view, the ideal governor was tolerant and inclusive, preserved "harmony in diversity," and was "broad-minded" and "liberal."

Three
Valuing virtuous people is the essence of governance.

Translation:
Master Mozi said, "Now, the nobles and high-ranking people who govern the states all want the states to become wealthy and populous, and to maintain good legal and political order. Yet in reality, the states have become poor rather than wealthy, they have become less populous rather than more, they have become chaotic rather than well-ordered. It seems that they have lost what they want and got what they dislike. Why is that?

"It is because the nobles and high-ranking people who govern the states fail to exalt the virtuous and to employ the capable

人之務，將在於眾賢而己。」

日：「然則眾賢之術將奈何哉？」子墨子言曰：「譬若欲眾其國之善射御之士者，必將富之，貴之，敬之，譽之，然後國之善射御之士，將可得而眾也。況又有賢良之士厚乎德行，辯乎言談，博乎道術者乎，此固國家之珍，而社稷之佐也，亦必且富之，貴之，敬之，譽之，然後國之良士，亦將可得而眾也。是故古者聖王之為政也，言曰：『不義不富，不義不貴，不義不親，不義不近。』是以國之富貴人聞之，皆退而謀曰：『始我所恃者，富貴也，今上舉義不辟貧賤，然則我不可不為義。』親者聞之，亦退而謀曰：『始我所恃者親也，今上舉義不辟疏，然則我不可不為義。』近者聞之，亦退而謀曰：『始我所恃者近也，今上舉義不避遠，然則我不可不為義。』遠者聞之，亦退而謀曰：『我始以遠為無恃，今上舉義不辟遠，然則我不可不為義。』逮至遠鄙郊外之臣，門庭庶子，國中之眾、四鄙之萌人聞之，

in governance. If a state has a lot of good officials, it will have strong governance; if a state has few good officials, it will have weak governance. Therefore, the job of high-ranking people is just to gather more virtuous people."

Someone said, "So how can one gather more virtuous people?"

Master Mozi replied, "Imagine if a ruler wants to acquire more good archers and good chariot drivers for his state, he will for sure enable them to become rich, treat them well, honor them and praise them. Then many good archers and charioteers will inevitably flock into the state. So, when there are good people who are of high moral integrity, eloquent in arguments, masterful in knowledge and skills, they should be cherished dearly as a state treasure and asset. Therefore, he should make them rich, treat them well, respect them and praise them, then numerous good people will definitely flock into the state. In the past when the sage kings ruled, they said, 'Do not make unrighteous people wealthy, do not make unrighteous people reputable, do not favor unrighteous people, do not be close to unrighteous people.' Then, when the rich and high-ranking people in the state heard this, they withdrew and deliberated, saying: 'I used to rely on my wealth and high rank, now the one above [a man's superior] upholds righteousness and does not discriminate against the poor nor the inferior; in this case, I cannot but become righteous.' Those who were close

皆競為義。是其故何也？曰：上之所以使下者，一物也，下之所以事上者，一術也。譬之富者有高牆深宮，牆立既，謹上為鑿一門，有盜人入，闔其自入而求之，盜其無自出。是其故何也？則上得要也。

「故古者聖王之為政，列德而尚賢，雖在農與工肆之人，有能則舉之，高予之爵，重予之祿，任之以事，斷予之令，曰『爵位不高則民弗敬，蓄祿不厚則民不信，政令不斷則民不畏』，舉三者授之賢者，非為賢賜也，欲其事之成。故當是時，以德就列，以官服事，以勞殿賞，量功而分祿。故官無常貴，而民無終賤，有能則舉之，無能則下之，舉公義，辟私怨，此若言之謂也。

「故古者堯舉舜於服澤之陽，授之政，天下平；禹舉益於陰方之中，授之政，九州成；湯舉伊尹於庖廚之中，授之政，其謀得；文王舉閎夭泰顛於罝罔之中，授之政，西土服。故當是時，雖在於

to the ruler also withdrew and deliberated, 'I used to rely on being close, now the one above upholds righteousness and does not discriminate against remoteness; in this case I cannot but become righteous.' Those who kept a distance also withdrew and deliberated, 'I used to think I could rely on nothing because I kept my distance, now the one above upholds righteousness and does not discriminate against distance; in this case, I cannot but become righteous.' So those officials in the remote countryside, those young people in the palace, the people of the state and those villagers living along the borders, all strived to become righteous. Why is this? It is said, 'There is only one thing that allows the one above to use his subordinates; there is only one skill that allows the subordinates to serve the one above. Take for an example, a rich man who lives within high walls and deep courts where there is only one door drilled into the wall. If a burglar made his way in, someone would close the door and search for him, and the burglar would have no way out. Why is this? Because the one above has got the key.'

"Therefore, the ancient sage kings governed by appraising morality and honoring virtues. Whether they were farmers, laborers or businessmen, if they were capable, they would be promoted, offered a high rank, rewarded with a good salary, assigned important jobs and granted the power of decision. It is said, 'If one's rank or position is not high then people will

厚祿尊位之臣，莫不敬懼而施，雖在農與工肆之人，莫不競勸而尚意。故士者所以為輔相承嗣也。故得士則謀不困，體不勞，名立而功成，美章而惡不生，則由得士也。」

是故子墨子言曰：「得意賢士不可不舉，不得意賢士不可不舉，尚欲祖述堯舜禹湯之道，將不可以不尚賢。夫尚賢者，政之本也。」（《尚賢上》）

【今譯】

墨子說：「如今王公大人治理國家，都希望國家富強，人民眾多，政治安定，但卻不得富強，反而貧困，人口不是眾多，反而減少，政治不能安定，反而混亂，完全失去了他所希望的，而得到他所厭惡的，這是甚麼原因？」墨子說：「這是因為王公大人中執政的人，不能在治理時尊崇賢人、使用能人。一個國家，如果賢良之士多，那麼國家的統治基礎就深厚；如果賢良之士少，那麼國家的統治基礎就薄弱。所以大人的急務，就是如何使賢人增多。」

not respect him; if one's salary is not high then people will not trust him; if one's decisions or orders are not final then people will not fear him.' Granting these three benefits to capable people was not intended as a gift to them, it was intended to enable them to get things done. Hence, at those times, one was ranked according to virtue, positioned according to service, rewarded according to effort, salaried according to contribution. Therefore, the officials were not always honorable, nor the people always inferior; capable people would be promoted, and incapable people would be dismissed. Righteousness was upheld, while personal resentments were dropped — this was the essence of governance.

"In the past [as examples], Yao promoted Shun from Yang of Fu Ze, entrusted him with governance, and the world was at peace. Yu promoted Yi from the central part of Yin Fang, entrusted him with governance, and the nine districts became unified. Tang promoted Yi Yin from the kitchen, entrusted him with governance, and his plans worked. King Wen promoted Hung Yao and Tai Tian among hunters and fishermen, entrusted them with governance, and the western states surrendered. Thus at that time, even those officials with high salaries and respected positions, they all served with modesty and awe; even farmers, laborers and businessmen, they were all eager to give encouragement and exalt virtue. Therefore, officials are supposed to support the ruler to inherit the state.

　　有人問：「使賢人增多的辦法是甚麼呢？」墨子說：「就好比要使一個國家善於射箭駕車的人增多，就必須使他們富裕，使他們顯貴，敬重他們，稱讚他們，然後國家善於射箭駕車的人就會增多。何況還有賢良之士，德行醇厚，口才善辯，學識廣博呢！他們確實是國家的寶貝、社稷的輔佐呀！也必須使他們富裕，使他們顯貴，敬重他們，稱讚他們，然後國家的良士也就會增多了。所以古時聖王治理政務，總要表示：『不讓不義的人富裕，不讓不義的人顯貴，不能信任不義的人，不讓不義的人接近（國君）。』所以，國內富貴的人聽到了，都退下來計議說：『當初我所依靠的是富貴，現在上面舉義而不避貧賤，那我不可不為義。』國君親信的人聽到了，也退回來計議說：『當初我所倚仗的是為國君所親信，現在上面舉義而不避疏遠，那我不可不為義。』接近國君的人聽到了，也退回來計議說：『當初我所倚仗的是與國君接近，現在上面舉義而不避遠方之人，那我不可不為義。』遠處的人聽了，也退回來計議說：『當初我以為與上面太疏遠而無所倚仗，現在上面舉義而不避遠，那我不可不為義。』一直到邊鄙郊外的臣僚，宮庭中的侍衛，

Hence, if there are good officials then one can plan without difficulty, save physical labor, win recognition and success, have good deeds known and bad things done away with. Then all are indebted to good officials."

Therefore, Master Mozi said [in finishing], "At favorable times one should not stop promoting virtuous officials, at unfavorable times one also should not stop promoting virtuous officials. If one wants to follow the Way inherited from Yao, Shun, Yu and Tang, one must not belittle the value of virtuous people. For valuing virtuous people is the essence of governance." ("Shang Xian I")

Contemporary interpretation:

Viewed from an historical perspective, democratization was a process that moved away from traditional oligarchic governance towards a governance based on the views of a majority of the people, or even all people. It gradually shifted from God-granted governance, to kingship or royal governance, then slowly to a governance with a broad base, allowing more people to participate in that governance. In medieval England, the Magna Carta transferred the rights of the king to the royal representatives of the House; later the creation of the Upper House and the House of Commons (especially the latter) made the communication between the upper and lower classes of people viable, so that the policies

城邑中的民眾，四野的農民聽了，都爭先為義。這是甚麼原因呢？這是因為君上用來支使臣下的，只有尚賢一種辦法；臣下用來侍奉君上的，也只有仁義一條途徑。就好比富人有高牆深院，牆立好了，僅只在上面開一個門，有強盜進來了，關掉他進入的那道門來捉拿他，強盜就無從逃出去了。這是甚麼原因？就在於國君抓住了要領。

「所以古時聖王為政，以德行排列位次，尊重賢能，即使是從事農業或工商業的人，只要有才能，就選拔他，給他高爵，給他厚祿，給他任務，給他決斷的權力，說：『如果爵位不高，民眾就不會尊重他；如果俸祿不厚，民眾就不會聽信他；如果沒有決斷權，民眾就不會畏懼他。』拿這三種東西給賢人，並不是對賢人予以賞賜，而是要把事情辦成。所以在這時，根據德行分封官職，根據官職處理政事，根據功勞決定賞賜，衡量各人的功勞而分配祿位。所以做官的不會永遠富貴，而民眾不會永遠貧賤。有能力的就選拔他，沒有能力的就罷黜他。出以公心，丟開私怨，說的就是這個意思。

made from above could reflect the opinions of the people from below. If we take a look at the modern electoral system, in the beginning only those gentlemen (male) with assets and status could vote. It was only later that the right to vote was gradually extended to ordinary workers, farmers, women and ethnic minorities (such as black people in the United States).

If we bear in mind this democratization process when reading "Shang Xian" in *Mozi*, we will be able to appreciate Mozi's greatness in proposing that in our choice of officials we should not care about their origins. Instead, we should recruit only capable people and entrust them with important roles.

Mozi was able to see that if a state "has a lot of good officials, the state will have strong governance; if a state has few good officials, the state will have weak governance." This is because good officials are virtuous, talented and competent, and they are also renowned people, outstanding people and excellent people from a specific region, where they always have a big group of admirers and followers (we call them "fans" nowadays). If you can gain support from them, you are at the same time gaining support from a big group of people. If these good people wholeheartedly support a ruler's policies, then their admirers and followers will also wholeheartedly support the ruler's policies. This explains why "the state will have strong governance": when the hearts of those in

「所以古時堯在服澤之陽提拔舜，將政事交給他，結果天下大治；禹在陰方之中提拔伯益，將政事交給他，結果天下統一；湯把伊尹從廚子當中提拔出來，把政事交給他，結果謀略成功；文王把閎夭、泰顛從獵人與漁夫中提拔出來，把政事交給他，結果西方諸侯都臣服了。所以在那時候，即使處在厚祿尊位的大臣，沒有一個不兢兢業業處理政事的；即使農夫工匠之輩，沒有不爭相勉勵而崇尚道德的。士是國君能憑藉他們的輔佐來繼承祖業的人。因此，得到了士，謀事就不會困難，身體就不會勞苦，功成名就，好事傳揚而惡行不生，都是因為有了士。」

所以墨子說：「得意之時不可不起用賢士，不得意之時也不可不起用賢士。如果想繼承堯舜禹湯之道，就不可不尊重賢才。尊重賢才，是政事的根本。」

【時析】

歷史地看，民主化進程就是從傳統的極少數人統治走向大多數人乃至全民統治，逐漸地由神權統治、君主統治和貴族統治，一步一步地擴大

positions of authority ("above") and those serving under them ("below") are united, the basis of the governance will be strong. In contrast, if only a few good people are involved in the political circle and the ruler can only hear the opinions of the inherited aristocratic class who in turn only care about their own interests, then the ruler will be distancing himself from a large group of good people and thus the majority of the people. As a result, the hearts of those above and those below will not unite, grievances will gradually accumulate and the basis of the governance will weaken.

Therefore, Mozi took "gathering capable people" as the critical mission for top officials, so that "the capable population can be increased" and the basis of governance can be broadened. The more capable people participate in the political game, the more stable a political regime will become.

Let's look at two of the oligarchic dictators of North Africa: Mubarak of Egypt and Gaddafi of Libya. Why did they suffer brutal deaths? Because during their long regimes they were surrounded by a close handful of family members or trusted aides who cared only for their own interests. Rarely was a good official included. Inevitably, governance gradually weakened and people's grievances inexorably rose over time.

It only needed a small flame to spark off a volcanic eruption.

統治的基礎，使更多的人參與到治理當中來。英國中世紀時期的《大憲章》將原本只屬於國王的權力擴大到貴族組成的議院，及後設立上下議院（尤其下議院）使得英國能夠溝通上下之情，上面的政策能夠反映下面的民意。就現代選舉制來說，最早能夠投票選舉的只是有財產、有身份的紳士（男性），到後來才逐步擴展到普通的工人和農民、婦女、少數民族（如在美國的黑人）。

從這個民主化過程來理解墨子《尚賢》篇中所提出的不問英雄出處（尤其階級出身），唯才是舉，委以重任的建議和措施，我們就能看出墨子的偉大之處了。

墨子看到，一個國家「賢良之士眾，則國家之治厚，賢良之士寡，則國家之治薄」。這是因為，賢良之士一般是有德性、有本事和能力，而且往往是一個地方的鄉紳、賢人、能人，他們身後總是有一大群欽佩者和追隨者（今天稱作「粉絲」），你贏得了他們的支持也就等於贏得了很多群眾的支持。如果這些賢良之士都衷心擁護國君的政策，那麼，他們的佩服者和追隨者也都會

To avoid this situation, how can "capable people be gathered" so that they can use their potentials to benefit the country? Mozi proposed four strategies: "Make them rich, treat them well, respect them and praise them." In other words, offer upright people a high salary, promote their social status, make them honorable and praise their efforts. In this way, a social ethos that values competence will form, and those who are virtuous, sensible, rational and skillful will be able to overcome their constraints in status, class, background, or locality and emerge in large numbers to serve the country in contributing to planning and policies. In view of the competitiveness of such people who have "come through the ranks," those who traditionally survived by relying on their background, wealth or relations will be obliged to improve their own conduct and capability in order to "work towards righteousness" (promote public interest). Mozi's proposal for valuing competence is all about breaking constraints based on descent, lineage, heritage and ranking, so that capable people can be recruited from a broad range of low-ranking "officials" and "outsiders." This is a means to broaden the governing foundation of a ruler while also being an important step towards democratization.

Once capable people are recruited, how can their potentials be fully utilized? Mozi suggested tangible ways to motivate them, that is, to offer them high positions, a high salary and the power of decision. Without these they could not gain the trust

心悅誠服地擁護國君的政策，所以「國家之治厚」，上下一心，統治基礎就會深厚。

反之，如果被吸納進統治圈子的賢良之士很少，國君只聽幾個世襲貴族的話，維護他們的利益，那就會脫離廣大賢良之士，也相當於脫離廣大群眾，結果是上下離心，民怨越來越多，統治基礎就會很薄弱。所以，墨子指出，當今王公大人的急務，只在「眾賢」而已，就是「擴充人才」，擴大統治基礎，讓更多的人才參與政治遊戲，使政權穩固。當代北非的幾個寡頭獨裁者，如埃及的穆巴拉克、利比亞的卡扎菲，最後為甚麼都不得善終？因為他們長期執政，身邊來來回回就那麼幾個家人和親信，只維護他們自己的利益，賢良之士很少，統治基礎越來越薄弱，人民的怨氣積壓很久了，一旦有個導火索，就會火山爆發。

那麼如何「眾賢」，使他們真正發揮才能，有益於國家呢？墨子提出了「富之，貴之，敬之，譽之」四招，就是高薪養廉，提高社會地位，享有名望。如此一來，就會形成尊重人才的社會風

of the people and would achieve nothing. For example, if they are always in the position of deputy and cannot make their own decisions, or if their predecessor always "governs from behind the curtain" for the newly appointed man, then how is it possible for subordinates to follow the new appointee's orders? They will not. It is important not to doubt a person's ability when assigning him to a task, otherwise it will be harmful for the boss as well as the employees.

Mozi proposed adopting both a "problem solving approach" — to focus on finding the best solutions to problems at hand — and a "competence-based approach" — to promote whoever is most capable for the job. In doing this, he no longer followed the traditional life-tenure system and nepotism (being respectful to honorable people and rewarding close relatives). Whoever is capable of solving problems will be promoted, and whoever fails to do so will be demoted; there is no guaranteed life-tenure. "Officials are not always honorable, and ordinary people are not always inferior," thus giving mobility to the social ladder and having no fixed classes of "children of officials," "children of the rich," "children of stars," "children of the poor," "the ants," "grassroots," etc. Once promoting the capable has become the norm, people will be motivated to try their best, and there won't be any "rent-seeking class" or the so-called "new generation of parasites" who seek nothing but their own diversion. In fact, what Mozi advocated in the idea

氣，那些有德行、有思想、有辯才、有技能的人才，就能突破地位、階級、出身、地域的局限，成批湧現出來，為國家出謀劃策做貢獻。在他們的競爭壓力下，那些以前靠着自己的出身、財富、關係混飯吃的人，也會想辦法提高自己的修養和能力，努力「為義」（增進公共利益）了。墨子的人才建議，重在打破血統、門閥、宗法、等級的限制，從廣大的低級的「士」和「賤民」階層中選拔人才，這實際上是擴大統治者的統治基礎的辦法，也是民主化過程中的重要一步。

人才選拔出來之後，如何盡其才呢？墨子提到了具體的用才之法，那就是給他們高職位、高薪水、一把手的決斷權，因為非如此不能信眾，不能把事情辦成。比如，若總是讓他們充當副職，不能說話算話，或者上一任總是在新一任後面「垂簾聽政」，那手下人還會聽他們的命令嗎？肯定不會。用人就要用而不疑，否則既害了老闆也害了人才。

墨子提出了圍繞着把事情辦好的就事論事的「唯事主義」和唯才是舉的「唯才主義」，不再

"the officials are not always rich, the people are not always inferior" is very close to the modern democratic system.

Who are those that Mozi regarded as "capable" or "good people"? Mozi mentioned three kinds of men: those who are very virtuous, those eloquent in arguments and those masterful in knowledge and skills. By "very virtuous," does he mean only personal morality, such as the virtues of propriety, righteousness, integrity and shame? According to what Mozi has said elsewhere, a virtuous person is he who "swiftly offers help to people when he has strength, devotedly shares with people when he has wealth, earnestly teaches people when he has grasped the Way," so that "those who are hungry can be fed, those who are cold can be clothed, those who work hard can find rest." Thus the "virtues" in Mozi's eyes are mainly envisaged as public virtues in the social realm, which is related to the "ethics of love" as required by his theology of "emulating heaven." Of course, the virtuous person should also give honest counsel to the ruler rather than acting as a yes-man; this may be called "public virtues in the political realm." By "eloquent in arguments," means those individuals who are good at rhetoric and argument, in particular those who are able to promote national policies and generate positive public opinions, so that people can come to a consensus and are willing to work together to make things better. By "masterful in knowledge and skills," he refers to those who are equipped

像傳統那樣搞終身制和裙帶制（親親尊尊）。誰只要有能力把事情辦好，誰就升，辦不好，就下降，沒有終身制。「官無常貴，民無終賤」，社會階級能夠上下流動，不會固化為「官二代」、「富二代」、「星二代」、「窮二代」、「蟻族」、「草民」等，只有唯才是舉，才能激發每一個人的上進心，也就不會有「食利階層」和只享安樂不做貢獻的「新生代寄生蟲」了。應當說，墨子的這種「官無常貴，民無終賤」的思想跟現代民主制是非常貼近的。

墨子所謂的「賢」或「賢良之士」，有哪些人呢？墨子提到了三類人：厚乎德行，辯乎言談，博乎道術者。「厚乎德行」，是否只是指私人道德，如禮、義、廉、恥一類道德呢？按照墨子在別處所說，一個人要有德，就要「有力者疾以助人，有財者勉以分人，有道者勸以教人」，有助於「饑者得食，寒者得衣，勞者得息」。可見墨子所說的「德」，主要是從社會公德上着眼，跟他的「法天」神學所要求的「愛的倫理」相關。當然，有德者還要對君主直言相諫，不做應聲蟲，這可以稱作「政治公德」。

with professional skills and who can produce results in a down-to-earth way. Many of the Mohists came from the grassroot classes of laborers, farmers and merchants, a lot of whom were "masterful of knowledge and skills." Many were inventors and weapon designers with one-of-a-kind talents. Mozi and Qin Hua-li are two such examples. The Mohist school's membership was radically different from that of the Confucian school, which was composed mainly of "scholars." No wonder Mozi repeatedly quoted from the classics, saying that the gifted politicians Yi Yin, Hong Yao and Tai Dian were a chef, a hunter and a fisherman.

When Mohists talk about "capable" or "good people," the "virtues" they have in mind are mainly "governance virtues" (management competence) instead of "personal virtues"; this is a bit different from the Confucians. To put it into a modern context, the moral expectations on state leaders of Confucians are more like the American evangelicals who expect the president to cherish his family, not give rise to sex scandals, have good personal conduct and be a reborn good Christian. In contrast, Mohists are more like the French and Italians who expect the president to do well in his governance of the country; as to whether he has illegitimate children or extra-marital affairs, they really don't care. Of course, owing to the overarching Western principle on the separation of powers, political power is independent of religion, meaning

「辯乎言談」，則是指口才好，有辯才，實際上當指有宣傳國家政策的能力，搞好社會輿論，讓人們產生共識，齊心協力把事情辦好。「博乎道術」，當指有各種專門技能，能踏踏實實辦實事者。墨家多出身工、農、商草根階級，他們當中「博乎道術」者為數不少，很多人都是身懷絕技的發明家和武器設計師。墨子和禽滑厘就是例子。墨家的構成，顯然跟以「士」為主體的儒家學派大異其趣。難怪墨子要反復地引經據典，說伊尹、閎夭、泰顛這些政治奇才，原先都只不過是廚子和獵戶罷了。

墨家所說的「賢」或「賢良之士」，他們的「德」主要是「治德」（管理能力）而不是「私德」，因此跟儒家有些不同。換了今天的語言說，就是在對國家領導人的道德要求上，儒家更像美國福音派，要求總統重視家庭、沒有緋聞、私德良好、是個重生了的好基督徒，而墨家更像法國和意大利人對總統的要求，你只要把國家治理好就行了，你有沒有私生子女、有沒有婚外情，我們不在乎。當然，由於西方總體上三權分立，政教分離，因此，國家元首的私德難以產生重大影

the personal conduct of the state leader has little impact on governance. Nonetheless, in some countries where theocracy and unified legislature and administration are still at work, the personal conduct of a country's leader will have a great, sometimes fatal, impact on the country. In recent years, we have witnessed how autocrats in the Middle East ended up ruining their families and being killed. Saddam Hussein, Hosni Mubarak and Muammar Gaddafi all dominated long periods of state governance, enabled their families and cronies to occupy top positions, undertook nepotistic capitalism or "socialism" and relentlessly suppressed opposition parties. By doing so they ultimately inflamed the people and brought about their own downfalls.

As proposed in "Shang Xian I", Mozi's doctrine on valuing capable people still offers a good proposal for modern-day corporate management and state politics. If we look at the historical development in China after Mozi's time, we can see how the Legalist school fully adopted Mozi's doctrine on valuing capable people. During the Qin dynasty, the Legalist school implemented a manpower policy that "promoted only those with competence," and rewarded those who made contributions. This policy broke through the original aristocratic ancestral system at the time, making Qin soldiers fearless in battle, farmers willing to exert themselves in opening up new lands, and capable and intelligent people from

響。但是，在政教合一、議行合一的國家，國家元首的私德卻會對國家產生重大的、有時是致命的影響。近幾年我們看到的中東獨裁者，之所以最後都家破人亡，如薩達姆、穆巴拉克、卡扎菲等人，跟他們長期把持國家政權、讓親友佔據重要位置、搞裙帶資本主義或「社會主義」、長期壓制反對派，導致民怨沸騰不無干係。

墨子在《尚賢上》裏提出的人才觀，對於今天的公司管理和國家政治，仍舊是有借鑒作用的。從中國後來的歷史來看，法家可以說是充分吸收了墨子的人才觀，法家在秦朝實行的人才政策，就是「唯才是舉」，論功行賞，打破了原先的貴族血統制，使得秦國士兵奮勇打仗，農民努力開闢荒田，周邊國家的才智之士爭先恐後地跑去秦國出謀獻策，為秦所用，經過數代有為國君的治理，到秦始皇時終於能一統天下。

四
天子唯能壹同天下之義，是以天下治也。

neighboring states to flock to Qin to offer counsel, wishing to be employed. After several generations of governance under accomplished rulers, Qin Shihuang (the First Emperor of Qin) was finally able to unify China.

Four

It is only the Son of Heaven who can unite the opinions of the world so that it can be run in good order.

Translation:

Master Mozi said, "In the past, when the first human beings appeared on earth, it was to a world without laws or government, so people varied in their opinions and 'everyone had different ideas.' One person would have one idea, two persons two ideas, ten persons had ten ideas; the more people there were, the more ideas there would be. People insisted on the correctness of their own ideas and rejected those of others, resulting in mutual disagreements. Fathers, sons and brothers within a family became hostile towards and estranged from each other. They could not stay peacefully together. People throughout the whole world harmed each other with water, fire and poisons. Those with strength to spare would not serve

【原文】

子墨子言曰：「古者民始生，未有刑政之時，蓋其語『人異義』。是以一人則一義，二人則二義，十人則十義，其人茲眾，其所謂義者亦茲眾。是以人是其義，以非人之義，故交相非也。是以內者父子兄弟作怨惡，離散不能相和合。天下之百姓，皆以水火毒藥相虧害，至有餘力不能以相勞，腐臭餘財不以相分，隱匿良道不以相教，天下之亂，若禽獸然。

「夫明虖天下之所以亂者，生於無政長。是故選天下之賢可者，立以為天子。天子立，以其力為未足，又選擇天下之賢可者，置立之以為三公。天子三公既以立，以天下為博大，遠國異土之民，是非利害之辯，不可一二而明知，故畫分萬國，立諸侯國君，諸侯國君既已立，以其力為未足，又選擇其國之賢可者，置立之以為正長。

「正長既已具，天子發政於天下之百

others, those with resources to spare let them rot instead of sharing them with others, those with good principles chose to hide them instead of teaching them to others. The whole world fell apart and people lived like beasts.

"Then the cause of the disorder came to light: it was the lack of governmental leadership. People searched around the whole world to select a good and capable person to become the Son of Heaven. When the Son of Heaven was appointed, only to find his strength was insufficient, good and capable people from around the world were selected to become the three Ministers. When the Son of Heaven and the three Ministers were appointed, it was realized that the world was so big that those people living in remote foreign territories were difficult to reach. It was difficult to explain to them clearly about right and wrong, and good and bad. The world was therefore divided into a multitude of states, and rulers to these states were appointed. When these state rulers were appointed but their strengths were found inadequate, good and capable people were again selected to become the top officials. When the top officials were all appointed, the Son of Heaven gave an order to the people of the world saying, 'Whenever you hear of something good or bad, report to the one above. What is judged right by the one above should be taken as right by all; what is judged wrong by the one above should be taken as wrong by all. If the one above makes any mistakes, he

姓，言曰：『聞善而不善，皆以告其上。
上之所是，必皆是之，所非必皆非之，上
有過則規諫之，下有善則傍薦之。上同而
不下比者，此上之所賞，而下之所譽也。
意若聞善而不善，不以告其上，上之所是，
弗能是，上之所非，弗能非，上有過弗規
諫，下有善弗傍薦，下比不能上同者，此
上之所罰，而百姓所毀也。』上以此為賞
罰，甚明察以審信。

「是故里長者，里之仁人也。里長
發政里之百姓，言曰：『聞善而不善，
必以告其鄉長。鄉長之所是，必皆是之，
鄉長之所非，必皆非之。去若不善言，
學鄉長之善言；去若不善行，學鄉長之
善行，則鄉何說以亂哉？』察鄉之所治
者何也？鄉長唯能壹同鄉之義，是以鄉
治也。

「鄉長者，鄉之仁人也。鄉長發政鄉
之百姓，言曰：『聞善而不善者，必以告
國君。國君之所是，必皆是之，國君之所

should be cautioned; if the subordinate does something good, he should be recommended to the one above. Those who unite with the one above and who do not form cliques with the subordinates are to be commended by the one above and praised by the subordinates. If one hears of something good or bad and does not report it to the one above, disputes what is judged as right by the one above, disputes what is judged as wrong by the one above, does not caution the one above about his mistakes, does not recommend subordinates to the one above when they are good, forms cliques with subordinates and will not unite with the one above, then he is to be punished by the one above and reprimanded by the people.' When the one above offered rewards and punishments on these grounds, they were regarded as very clear-sighted and trustworthy.

"At that time, the village chief was the benevolent man of the village. In his orders to the village people he said, 'Whenever you hear of something good or bad, report it to the district chief. What is judged right by the district chief should be taken as right by all; what is judged wrong by the district chief should be taken as wrong by all. Get rid of your bad words and learn kind words from the district chief; get rid of your bad conduct and learn good conduct from the district chief. If you do this, how can the district be in disorder?' Looking closely, what makes good governance of a district? It is only

非，必皆非之。去若不善言，學國君之善言，去若不善行，學國君之善行，則國何說以亂哉？」察國之所以治者何也？國君唯能壹同國之義，是以國治也。

「國君者，國之仁人也。國君發政國之百姓，言曰：『聞善而不善。必以告天子。天子之所是，皆是之，天子之所非，皆非之。去若不善言，學天子之善言；去若不善行，學天子之善行，則天下何說以亂哉？』察天下之所以治者何也？天子唯能壹同天下之義，是以天下治也。

「天下之百姓皆上同於天子，而不上同於天，則菑猶未去也。今若天飄風苦雨，溱溱而至者，此天之所以罰百姓之不上同於天者也。」

是故子墨子言曰：「古者聖王為五刑，請以治其民。譬若絲縷之有紀，罔罟之有綱，所連收天下之百姓不尚同其上者也。」（《尚同上》）

the district chief who can unite the opinions of the district so that it can be run in good order.

"The district chief was the benevolent man of the district. In his orders to the people of the district, the district chief said, 'Whenever you hear of something good or bad, report it to the ruler of the state. What is judged right by the ruler of the state should be taken as right by all; what is judged wrong by the ruler of the state should be taken as wrong by all. Get rid of your bad words and learn kind words from the ruler of the state; get rid of your bad conduct and learn good conduct from the ruler of the state. If you do this, how can the state be in disorder?' Looking closely, what makes good governance of a state? It is only the ruler of the state who can unite the opinions of the state so that it can be run in good order.

"The ruler of the state was the benevolent man of the state. In his orders to the people, the ruler of the state said, 'Whenever you hear of something good or bad, report it to the Son of Heaven. What is judged right by the Son of Heaven should be taken as right by all; what is judged wrong by the Son of Heaven should be taken as wrong by all. Get rid of your bad words and learn kind words from the Son of Heaven; get rid of your bad conduct and learn good conduct from the Son of Heaven. If you do this, how can the world be in disorder?' Looking closely, what makes good governance of a world?

【今譯】

墨子說：「古時人類剛誕生，還沒有刑法政治的時候，如人們所說的『意見因人而異』。所以一人有一種意見，兩人有兩種意見，十人就有十種意見。人越多，所謂意見也就越多。人人都以為自己的意見對而別人的意見錯，因而相互攻擊。

「所以家中父子兄弟間生出怨恨，家人離心，不能和睦相處。天下的百姓，都用水火毒藥相互殘害，以致有餘力者不能幫助別人，有餘財者寧願讓它腐爛也不分給別人，有好的道理也自己隱藏起來，不肯教給別人。天下亂糟糟的，有如禽獸一般。

「明白了天下大亂的原因，是由於沒有行政長官，所以人們就選擇賢能的人，立為天子。立了天子之後，因為他的力量還不夠，所以又選擇天下賢能的人，立為三公。天子和三公都立了，又認為天下地域廣大，對遠方異邦的人民以及是非利害的辨別，不能一一瞭解，所以又把天下劃分為萬國，然後設立諸侯國君。

It is only the Son of Heaven who can unite the opinions of the world so that it can be run in good order.

"If the people of the whole world unite with the Son of Heaven and yet are not united with heaven itself, then we are not yet done away with hazards. Now suppose violent storms and heavy rains keep hammering down from heaven, they should be interpreted as the way heaven punishes the people for not uniting with heaven."

Hence, Master Mozi said, "In the past, the sage kings established the five penal codes in order to govern the people. Resembling how threads of silk are tied into skeins, or how the fishing net is fastened to a rope, they are used to tighten the grip on those people who do not unite with the one above." ("Shang Tong I")

Contemporary interpretation:

Mozi's "Shang Xian" has received almost unanimous commendation from modern readers, but his "Shang Tong" has caused endless controversies.

The first question up for discussion is from this passage: "the cause of the disorder came to light — it was the lack of governmental leadership. So, people searched around the whole world and selected a good and capable person to

「諸侯國君已立，又因為他們的力量還不夠，就在他們國內選擇一些賢能的人，立為行政長官。行政長官設立之後，天子就向天下的百姓發佈政令，說：『你們聽到善和不善的，都要報告給上面。上面認為對的，大家必須認為對；上面認為錯的，大家必須認為錯。上面有過失，就應該規諫，下面有好人好事，就應當推薦給國君。是非與上面相同，而不與下面結黨，這是上面所讚賞，下面所稱譽的。假如聽到善與不善，卻不向上面報告；上面認為對的，也不認為對，上面認為錯的，也不認為錯；上面有過失不能規諫，下面有好人好事不能向上面推薦；與下面結黨而不與上面一致，這是上面所要懲罰，也是百姓所要非議的。』上面根據這些方面來行使賞罰，就必然十分審慎、可靠。

「所以里長就是這一里之內的仁人。里長發佈政令於里中的百姓，說：『聽到善和不善的，必須報告給鄉長。鄉長認為對的，大家都必須認為對；鄉長認為錯的，大家都必須認為錯。去掉你們不好的話，學習鄉長的好話；去掉你們不好的行為，學習鄉長的好行為。那麼，鄉里怎麼會

become the Son of Heaven." So, what is meant by "selected"? Does it mean selected "by popular vote" among the people, or through other means, like being "selected" from "heaven's will"? In that case, it would be impossible to have "democracy by vote" as we do nowadays, so we should not expect the Son of Heaven to be "selected by popular vote."

Since Mozi talked a lot about the governance of the sage kings of the past, we can draw on his other writings for reference.

In "Fa Yi" it is said, "The sage kings of the past — Yu, Tang, Wen and Wu — loved the people of the world. They took the lead in worshipping heaven and paying tributes to the spirits and in doing so benefited a lot of people. Heaven therefore blessed them and appointed them as the Sons of Heaven." In "Shang Xian II" we have, "In the past, the Three Dynasties' sage kings — Yao, Shun, Yu and Tang — loved the people of the world, they took the lead in worshipping heaven and paying tributes to the spirits and benefited a lot of people; therefore heaven blessed them and appointed them as the Sons of Heaven." "Tian Zhi III" states, "In the past, the sage kings — Yao, Shun, Yu, Tang, Wen and Wu — loved the world all-embracingly... because they loved what it loved and benefited what it would benefit. Heaven thus bestowed them with awards, put them in superior positions and appointed them as the Sons of Heaven."

說混亂呢？』考察這一鄉得到治理，其原因是甚麼呢？是由於唯有鄉長能夠統一全鄉的意見，所以鄉就治理好了。

「鄉長是這一鄉的仁人。鄉長發佈政令於鄉中百姓，說：『聽到善和不善的，必須把它報告給國君。國君認為對的，大家都必須認為對；國君認為錯的，大家都必須認為錯。去掉你們不好的話，學習國君的好話；去掉你們不好的行為，學習國君的好行為。』那麼，國家怎麼能說混亂呢？考察一國得到治理，其原因是甚麼呢？是因為國君能統一全國的意見，所以國家就治理好了。

「國君，是這一國的仁人。國君向全國百姓發佈政令，說：『聽到善和不善的，必須報告給天子。天子認為對的，大家都必須認為對；天子認為錯的，大家都必須認為錯。去掉你們不好的話，學習天子的好話，去掉你們不好的行為，學習天子的好行為。』那麼，天下怎麼能說混亂呢？考察天下治理得好，其原因是甚麼呢？是因為天子能夠統一天下人民的意見，所以天下就治理好了。

It is clear from these passages that Mozi believed that Yao, Shun, Yu, Tang, Wen and Wu were appointed as the Sons of Heaven because they acted in accordance to "heaven's will"; they practiced the policy of "three beneficences" (serving the interests of heaven, the spirits and men) and loved all-embracingly the whole world. They were therefore recognized and adored by heaven to the extent that heaven endorsed and appointed them as "the Sons of Heaven." Apparently, this was a kind of "heavenly endowed sovereignty." According to Mozi, "heaven" is an entity with intentions, emotions and the power to judge and enact rewards and punishments, and "the Son of Heaven" is the person who can grasp, understand and implement "heaven's will." So "the Son of Heaven" is actually the one who unites the state and the religion, connecting the religious authority with the political authority, in other words, uniting the role of the ruler with the teacher. For example, as the Son of Heaven, Tang of the Shang dynasty was reprimanded by heaven through a seven-year drought for his failures; he had to admit to these and prayed for rain in the mulberry woods. This is an example that illustrates theocracy in practice in the past. Mozi approved highly of "the deeds of the sage kings of the past" and even took them as one of his "three exemplars"; it follows therefore that he also thought highly of the power of such a theocracy that united the role of the ruler and the teacher to create "good man politics" or "philosopher king politics."

「天下的老百姓都向上統一於天子。如果不向上統一於天，那麼災禍還不能完全去掉。假如現在天刮着大風，下着暴雨，頻頻而至，就可以視為上天在懲罰那些不向上統一於天的百姓。」

所以墨子說：「古時聖王制定五種刑法，用來治理人民，就好比絲線有紀（絲頭的總束）、網罟有綱一樣，是用來收緊那些不向上統一於上級的老百姓的。」

【時析】

墨子的《尚賢》在現代幾乎得到了眾口一詞的稱讚，他的《尚同》卻引起了不斷的爭議。

第一個問題，「天下之所以亂者，生於無政長。是故選天下之賢可者，立以為天子」。這裏的「選」，到底是老百姓自己「民選」出來的，還是以別的方式，比如靠「天」的意志「選」出來的？當時還不可能有今天的「票選民主」，因此天子不太可能是「民選」出來的。墨子喜歡談古聖王時代的政事，我們要參考他在別的地方的說法。

During the Republican years of China, as also nowadays, some scholars (such as Feng Youlan) have accused Mozi of advocating theocratic politics. They are not without grounds. The problem is how do we understand what Mozi meant in concrete terms when he said "the Son of Heaven" should unite with "heaven," in other words, with "heaven's will"?

The second question we face is, what was Mozi attempting when he talked of a level-by-level centralization of power towards the Son of Heaven? Was he advocating an autocratic dictatorship? If we look into Mozi's original intentions, we will know that in writing "Shang Tong" he wanted to identify the causes behind the chaotic situation brought about during the Spring and Autumn period by inter-state rivalry, as well as the battles between different schools of thought. He believed that the root of the problem rested with the nobles and high-ranking people who betrayed the moral leadership of the past and sought only to satisfy their private interests (had their own ideas). In doing so, they formed interest groups and ignored the common interest of society, thus causing confrontation and chaos between the superior and subordinate groups. Mozi hoped to reconnect the two: to inform the superiors of what happens below, and to enable orders from the superiors to be duly executed by the subordinates, so that the world could be run smoothly and peacefully. Mozi took "heaven's will" as the ultimate ground that justified political legitimacy. He claimed

《法儀》說：「昔之聖王禹湯文武，兼愛天下百姓，率以尊天事鬼，其利人多，故天福之，使立為天子。」《尚賢中》說：「昔三代聖王堯舜禹湯，兼愛天下之百姓，率以尊天事鬼，其利人多，故天福之，使立為天子。」《天志下》說：「昔也三代之聖王堯舜禹湯文武之兼愛天下也……天以為從其愛而愛之，從其所利而利之，於是加其賞焉，使之處上位，立為天子。」

可見，在墨子看來，堯舜禹湯文武這些人能夠被立為「天子」，是因為他們順「天志」而行，實行「三利」政策（利天利鬼利人），兼愛天下，因此得到了天的認可和寵愛，天承認並立他們為「天子」（天的兒子）。無疑，這是「君權天授」論。

由於墨子的「天」是有意志、有情感、能進行審判賞罰的「天」，而「天子」則必須領會、體悟並執行「天意」，因此，「天子」的身份實際上是政教合一，政權與教權合一，或者說，君師合一。比如，商湯作為「天子」，在「天」降七年旱災以示他犯了錯誤時，便要在桑林認罪祈

that if "the Son of Heaven" could follow heaven's will, then his orders could be followed and executed respectively by the rulers of the states, the district chiefs, the village chiefs, as well as by individuals. The whole world would then be united with just one idea, and everyone could "emulate heaven": when people can love each other all-embracingly and serve in each other's interests, the world will become a human paradise. This original idea was of Mozi's conception.

However, in reality would this create an opportunity for autocratic dictatorship? Certainly. First, "the Son of Heaven" himself could be a problem. If we say the first two generations of Sons of Heaven during the Xia, Shang and Zhou dynasties were able to respect heaven and love their people, when it came to the third and fourth generations, they were already losing their grip on "heaven" and "people"; therefore, it would be an unlikely option to invest in them the hope of creating a human paradise. Besides, even though Mozi claimed that it is "the will of heaven" to have people love each other and act in mutual interest, whether the Sons of Heaven would agree with him is yet another question. What is more, even if they acknowledge the potential of the idea, in practice they may not be able to carry it through, or attain Mozi's intended standards. It also begs the question of how did the Sons of Heaven receive their orders from heaven? If we look at the stories of the "sage kings of the past," they often took severe draughts or torrential

雨，這是古代政教合一的例證。

墨子對於「古者聖王之事」極為贊同，列為他的「三表」之一，因此，他對於這種政教合一、君師合一的「賢人政治」、「哲學王政治」是贊同的。民國時期和現代有些學者（如馮友蘭）指責墨子搞神權統治，也不是完全沒有根據。問題在於如何理解墨子所說的「天子」上同於「天」的具體內容，即「天意」到底為何。

第二個問題，墨子要將權力一層層集中到天子那裏，是不是要搞專制獨裁？從墨子的本意來說，他寫《尚同》是針對春秋列國相爭、各家相殘的亂象，認為其根源在於當時王公大人反古聖賢之道，各有私利（各有一義），結成利益集團，不顧社會整體利益，從而陷入上下不同義的亂局。

墨子希望能打通上下，下情上達，上令下行，以使天下暢通平和。墨子以「天志」為政治合法性的最終根據，認為如果「天子」能順天之意，其令能得到國王、鄉長、里長、個人的一級級的

storms as signs of warning or judgment of what they did. And yet as Confucius said, "How does heaven speak? How does heaven speak?" There is always a degree of mystery involved in the particular rewards and punishments taken as being conferred by heaven. The interpretations of "heaven" by "the Sons of Heaven" involve such a degree of subjectivity that any of the attempts to understand heaven's will this way can easily go wrong. If all the powers are put into the hands of the Son of Heaven, the chances for him to make mistakes or to abuse his position of power are just too high. So much so that it would be difficult to prevent him from pursuing an autocratic dictatorship.

In view of this, did Mozi come up with any effective solution to keep the Son of Heaven's power under control? First of all, Mozi considered that ultimate power was not "united with" the Son of Heaven but united with "heaven." In other words, heaven always existed above the Son of Heaven. We may also draw from what Mozi said in "Fa Tian": "Among men, neither the rulers, the parents, nor the teachers deserve to be emulated because benevolent ones are rare, and they often make mistakes and create problems." Therefore, from Mozi's point of view, the Son of Heaven does not own any ultimate status, and Mohism does not advocate "idolatry," neither does it support centralization of power upon the Son of Heaven. When heaven causes natural disasters like droughts,

聽從和執行，天下一義，那麼，人人都能「法天」——兼相愛、交相利，人間就變成樂土了。這是墨子的本意。

但是，在客觀上，會不會有專制獨裁的可能？當然有。首先，「天子」就往往出問題。如果說夏商周的第一代第二代天子可能還敬天愛民，到第三代第四代可能就跟「天」和「民」脫節了，因此，把建設人間樂土的希望繫在他們身上，很不保險。另外，雖然墨子認為「天志」就是希望人們兼相愛、交相利，但天子是否也認為「天志」就是如此，就成問題了，有時他們雖然認識到了，在實踐時也可能半途而廢或者根本達不到墨子的標準。

還有，天子如何得到天的命令呢？從「古者聖王」的事跡來看，他們往往是通過天大旱、天大雨來判斷天是在警告和審判自己，但正如孔子所說，「天何言哉，天何言哉」，天的具體賞罰常常帶有神秘性，「天子」對「天」的解讀，實在太具有主觀性了，這很容易導致天子在領會天意時出錯誤。倘若人間大權都集中在天子那裏，

rainstorms or plagues, etc., the Son of Heaven should be on the alert because these are warnings from heaven asking him to confess and pray to heaven, and reflect upon the mistakes he made in his governance as well as his attitude towards the people. He must mend his ways to regain heaven's love. Thus, Mozi put constraints on the Son of Heaven with "heaven." Yet does "the Son of Heaven" alone own the right to communicate with and interpret "heaven"? Has he become the "sole connection with heaven" so that other people are excluded from interacting with "heaven"? Mozi offered no answers to these questions.

If we refer to the Old Testament, we will see that even when David and Solomon became the kings of the Israeli people, the prophets at the time kept criticizing, counseling and restraining them. These "prophets" were able to communicate with God, so when God was not satisfied with David or Solomon, He would send messages to the prophets and ask them to criticize the kings, reveal their wrongs and persuade them to mend their ways. This means that in the past in Israel, the state and the religion were separate, the ruler and the teacher were independent of each other. Even David and Solomon, who had both been endorsed by God (they had been anointed with oil) and were conferred with "divine sovereignty," did not solely own the rights to communicate with and interpret God as they were not the one and only "Son of Heaven."

天子犯錯誤和濫用權力的機會實在太大了,很難保證他就不會搞專制獨裁。

那麼,墨子是不是想到了制約天子權力的辦法?這些辦法會不會有效果呢?首先,墨子並未將最終權力「上同」於天子,而是上同於「天」,就是說,在天子之上還有天。結合墨子在《法天》中所說的,人間的君、親、師不足以為法,因為他們當中仁者寡,而且經常犯錯誤出問題,所以,天子對於墨子來說並不具有終極地位,墨家對天子並沒有搞「偶像崇拜」,也談不上權力一統於天子。

當天降大旱、大澇、瘟疫等災害時,天子就要小心了,因為這是天在警告他,他一定要悔罪、向天祈禱,反省執政的錯誤、對待百姓的態度,以修改錯誤,挽回天寵。墨子用「天」來制約天子,但「天子」是不是壟斷了對「天」的溝通權和解釋權?是不是「絕地天通」,不讓其他人染指與「天」的交流?墨子對此沒有說明。

如果看一下《舊約》就會發現,大衛、所羅

Mozi however saw the "sage kings," such as Tang of the Shang dynasty, as those who united the state and religion, as well as having the roles of ruler and teacher. Can we say that Mozi failed to assign someone who would function like the "prophets" — someone who could monitor, correct, criticize and caution the Son of Heaven? No! As seen from the passage, the Son of Heaven ordered people to "caution the one above when he makes mistakes," so if "a mistake made by the one above" is recognized but is not acted upon, the subordinate witnessing it should be punished and be reprimanded by others. This clearly shows that the level-by-level progression of "unity" makes it obligatory for subordinates to point out the mistakes of their superiors, and this necessarily involves monitoring the Son of Heaven.

In "Qin Shi" and "Shang Xian," Mozi made daring to criticize one of the requirements of the "capable official." He spoke against ministers who had a servile attitude to the ruler, and he considered the existence of these yes-men as having no value. He applied the same principle also to the Son of Heaven. Mozi made "admonishment" a part of the political system so that the Son of Heaven was able to objectively assess a situation to ensure proper governance was carried out. As we have mentioned before, Mozi was a grassroots thinker and did not opt for "revolution," proposing instead "reformative" measures. In "Shang Xian" he urged the ruler to be fair to

門雖然做了以色列人的國王，但是仍有「先知」在批評、直諫、制約他們，這些「先知」能夠與上帝溝通，上帝如果對大衛、所羅門不滿，就會傳話給這些先知，讓他們去批評、揭露國王的罪過，使之改邪歸正。這就是說，在古代以色列人那裏，政教是分離的，君師是分立的，雖然大衛、所羅門是上帝所承認（膏過油）的，稱得上「君權神授」，但是國王本身還不是唯一的「天子」，也沒有壟斷對「天」的交往權和解釋權。

而墨子的商湯這樣的「聖王」似乎是政教、君師合為一體。但是，能不能說墨子就沒有安排在功能上類似於「先知」的人，來監督、糾正、批評、直諫天子呢？有的！天子要求人們都要「上有過則規諫之」，如果發現「上有過」卻不規諫之，那是要受罰的，要受到人們議論的，可見，在一級級的「上同」裏，指出上面的錯誤已是下級的一個義務了，這也必然包括了對天子的監督。

在《親士》、《尚賢》等篇裏，墨子對於「賢士」的要求之一就是要勇於直諫，他反對臣子對

all "capable people" regardless of class and background, suggesting they should be absorbed into the ruling team in an effort to make the political leadership more representative. In "Shang Tong" he also talked about how "admonishment" and criticism should be part of the political system, so that any criticism or disagreement could be regularized and institutionalized. His point was to enable the Son of Heaven or the ruler to gain self-corrective awareness in any decisions he made. If we consider that the predominant political system at the time was "do-as-the-boss-tells-you," Mozi's proposal was a truly outstanding one. We can even say that to suggest taking dissonance and differences into the political system was in fact a germinating idea for a moderate form of constitutionalism.

When we discuss "Shang Tong," it is better to read it together with "Shang Xian" and "Qin Shi," as well as "Geng Zhu," which all chronicled "the deeds of Mozi." These show that in Mozi's view the "Son of Heaven" should not just be a "good enough" benevolent person with high aspirations, but that he should also subject himself to sanctions by "heaven" and scrutiny by the spirits and the gods. Furthermore, he should accept regular criticism and honest advice from loyal and admonitory ministers. Through open debate on "disagreements" and other opinions, the Son of Heaven could learn and benefit from different perspectives, be inspired by collective wisdom, obtain consent from a majority of

國君唯唯諾諾，認為那種只能做應聲蟲的部下是沒有存在價值的，對天子當然也應該如此。墨子將「規諫」納入了政治體制之內，這樣好讓天子客觀地掌握實情，進行治理。

我們說過，草根思想家墨子沒有「革命」只有「改良」的想法，在《尚賢》篇裏他爭取讓國君對各階級出身的「賢士」一視同仁，將他們納入統治隊伍，從而擴大統治者的合法性。在《尚同》篇裏他實際上也將對天子、國君的「規諫」和批評納入了政治體制之內，使得批評與異議常規化和體制化，從而使得天子和國君的決策具有一定的自我糾錯的能力，在當時普遍的「一把手」說了算的政治制度中，應當說，墨子的這個建議是很了不起的。這種把異議與不同的看法容納進政治體制內的提議，甚至可以說有一點溫和的憲政主義的萌芽了。

在討論《尚同》時，應該將它和《尚賢》與《親士》，以及作為「墨子行傳」的《耕柱》等篇章聯繫起來看。可以說，墨子的「天子」除了本身應該是「賢可」之仁人志士外，還要上面受

the people and finally reach consensus. "It is only the Son of Heaven who can unite the opinions of the world"; "the whole state is united like one person." In this way, the implementation of policies would be smooth and speedy: "what is judged right by the Son of Heaven should be taken as right by all; what is judged wrong by the Son of Heaven should be taken as wrong by all." Besides, the Son of Heaven in the capacity of the son of "heaven" is a person who loves all-embracingly and serves the interests of all. In other words, it is his obligation to "promote the interest of the world, and save the world from calamities." Hence, from Mozi's political point of view, "to align with" the Son of Heaven would not degenerate into a form of dictatorship; on the contrary, such politics matched well with "heaven's will." The rationale for Mozi's thinking was that the king of the Zhou dynasty was so vulnerable at the time that all the vassal state rulers ignored him; they did whatever they wanted and fought each other, creating great chaos in the world. Mozi's intention was to unite "all the ideas of the world" through the Son of Heaven, so that chaos and confrontation could come to an end and the world could regain peace and order.

The third question arises in "Shang Tong II" where Mozi says that the Son of Heaven has many ears and eyes and is so well informed that sometimes he knows of what has happened before even neighbors of those involved do. Doesn't this

到「天」的制裁和鬼神的監督，下面受到直諫之臣的制度化的「挑錯」和諍諫。這樣，通過對「異議」和不同意見的討論，反復磋商，天子的決策就能集思廣益，凝聚眾智，並獲得大多數人的同意，從而達成全民共識。

「天子唯能一同天下之義」，「全國團結如一人」，執行起來就會雷厲風行，「天子之所是，皆是之，天子之所非，皆非之」，而天子作為「天」之子，是以兼愛交利，即「興天下之利，除天下之害」為己任的，因此，這種「上同」於天子的政治，在墨子看來，非但不是獨裁，反倒是符合「天志」的理想政治。這是因為，在墨子的時代，周天子已軟弱無力，諸侯國根本不把他放在眼裏，各行其是，互相爭鬥，搞得天下大亂。墨子想將「天下之義」統一到天子那裏，實際上是想止息紛爭亂象，重歸天下太平。

第三個問題，墨子在《尚同中》說，天子耳目眾多，消息靈通，甚至當事人鄰里都不知道的事，天子卻已經知曉，這是不是在搞特務統治，

suggest a governance built upon a network of spying and "tipping off"? Let us examine the original text.

"Therefore, the sage kings of the past made use of the principle of unity for selecting top officials, so that rapport could be established between the one above and the subordinates. When the one above overlooked any tasks or missed any benefits, the subordinates would take note and put a remedy in place for the benefit of the one above. When grievances and complaints accumulated among subordinates, the one above would know and deal with them. So, if thousands and thousands of miles away there was a person doing good, his family members might not know of it and his fellow villagers might not all hear of it, and yet the Son of Heaven would have known and have rewarded him. If thousands and thousands of miles away, there was a person doing bad things, his family members might not all know of it and his fellow villagers might not all hear of it, and yet the Son of Heaven would have known and have punished him. Hence, the people around the whole world were all fearful, shocked and alarmed; they dared not act evilly or violently, saying that the Son of Heaven had the eyesight and hearing of a god. The former kings said, 'He is not a god, but he can make use of others' ears and eyes to help him see and listen, make use of others' lips to help him speak, make use of others' minds to help him think, and make use of others' limbs to help him act.' If many people help him

告密政治？我們來看原文。墨子說：「故古者聖王唯而審以尚同，以為正長，是故上下情請為通。」上有隱事遺利，下得而利之，下有蓄怨積害，上得而除之。是以數千萬里之外，有為善者，其室人未徧（遍）知，鄉里未徧（遍）聞，天子得而賞之。

數千萬里之外，有為不善者，其室人未徧（遍）知，鄉里未徧（遍）聞，天子得而罰之。是以舉天下之人，皆恐懼振動惕栗，不敢為淫暴，曰：「天子之視聽也神。」先王之言曰：「非神也，夫唯能使人之耳目助己視聽，使人之吻助己言談，使人之心助己思慮，使人之股肱助己動作。」助之視聽者眾，則其所聞見者遠矣。助之言談者眾，則其德音之所撫循者博矣。助之思慮者眾，則其談謀度速得矣。助之動作者眾，即其舉事速成矣。

後人說墨子搞特務統治的一個字面證據是，墨子說天子「使人之耳目助己視聽」，其實這不過是引自《尚書》一類的古話。《尚書》說「臣作朕股肱耳目」，其意是做臣下的，相當於延長

see and listen, then he can see and listen from afar. If many people help him speak, then his kind words can comfort a wide audience. If many people help him think, then he can plan swiftly and put things into action. If many people help him act, then his measures can be accomplished quickly.'"

When later generations accused Mozi of imposing "rule by spies," they were referring to the words in the above passage: Mozi said the Son of Heaven "can make use of others' ears and eyes to help him see and listen." This is actually a phrase taken from the *Book of Documents*: "The minister serves as my limbs, my ears and my eyes," meaning that ministers serve as the ruler's extended ears and eyes so that they can inform him in a timely manner of the public's hardships, grievances and opinions. The use of "ears and eyes" here was not intended to imply the later-derived meaning of placing special agents everywhere to spy on people's secrets or wrongdoings. Since Mozi "values unity" and seeks to establish a united order for the world, it is essential for a ruler to have a clear understanding of the common people's circumstances. Only when he is accurately informed about the circumstances, can he identify the critical issues, come up with the best solutions, implement effective measures and satisfactorily solve various problems at hand. If by "make use of others' ears and eyes to help one see and listen" Mozi meant using one's ministers' ears and eyes to understand the hardships of

了君上的耳目，把民間疾苦、怨聲、輿情及時地讓君上知曉。這裏「耳目」並不是後來衍生出的到處打探秘密消息的特務間諜的意思。

既然墨子「尚同」，要讓天下有統一的秩序，把握和瞭解民間的實際情況就非常重要，這樣才能獲得正確的資訊，對症下藥，想好辦法，再通過強有力的執行，順利地解決各方面的問題。如果「使人之耳目助己視聽」是通過臣下的耳目而瞭解人民疾苦，其功能近似於今天的新聞報導、情報資訊部門；那麼，「使人之吻助己言談」，其功能近似於替君上宣傳國家政策的宣傳部；「使人之心助己思慮」，其功能就近似於今天的智囊團和決策部門；「使人之股肱助己動作」，其功能就近似於今天的各個部委具體執行中央的各大決策。

這樣，由於天子對於人民的疾苦非常瞭解，知道最近發生了甚麼問題，本着「興天下之利，除天下之害」的「天志」，就可以迅速地得到資訊情報，通過集體討論把握問題所在，並找到解決的計策，然後通過職能部門加以執行。

the people, it is describes a function similar to today's news agencies and information departments. Similarly, "make use of others' lips to help one speak" looks much like today's publicity machines responsible for publicizing government policies. "Make use of others' minds to help one think" is perhaps comparable to today's think-tanks and policy decision departments; "make use of others' limbs to help one act" is not unlike various contemporary ministries and commissions responsible for executing major policy decisions made by the central government. In this way, the Son of Heaven could have a thorough understanding of the hardships of his people and learn about the current issues bothering them. Keeping in mind that "heaven's will" was to "promote the interests of the world, save the world from calamities," he could be expediently informed, get to the core of problems in collective discussion, devise solutions and have them executed through a consolidated effort by the operational departments. As to whether the Son of Heaven might know in advance of a person's family members or fellow villagers about what good or bad things he or she had done, that he did would be of no surprise. Those who do bad things will not want their family or fellow villagers to know of them. This is the basis of "neighborhood watch." Those who do good things with a pure heart would not have done them for reward, so they will not go around telling people about their good deeds. It would not be surprising therefore if their families or fellow villagers

　　至於有的人做了好事或壞事，在其家人或鄉人都未知道的情況下就被天子知道了，也不奇怪。做壞事的人本來也不願意家人或鄉人知道，因此需要有人檢舉揭發。做好事的人如果是真心做好事，而不是為了獎賞做好事，那麼也不會到處宣揚自己做了好事，因此其家人或鄉人不知道也不奇怪。當然，好事的受益人（如被救者、被幫助者）會宣揚好人好事，但總有一個傳播的過程，並不總能很快就讓所有人知道好人好事。而根據墨子「尚同」的制度設計，下級官員有義務向上級報告最新的民情，這裏面就包括了好人好事、壞人壞事，因此，上級比做好事或壞事者家人或鄉人更快知道事情，也並不奇怪。即如今天，新聞媒體所報導的我們身邊的好事或壞事，又有多少是我們耳聞目睹的呢？很少。還不是經過了資訊處理中心（在古時就是上級，直至天子一級）的公佈？所以，從墨子的本意來說，無非是說，「天子」像「天」一樣耳目靈敏，通過借助於臣下和人民的力量，能迅速地發現問題、解決問題，使天下大治。墨子沒有一個地方說到「天子」要通過「秘密警察」搞情報，因為一切都是一級級「尚同」，資訊的流動程式是公開的；也沒有說

do not know about such good conduct. Certainly, those who benefit from good deeds (after being rescued or helped, for example) will try to make the good man known to others, but it takes time for news to be disseminated, so not everyone will know about the good person and his deeds at once. In Mozi's system of "valuing unity," subordinates are obliged to report to superiors about the most updated public sentiment, which includes news of good people and good deeds, as well as that of bad people and bad deeds. In an era before electronic communication, it was inevitable then for officials to have information ahead of the family or fellow villagers of those involved. Even today, how many reports on news media of good or bad deeds around us have we witnessed in person? Very few. Aren't they instead mediated reports from information processing centers (a modern version of the reporting system used by the Son of Heaven in the past)? Therefore, we can say that Mozi's intended meaning was that "the Son of Heaven" had ears and eyes as keen as "heaven" and was able to draw on the power of the ministers and people to swiftly discover pressing issues, solve problems and return the world to order. Nowhere did Mozi suggest "the Son of Heaven" should get intelligence through "secret police." Since "subordinates aligned themselves with the one above" level by level, the conveyance of information would be open. Neither did Mozi advocate gossiping or telling tales; on the contrary, he stressed unifying the channels for collecting information

過要人們互相打小報告，搞揭發檢舉，反而強調
情報收集的統一程式，由各級向上通報資訊，統
一處理。

墨子針對他那個時代天下大亂的問題，開出
藥方，提出權力層層集中，最後集中於天子（集
權不等於獨裁），從而達到天下大治的目的。他
的本意是良好的，但是客觀效果如何呢？當秦漢
通過武力統一中國，「天子」獨攬大權時，他們
能體現「天志」嗎？我們看到中國陷入了長達兩
千年的「王朝循環」，每隔二三百年就改朝換代
一次，每個朝代的第一、二代「天子」因為是從
民間辛辛苦苦「打天下」而來，因此清楚民間疾
苦，他們會快速地瞭解各地實情，通過與一起「打
江山」的同樣出身民間的大臣進行不乏民主精神
的集體討論協商，制定解決問題的政策，並能夠
有力地執行政策。

一般來說，每個朝代的開國君主都是比較符
合墨子的「天子」的標準的。但每個朝代經過
數代君主之後，往往就會「上下脫節」，小皇帝
們都「生於深宮」，錦衣玉食，哪裏會知道民間

so that a man in a position of authority could gather all the information needed and process it as a whole.

Facing the chaotic situation of the world of the time, Mozi's remedy was to have power centralized progressively from the bottom up to finally reach the hands of the Son of Heaven (centralization of power is not dictatorship) in order to have the whole world put back in good order. Mozi made his proposal with the best of intentions, but what was the actual outcome? When the rulers of Qin and Han unified China by force and had exclusive control of power as "Sons of Heaven," did they succeed in actualizing "heaven's will"? The reality is that China was trapped in a "dynastic cycle" for two thousand years where political leaders and dynasties changed every two or three centuries. With each dynasty, the first or second generations of the "Son of Heaven" knew deeply about the hardships of the people because they themselves had also endured hardships as commoners during their "fights over the world." They would have swiftly collected information about the situation of different regions, held discussions with their ministers — who were also commoners assisting in the "fight over the world" — in a manner not without democratic spirit, made decisions on what policies to adopt, and then had the policies executed forcefully. In general, the founding rulers of every dynasty were those who matched well with the standards of the "Son of Heaven" set by Mozi.

疾苦，以王公大臣、官僚群體為代表的利益集團只顧盤剝百姓，歷代積累，民怨加深。為維護統治，維持穩定，皇帝集團只好加增苛捐雜稅，維持龐大的軍隊、警察等國家暴力機器，並養活、增加秘密警察機關（如明朝的東廠西廠錦衣衛），實行特務統治，但最終仍舊是無法挽救頹勢。人民起義，舊朝傾亡，新朝湧現，能夠代表「天意」的「從民間崛起」的「新天子」打下江山，成為新朝「太祖」，於是開始新一輪王朝循環。

墨子的「尚同」理想，仍不乏「賢人政治」或「哲學王政治」的色彩，在這思路下治理的好壞高度依賴於「天子」的道德品質和能力。「文景之治」、「貞觀之治」、「康乾盛世」中聽得進不同意見、瞭解民情的皇帝，可以說是墨子「尚同」理想中「天子」的標準。隋煬帝、崇禎帝、慈禧太后這樣的主子當然就不符合墨子的「天子」標準，而是對那個標準的扭曲。秘密警察和特務統治是對墨子真正意義上的「天子」耳目的一個扭曲，因為它把墨子提倡的一個公開透明的程式變成秘密不能見光的陰謀了。

However, after several generations of rulers, those in power would become "disengaged from those below": the little emperors were all "born in the exclusiveness of the royal court." They dressed well, ate well and knew nothing about the hardships of the common people. At the same time, the nobles and the ministers, and other interest groups represented by the bureaucracy, only sought to accumulate wealth for themselves at the expense of people's welfare. Thus after years of exploitation, popular grievances grew. Yet as the state only cared about safeguarding governance and securing stability, the emperor's cronies were obliged to levy heavy taxes on the people to keep the state-run violence machine running, and to feed and expand the secret police agencies. This is exemplified by the Eastern Depot, the Western Depot and the Embroidered Uniform Guard or Jinyiwei in the Ming Dynasty. In the end, rule by spies was imposed. Eventually, however, it failed to rescue the state from its downward spiral, sparking off popular uprisings and bringing about the collapse of the old regime. Then a new regime emerged, a "new Son of Heaven" representing "heaven's will" "rose from among the people" and won the world over, becoming the "First Emperor" of the new dynasty, thus starting a new round of the dynastic cycle.

Mozi's ideal of "subordinates aligning themselves with the one above" favors "good man politics" or "philosopher king

五

上有過則微之以諫，己有善則訪之上，而無敢以告。

【原文】

　　魯陽文君謂子墨子曰：「有語我以忠臣者，令之俯則俯，令之仰則仰，處則靜，呼則應，可謂忠臣乎？」子墨子曰：「令之俯則俯，令之仰則仰，是似景也。處則靜，呼則應，是似響也。君將何得於景與響哉？若以翟之所謂忠臣者，上有過則微之以諫，己有善則訪之上，而無敢以告。外匡其邪，而入其善，尚同而無下比，是以美善在上，而怨讎在下，安樂在上，而憂慼在臣。此翟之所謂忠臣者也。」（《魯問》）

【今譯】

　　魯陽文君對墨子說：「有人告訴我怎樣才算是忠臣，叫他低頭就低頭，叫他抬頭就抬頭，坐着就安安靜靜的，喊他就答應，這可以叫做忠臣嗎？」墨子說：「叫他低頭就低頭，叫他抬頭就

politics." According to this thinking, the quality of governance depends greatly on the moral qualities and capability of the "Son of Heaven." The "good rule of Wen and Jing," the "good rule of Zhenguan," or the "Kangqian period of prosperity," in which emperors listened to different opinions and had a deep understanding of public sentiment, speak well for the standards of the "Son of Heaven" in Mozi's ideal of "subordinates aligning themselves with the one above." Rulers such as Emperor Yang of Sui, Emperor Chongzhen or Empress Cixi obviously did not live up to the standards of the "Son of Heaven" defined by Mozi. Maintaining secret police and rule by spies was a distortion of the true meanings of "ears and eyes" of the "Son of Heaven" because the system turned the public and transparent mechanism as seen by Mozi into a secretive and dark conspiracy.

Five
When the one above makes a mistake, he [a loyal minister] will look for an opportunity to caution him; when he has a good idea, he discusses it with the one above and refrains from telling others about it.

抬頭，這就好像影子。坐着安安靜靜，喊他就答應，這就好像回聲。你從影子和回聲那裏能得到甚麼呢？我所說的忠臣卻是這樣的：國君有過錯，就尋找機會加以勸諫，自己有好的見解就與國君商議，不告訴別人。匡正國君的偏邪，使其走入正道，（他）上跟國君保持一致，不在下面結黨營私，因此，美名歸於上面，怨仇卻由下面擔當，安樂歸於上面，而憂戚由臣下擔當。這才是我所說的忠臣。」

【時析】

墨子在《尚同》篇裏對理想的「君上」作了描述，在這裏他則對理想的「忠臣」作了描寫。他看不起那種唯唯諾諾，只做國君影子和回聲的臣子，認為他們沒有起到應有的作用。墨子所理解的忠臣，一要直諫，不使國君犯錯；二要為國君排憂解難，出謀劃策，事成後功勞歸國君，失敗歸自己；三要保持對國君的忠誠，不結黨營私搞利益集團架空國君。忠臣建言時還要考慮到國君的面子，只對國君一個人說，不要事先嚷嚷讓天下人都知道這主意出於自己。確實，這樣的忠臣是真正為國君的長遠利益着想的人，明事理的

Translation:

Prince Wen of Lu Yang said to Mozi, "Someone told me how I can spot a loyal minister: when I order him to bow, he bows; when I order him to lift up his head, he lifts up his head; when he retreats, he sits in silence; when he is summoned, he answers. Is this really how a loyal minister should be?"

Master Mozi said, "When you order him to bow, he bows; when you order him to lift up his head, he lifts up his head. It looks as if he might be your shadow. When he retreats, he sits in silence; when he is summoned, he answers. It looks as if he might be your echo. What can you get from a shadow or an echo?

"For me, a loyal minister acts like this: when the one above makes a mistake, he will look for an opportunity to caution him; when he has a good idea, he discusses it with the one above and refrains from telling others about it. He corrects the one above when he goes astray, he guides him in the righteous path; he aligns with the one above and forms no cliques with his subordinates. Hence, reputation and greatness go to the one above, grievances and discontent vented with the subordinate; the one above is happy and contented, while the minister bears the worries and the sorrows.

"This is how I consider a loyal minster should be." ("Lu Wen")

國君都會器重的。即使放在今天的公司企業管理中，能不結黨營私、敢於直言得罪領導、同時又樂於為領導當「替罪羊」從而增加集團凝聚力的人才，也非常難得。

Contemporary interpretation:

In "Shang Tong," Mozi describes how an ideal "ruler" should act. In this passage, he describes how an ideal "loyal minister" should convey himself. He despises the "yes-man" kind of minister who acts only like the ruler's shadow or echo when he thinks he is not doing what he should. According to Mozi, a loyal minister must first be someone who honestly counsels the ruler not to make mistakes; second, he must be able to ease worries and solve problems for the ruler — but while he is good at offering proposals and strategies, he will not claim any merit if they succeed, and he will bear all the responsibility if they fail; third, he must be loyal solely to the ruler, he will not form cliques or interest groups for his own benefit and override the power of the ruler. When a loyal minister offers any advice, he must be careful to maintain the face of the ruler, so he should advise him in private and avoid speaking up before others and boasting about his own ideas. Indeed, such loyal ministers should be those who genuinely care about the long-term interests of the ruler, and any sensible ruler should treasure their assistance.

Even today, it is still a rare treasure in corporate management to have someone who has no desire to form a coterie or to advance private interests, who dares to offend the leader with honest advice and at the same time is willing to serve as the "scapegoat" for the leader for the sake of team cohesion.

簡樸生活 *Living a Simple Life*

一

用財不費，民德不勞，其興利多矣。

【原文】

聖人為政一國，一國可倍也；大之為政天下，天下可倍也。其倍之非外取地也，因其國家，去其無用之費，足以倍之。聖王為政，其發令興事，使民用財也，無不加用而為者，是故用財不費，民德不勞，其興利多矣。

其為衣裘何？以為冬以圉寒，夏以圉暑。凡為衣裳之道，冬加溫，夏加清者，芊組不加者去之。其為宮室何？以為冬以圉風寒，夏以圉暑雨，有盜賊加固者，芊組不加者去之。其為甲盾五兵何？以為以圉寇亂盜賊，若有寇亂盜賊，有甲盾五兵者勝，無者不勝。是故聖人作為甲盾五兵。凡為甲盾五兵加輕以利，堅而難折者，芊組不加者去之。其為舟車何？以為車以行陵陸，舟以行川谷，以通四方之利。凡為

One
Resources are not wasted, people gain rather than suffer from their labor, thus he brings about many benefits.

Translation:

When a sage governs a state, the wealth of the state will double; when he extends his rule to the world, the wealth of the world will double. The increase does not come through annexing lands from other states, but through doing away with unnecessary expenses in the state so that its wealth becomes twice as much. When the sage governs, whether in issuing orders, initiating projects, hiring people as well as spending, he never does anything unproductive. Resources are not wasted, people gain rather than suffer from their labor, and thus he brings about many benefits.

Why does he make clothes and fur coats? To keep out the winter cold and the summer heat. The purpose of clothing is to keep us warm in winter and cool in summer. Anything decorative or not serving these purposes should be eschewed. Why does he build houses and residences? To keep out the cold and wind from winter, the heat and rain from summer and to guard against the thieves. Anything decorative or

舟車之道，加輕以利者，芊軱不加者去之。凡其為此物也，無不加用而為者，是故用財不費，民德不勞，其興利多矣。

　　有去大人之好聚珠玉、鳥獸、犬馬，以益衣裳、宮室、甲盾、五兵、舟車之數於數倍乎！若則不難，故孰為難倍？唯人為難倍。然人有可倍也。昔者聖王為法曰：「丈夫年二十，毋敢不處家。女子年十五，毋敢不事人。」此聖王之法也。聖王即沒，於民次也，其欲蚤處家者，有所二十年處家；其欲晚處家者，有所四十年處家。以其蚤與其晚相踐，後聖王之法十年。若純三年而字，子生可以二三年矣。此不惟使民蚤處家而可以倍與？且不然已。（《節用上》）

【今譯】

　　聖人在一國施政，一國的財富可以加倍增長；大到施政於天下，天下的財富可以加倍增長。這種財富的加倍，並不是向外掠奪土地，而是根據國家的情況，省去無用之費，因而足以加倍。聖

not serving these purposes should be eschewed. Why does he make armor, shields and the five weapons? To keep out enemies and thieves. Those with armor, shields and the five weapons will win; those without will not. Therefore, the sage makes armor, shields and the five weapons. In principle, armor, shields and the five weapons are best if they are lightweight and sharp. They also need to be strong and unbreakable. Anything decorative or not serving these purposes should be eschewed. Why does he make boats and carts? Carts are made to ride in the hills and on land; boats are made to navigate rivers and gorges so as to facilitate transport in all directions. In principle, boats and carts are best if they are lightweight. Anything decorative or not serving this purpose should be eschewed. All these things are made with a practical purpose in mind. Resources are not wasted, people gain rather than suffer from their labor, and thus he brings about many benefits.

Besides, if the nobles and high-ranking people can forgo their coveted jewelry, birds and beasts, dogs and horses, then the production of clothes, houses, armor and shields, the five weapons, as well as boats and carts can be multiplied many times! To do this is not difficult. What, then, is difficult to increase "multifold"? It is only the population that is difficult to multiply this way. Nonetheless, there are still ways it can be done. In the past, the sage king made it obligatory that "by the

王施政，發佈命令、興辦事業、使用民力和財物，沒有不是有益於實用才去做的，所以使用財物不浪費，民眾有所得而不勞苦，他興起的利益很多。

　　他縫製衣裘做甚麼呢？冬天用以禦寒，夏天用以防暑。凡是縫製衣服的原則，冬天能增加溫暖、夏天能增加涼爽，就大力發展；反之，就去掉。他建造房子做甚麼呢？冬天用以抵禦風寒，夏天用以防禦炎熱和下雨。盜賊侵入時能夠加固防守的，就增益它；反之，就去掉。他製造鎧甲、盾牌、戈矛和各種兵器做甚麼呢？用以抵禦外寇和盜賊。如果有外寇盜賊，擁有鎧甲、盾牌和各種兵器的就勝利，沒有的就失敗。所以聖人製造鎧甲、盾牌和各種兵器。凡是製造鎧甲、盾牌和各種兵器，能增加輕便鋒利、堅而難折的，就增益它；不能增加的，就去掉。他製造車、船是為了甚麼呢？車用來行陸路，船用來行水道，以此溝通四方的利益。製造車、船的原則，能增加輕快便利的，就增益它；不能增加的，就去掉。他製造這些東西，無一不是增加實用才去做的。所以用財物不浪費，民眾有所得而不勞累，他興起的利益有很多。

302

age of twenty, no men were allowed to be unmarried; by the age of fifteen, no women were allowed to be unwedded." This is the rule of the sage king. Once the sage king passed away, the people became lax, so those who wanted to get married early did so as soon as they reached twenty; those who wanted to get married later did so up until the age of forty. If the ages of the early weds and the late weds are averaged out, there is a ten-year lag compared with that under the sage king's rule. If all married couples bear a child every three years, then two to three more children will be born. Isn't it true that if people are urged to get married at an early age, then the population will increasingly multiply? It is only that we no longer do so these days. ("Jie Yong I")

Contemporary interpretation:

Mozi's maxim of "moderation in use" is equivalent to the "energy saving," "environmentally friendly" lifestyle advocated today that aims to achieve a "doubling of income" through opposing wasteful extravagance. He explained clearly how to double the GDP of a state: rather than having an "outward expansion approach" of development, an "inward approach" of development should be adopted. That is to say, the imperial and colonial ways of outward plunder should not be followed (because that contradicts his claim for "all-embracing love" and "against attack"); instead, inward development should be pursued. Yet his idea of "inward"

　　又去掉王公大人喜歡搜集的珠玉、鳥獸、犬馬，用來增加衣服、房屋、甲盾、兵器、車船的數量，使之成倍增加，這也不難。甚麼是難以倍增的呢？只有人是難以倍增的。然而人也有可以倍增的辦法。古代聖王制訂法則，說：「男子年到二十，不許不成家，女子年到十五，不許不嫁人。」這是聖王的法規。聖王既已去世，聽任百姓放縱自己，那些想早點成家的，有時二十歲就成家，那些想遲點成家的，有時四十歲才成家。拿早的與晚的相平均，與聖王的法則差了十年。如果婚後都三年生一個孩子，就可多生兩三個孩子了。這豈不是讓百姓早成家就可以使人口倍增了嗎？然而如今並不這麼做。

【時析】

　　墨子所說的「節用」，相當於今天所提倡的「節能」、「環保」生活，通過反奢侈而實現「收入倍增」。他說的很明確，讓一國 GDP 成倍增加，不能採取「對外擴張式」發展，而應採取「內向式」發展。不能採取向外掠奪的帝國主義和殖民主義的方法（因為這與「兼愛」「非攻」矛盾），而須靠內部挖潛。但他的「內向式」發展，

development was not that of the "involution" of development adopted during the Ming and Qing dynasties when the population increased exponentially while no outward expansion was undertaken. "Involution" of development at that time sought to adopt an intensive farming strategy, increasing the per unit yield from farming operations (rather than increasing the area of land) to be able to sustain an increasing population. In his "inward" development model, Mozi saw the suppression of the culture of extravagance as a priority so that expenditure on luxury items by the rich could be diverted to make necessities for the common people. Mozi's "moderation in use" represented a "pragmatic" philosophy of wealth held by the "underprivileged" of the time. His views are still applicable to the modern world where the gap between the rich and the poor is very wide. As we all know, in many countries the money spent on a single meal by government officials or the rich would be enough to maintain a school in a remote region for several years. If such money spent on extravagant meals could be saved through legal or philanthropic means and used to serve the poor, wouldn't it benefit more people so that the gross national "happiness index" could be maximized?

If we take a look at the global lifestyle trends in recent years, the green economy, the zero carbon emission economy and environment-friendly lifestyles have all come into vogue. At

跟明清時期中國因為人口大增而不對外擴張時採取的「內捲式」發展不同。「內捲式」發展是對農田採取精耕細作，提高農作物的單位產量，以養活更多的人口。在墨子這裏，首先重視的還是抑制奢侈風氣，讓富貴人士把買奢侈品的費用省下來，用於生產平民必需的實用品。墨子「節用」代表了當時的「賤民」的「實用」財富觀。他的觀點在貧富懸殊的今天仍然具有現實意義。我們知道在很多國家，往往官員或富人一頓飯的酒飯錢就相當於偏遠地區一個小學數年的費用，如果能通過法律和慈善的辦法把這些酒飯錢省下來用到窮困地區，實際上不就是使更多的人獲利，從而增加了人民的「幸福指數」嗎？

從國際生活形態來看，近些年綠色經濟、零碳排放經濟、環保生活觀的興起，實際上也在更高層次上向着「簡樸生活」回歸。比如在「食」上，原先為了追求味道的鮮美、色彩的鮮豔，發明了很多食品添加劑、顏色添加劑，雖然吃起來味道豐富了，食品看起來也悅目了，但實際上卻是以損害健康、破壞環境為代價的。墨子的「節用」生活雖然目的最終是為了國家富強，而不是

a deeper level, these can actually be regarded as a return to a "simple lifestyle." Take "food" as an example. People used to seek richness in flavors and vibrancy in colors, and therefore invented many artificial flavorings and colorings. With time, the flavors have become richer and the foods are more pleasing to our eyes; yet in reality they are harmful to our health as well as to our environment. Even though Mozi's ultimate aim in living a "frugal" life was to make the state wealthy and powerful — unlike Zhuangzi whose aim was to recover the qualities of the natural "flavors" — the significance of his idea is still undeniable.

In the contemporary global economic realm, China and India are two countries with vast populations and vigorous economic development. If they adopted the same lifestyle as their American and European counterparts did in the past, the per capita consumption of resources and energy would be huge and definitely cause a real concern as to whether our incessant demands for resources and energy would overburden Mother Nature. Of the world's population of 7 billion, Western developed countries account for no more than 1 billion, and the combined population of China and India add up to more than 2 billion. Since Western countries have already consumed much of the earth's resources, if the 2 billion population of China and India are going to consume the remaining resources on a par with their Western

像老莊那樣恢復「味道」天然的面貌，但仍有其價值。

在當今的世界經濟版圖上，中國和印度這兩個人口大國經濟發展正蒸蒸日上。如果在生活方式上，他們也走上歐美發展的老路，即每個人都消耗大量的物資和能源，那麼，地球能否負荷人類的物資和能源需求都會成問題。現在全球有70億人口，發達國家歐美加起來不會超過10億人，中印兩國加起來人口超過20億。歐美已經消耗了地球大部份的資源，如果中印兩國20億人口按歐美人均標準來消耗地球的資源，恐怕地球生態危機會惡化。到時從石油、糧食、海洋食物（魚類）到水資源甚至空氣等，恐怕都會搶個你死我活。在這個時候，一方面歐美人應該使自己的生活重歸簡樸，另方面中印等新興大國應該避免重走歐美現代化過程「先污染再治理、先浪費再收斂」的老路，並有責任探索其他的既注重生活品質和幸福感同時又不過分浪費地球資源的新的生活方式。比如，由於中印兩國人口眾多而密集，可以側重於發展公共交通和自行車這類無污染交通工具，抑制發展私家車。這相當於明清

counterparts, the ecological crisis can only worsen. When that happens, people might find themselves fighting for natural resources such as petroleum, food (whether from land or the ocean), water and air. In the face of this, it is beholden on people in Europe and America to return to a simpler lifestyle, while major developing countries like China and India should avoid their old paths of "pollute then remedy, waste then restrain." They should, instead, assume responsibility for exploring alternative lifestyles that cherish a quality of life and feelings of happiness without overly exploiting natural resources. For example, China and India in an effort to offset the environmental degradation caused by their enormous populations and dense living conditions should develop non-polluting public transportation and encourage the use of bicycles to limit the number of private vehicles on the roads. This would be comparable to the Ming and Qing dynasties' adoption of agrarian "involution" to promote China's agricultural output. In other words, increasing the uptake in public transportation now would reduce public hazards such as traffic jams and pollution. Disappointingly, in an effort to raise the country's GDP the Chinese government in the twentieth century promoted heavily the use of private vehicles. These ran on dirty fuels, causing serious pollution problems in super cities like Beijing and Shanghai. They became "cities of fog," their roads swamped with cars. The situation was exacerbated by emissions from thousands of poorly built

之間中國農業的「內捲式發展」，就是提高公共交通工具的使用率，從而減少污染等公害。可惜，中國政府近年來為了拉動GDP，反而大力發展私家車，搞得北京、上海這樣的超級城市污染嚴重，成為「霧都」，馬路也成了停車場，這正是在走當年倫敦、紐約、曼谷等城市的老路。在發展太陽能和風能等無污染的自然能源上，中國政府倒是很積極，但由於目前這些新興能源成本很昂貴，只是在一些地方進行試點。假如將來能普遍展開，倒可以說是在走一條新路。

至於奢侈品，墨子從當時的社會現狀和生產力水準出發，是主張抑制的。但是在發展社會經濟的過程中，奢侈品的作用是不能一概而論的。就人的天性而言，喜新厭舊、追求精緻是自然的心理現象，在商品的設計和發明上，有時就難免出現精美「無用」的奢侈品。照墨子的實用主義觀點，衣服能禦寒就行了，何必在上面繡那麼多花紋呢？陶瓷能用來喝水、吃飯、盛東西就行了，何必畫上精美的山水人物圖像，而且要精益求精，直到把它做成只能觀賞不能使用的藝術品呢？當代藝術家吳冠中說過，文盲不可怕，美盲

factories, reminiscent of London and New York many decades before and later Bangkok. The Chinese government, however, has recently worked hard to develop clean natural resources, such as solar power and wind power. But the current high cost of these alternatives means that they are still under trial at a few piloting sites only. If their use can in the future be made universal, there may yet be hope.

While Mozi opposed the acquisition of luxury goods because of the social circumstances and poor economic situation of his time, no easy conclusion can be drawn on his attitude to luxury goods in themselves. It is human nature and thus a natural psychological phenomenon to favor new things over the old and be attracted to fine objects. It is also unavoidable for "useless" delicate luxury goods to be created during the development of commercial products. Mozi's pragmatic stance was that the purpose of clothes was to keep us warm, so why bother with embroidering them? Pottery was used for serving drinks and food as well as containing items, so why bother decorating them with beautiful scenery or portraits and seeking to refine them further until they become aesthetic pieces devoid of any practical use? Contemporary Chinese painter Wu Guangzhong said that being illiterate is not awful, lacking aesthetic taste is. Beauty is one of the highest spiritual pursuits of humans (the others are truth and goodness) and as such is indispensable and also always associated with refinement. In

才可怕。美是人類追求的最高精神境界之一（其他是真、善），不可或缺，而美總是與精緻有關。其實「奢美」可滿足心靈的需要，且與「實用」並肩而行，在中國發掘出來的最早的陶器中，就不乏畫着優美人面的作品，在當時它們也算得上奢侈品了。由於私有制下人們的富有程度不同，那些有錢人能買得起費時費力、做工精緻的產品，也就順理成章。而且，奢侈品作為一個產業，也能夠拉動經濟，增加從業人員，因此墨子之反對奢侈，只在當時社會處境下具有積極意義，不能放在任何時代、任何處境中一概而論。

二

以厚葬久喪者為政，國家必貧，人民必寡，刑政必亂。

【原文】

……細計厚葬，為多埋賦之財者也。計久喪，為久禁從事者也。財以成者，扶而埋之，後得生者，而久禁之，以此求富，

fact, "luxurious beauty" can satisfy spiritual needs and is a partner to "practicality." Some pre-historic pottery artefacts excavated in China in recent years were found painted with beautiful human faces and can be considered luxury goods of the time. In a capitalist system, in which people are divided by wealth, it is usually only the rich who can afford to buy finely crafted goods that have involved much time and effort in their creation. However, luxury goods as an industry stimulate the economy and expand the workforce. For this reason, the significance of Mozi's opposition to extravagance should be seen in the context of the social circumstances prevailing at the time he lived. It should not be extrapolated to other periods.

Two

If one governs allowing elaborate funerals and a prolonged mourning period, the state will become destitute, the population will decline, and law and order will deteriorate.

Translation:
If we consider the rituals of elaborate funerals, it is clear that significant wealth is buried along with the deceased. Having a prolonged mourning period means that people are kept away

此譬猶禁耕而求穫也，富之說無可得焉。
……

　　今唯無以厚葬久喪者為政，君死，喪
之三年，父母死，喪之三年，妻與後子死
者，五皆喪之三年……此其為敗男女之交
多矣。以此求眾譬猶使人負劍，而求其壽
也。眾之說無可得焉。是故求以眾人民，
而既以不可矣。欲以治刑政，意者可乎？
其說又不可矣。今唯無以厚葬久喪者為
政，國家必貧，人民必寡，刑政必亂。若
法若言，行若道，使為上者行此，則不能
聽治，使為下者行此，則不能從事。上不
聽治，刑政必亂，下不從事，衣食之財必
不足。若苟不足，為人弟者，求其兄而不
得，不弟弟必將怨其兄矣，為人子者，求
其親而不得，不孝子必是怨其親矣，為人
臣者，求之君而不得，不忠臣必且亂其上
矣。是以僻淫邪行之民，出則無衣也，入
則無食也，內續奚吾，並為淫暴，而不可
勝禁也。是故盜賊眾而治者寡，夫眾盜賊
而寡治者，以此求治，譬猶使人三（還）

from work for a long time. Wealth is created, yet it is taken away and buried; the surviving family of the deceased should get back to work, yet they are kept away from work for a long time. Trying to seek wealth in this way is like trying to ban farming and yet still expect a harvest. It is impossible to seek wealth in this way.

Now the state is governed in a way that allows elaborate funerals and a prolonged mourning period. When the ruler dies, there will be three years of mourning; when parents die, there will be three years of mourning; when one's wife or eldest son dies, there also will be three years of mourning. All five deaths require one to observe a three-year mourning period. A lot of men and women are thus forbidden to have sex. Trying at the same time to seek an increase in population is like making a man throw himself on his sword and wishing him longevity. It is impossible to increase the population in this way. .

It is thus impossible to improve population numbers by having elaborate funerals. Perhaps they have a better effect on improving law and order. Again, that is not possible.

Instead, if one governs allowing elaborate funerals and a prolonged mourning period, the state will become destitute, the population will decline, and law and order will

而毋負己也，治之說無可得焉。（《節葬
下》）

【今譯】

　　仔細計算厚葬之事，實是大量埋掉錢財；計
算長久服喪之事，實是長久禁止人們做事。財產
已形成了的，掩在棺材裏埋掉了；喪後應當生產
的，又被長時間禁止。用這種做法追求財富，就
好比禁止耕田而想求收獲一樣，求富的主張是無
法實現的……

　　如今以厚葬久喪的原則去治理國家，國君死
了服喪三年，父母死了服喪三年，妻與嫡長子死
了，又服喪三年，五者都服喪三年……這樣就會
大大妨礙男女之間的交合。用這種辦法追求增加
人口，就好像讓人伏在劍刃上尋求長壽。人口增
多的說法不可實現。所以用厚葬來使人口增多，
是不可能了。那以此來治理刑事政務，也許可以
吧？又是不行的。以厚葬久喪的原則治理政事，
國家必定貧窮，人口必定減少，刑政必定混亂。
假如效法這種意見，實行這種主張，使居上位者
依此而行，就不能治理；使在下位者依此而行，

deteriorate. If such a practice is adopted with funerals, then the one above [a man's superior] following this ritual will not be able to attend to governance, and those below him who follow it will not be able to work. If the one above does not attend to governance, law and order will unavoidably deteriorate; if those below him do not work, there will inevitably be a shortage of clothes and food. When faced with a shortage of such necessities, younger brothers will seek help from their elder brothers. If this is done in vain, insolent younger brothers will criticize their elder brothers. If the sons seek help from their parents in vain, impious ones will strongly reproach their parents. If officials seek help from their ruler in vain, disloyal ones will certainly rebel against their superior. As a result, people who have no clothes to wear when going out and no food to eat at home will feel humiliated, and the evil and wicked among them will gang up to do bad and ruthless things. As their numbers grow, it will become simply impossible to stop them. In the end, robbers and thieves will be so numerous that maintaining public order will be a rare thing.

To govern a state by increasing the number of robbers and thieves and weakening public order is like asking a person to turn around three times and stop without turning his back to you. It is impossible to achieve good governance in this way. ("Jie Zang III")

就不可能從事生產。居上位的不能治理政事，刑事政務必定混亂；在下位的不能從事生產，衣食之資必定不足。假若不足，做弟弟的向兄長求索而沒有所得，不恭順的就必定怨恨他的兄長；做兒子的求索父母而沒有所得，不孝的就必定怨恨他的父母；做臣子的求索君主而沒有所得，不忠的必定要背叛他的君主。因此品行淫邪的百姓，出門沒有衣穿，回家沒有飯吃，內心懷恥辱之感，就會一起去做邪惡暴虐之事，多得無法禁止。因此盜賊眾多而治安好的情況很少。倘使盜賊增多而治安不佳，用這種做法尋求治理，就好像把人旋轉多圈，而要他不背向自己一樣，使國家治理的說法根本不可能實現。

【時析】

　　墨子的時代，流行厚葬的習俗，棺材裏放上珠寶，死者親屬要服喪數年，導致一系列問題出現。墨子反對厚葬，是站在當時平民的立場上反對王公諸侯在喪事上的奢侈浪費。他認為厚葬浪費錢財，減少人口（因為守喪數年會導致不能生產），對社會、國家不利。當時王公諸侯厚葬能夠到甚麼地步？1978 年後中國湖北省隨州發掘

Contemporary interpretation:

During Mozi's time, it was customary to have elaborate funerals: valuables were put into the coffin and the grieving family had to observe a mourning period of several years. Such practices led to many problems. Mozi's objection to elaborate funeral customs was from the common person's stance: he was critical of the nobles and vassal rulers squandering wealth on funeral customs. Mozi thought that elaborate funerals were a waste of both money and human resources, as people could not be productively engaged during the mourning period and bring benefit to the state.

How elaborate could a funeral be for nobles and vassal state rulers at the time? In 1978, the Tomb of Marquis Yi of Zeng was excavated in Suizhou, in China's Hubei Province. Marquis Yi of Zeng lived during the same period as Mozi, and archaeologists believe he was the ruler of the small state of Sui located next to the state of Chu. Excavation of this tomb yielded two sets of chime bells, totaling a hundred bells, and a variety of lutes (*qin* and *xe*) were also found. The tomb was like a large-scale subterranean music palace. In order to play the instruments and create music, a great number of strong boys and young girls were necessary. Also found in the tomb were twenty-one small, colorfully painted coffins containing the corpses of women, mostly aged about eighteen to twenty years. They had been buried alive. In life, they had probably

出了曾侯乙墓。這個曾侯乙跟墨子是同時代的人，
考古學家認為他就是當時楚國旁邊的一個小國隨
國的王侯。他的墓裏出土了兩套編鐘，足一百件，
以及各種琴瑟，相當於一個大型的地下音樂宮殿。
要演奏和敲動這些樂器，非得整團的青春少女和
壯力小夥不可。墓中還有人殉，二十一個彩繪小
棺中所殮者大多為十八至二十歲的女性，她們生
前應該是為這位王侯奏樂的樂工，即「撞巨鐘，
擊鳴鼓，彈琴瑟，奏竽笙」者。墓中還有大量青
銅兵器。隨國在當時還只是一個小國，由此可見，
如果是大國國君死了，厚葬能達到甚麼程度。這
就不止是死人跟活人爭財富，還是跟活人爭活人
了。難怪墨子要極力反對厚葬。

今天人們對待葬禮的態度其實跟墨子是比較
接近的。由於現在人口越來越多，如果再實行傳
統的土葬，死人勢必會佔用很多土地，影響到活
人的生計，因此，現在一般實行火葬，骨灰放在
公墓裏，或葬在偏僻少人的山地。就此而論，說
墨子的節葬論有現代元素也不為過。不過現在的
問題是，即使火化，公墓的費用也越來越高，所
以有不少網友呼籲，政府在抑制房價，讓人們「住

served as musicians for the ruler, responsible for "striking the bells, banging the drums, and playing the lutes and the pipes." There were also numerous bronze weapons in the tomb. The state of Sui was only a small state at the time, so one can imagine how elaborate a funeral might be when the ruler of a big state passed away. The deceased had not only robbed wealth from people when living, but had also snatched the lives of the living and entombed them with his death. No wonder Mozi opposed elaborate funerals so fervently.

Nowadays, people share similar views to Mozi on how funeral customs should be conducted. Population numbers have risen substantially and if we were to keep to traditional burial customs, vast areas of land would be needed for the deceased. This would affect the provision of sustenance for the living. Cremation has thus become a common practice in China, the ashes of the deceased being placed in a public columbarium or in some cases buried in remote hillside areas. In this respect, we may say that Mozi's advocacy of simplifying funeral customs pre-dates certain modern practices. Nevertheless, even with the use of cremation and a public columbarium, funeral expenses continue to rise. This has caused many netizens to call on the government to do its part: while keeping housing prices down so that people can "afford to buy a home," it should also properly regulate funeral services so that people can "afford to buy a resting place"!

得起」的同時，也要管理好殯儀業，讓人們「死得起」。

三
虧奪民衣食之財，仁者弗為也。

【原文】

子墨子言曰：「仁之事者，必務求興天下之利，除天下之害，將以為法乎天下。利人乎，即為；不利人乎，即止。且夫仁者之為天下度也，非為其目之所美，耳之所樂，口之所甘，身體之所安，以此虧奪民衣食之財，仁者弗為也。」是故子墨子之所以非樂者，非以大鐘、鳴鼓、琴瑟、竽笙之聲，以為不樂也；非以刻鏤華文章之色，以為不美也；非以犓豢煎炙之味，以為不甘也；非以高臺厚榭邃野之居，以為不安也。雖身知其安也，口知其甘也，目知其美也，耳知其樂也，然上考之不中聖王之事，下度之不中萬民之利。是故子墨子曰：「為樂，非也。」（《非樂上》）

Three
A benevolent man refuses to rob people of money they have saved for clothes and food.

Translation:

Master Mozi said, "When a benevolent man is at work, he will definitely seek to promote the interests of the world and save the world from calamities; in doing so, he will become a model for the world. He does whatever benefits people; he avoids whatever is detrimental to people. When a benevolent person takes the interests of the world into consideration, he does not do so for things that are beautiful to the eyes, pleasant to the ears, delicious to the palate, comfortable to the body; a benevolent man refuses to rob people of money they have saved for clothes and food for such things." Hence, Master Mozi was against music, not because he thought the sounds of big bells, the drums, the lutes and the pipes were not pleasant; not because he thought artefacts of sculpture, carving and ornamentation were not beautiful; not because he thought the taste of the fried and broiled meat of cattle was not delicious; not because he thought living in high towers, grand pavilions and tranquil villas was not comfortable. Surely, his body knew the comfort, his palate knew the good taste, his eyes knew the beauty and his ears knew the pleasure. But when he considered those above, he found these luxuries

【今譯】

墨子說：「仁人做事，務必謀求天下的福利，去除天下的禍害，以此作為天下的楷模。對人有利的，就去做；對人無利的，就停止。仁人替天下考慮，並不是為了眼睛能看到美麗的東西，耳朵能聽到快樂的聲音，嘴巴能嘗到美味，身體能享受舒適的感覺。為了這些而掠取民眾的衣食財物，仁人是不做的。」墨子之所以反對音樂，並不是認為大鐘、響鼓、琴、瑟、竽、笙的聲音不悅耳，並不是認為雕刻、紋飾的色彩不悅目，並不是以為烹調出的禽畜佳餚不悅口，並不是認為居住在高樓深院中身體不舒服。雖然身體感到舒適，嘴裏感到香甜，眼睛感到美麗，耳朵覺得快樂，向上考察，不符合聖王的事跡；向下考慮，不符合萬民的利益。所以墨子說：「搞音樂是不對的！」

【時析】

墨子非樂，有他的針對性。他針對的是當時王侯的沉溺音樂，耗費民財民力。在《非樂上》裏，墨子提到了跟他同時代的大國齊國的國王齊康公。這個國王是個昏君，他「淫於酒、婦人、

not in accordance with what the sage kings did; and when he considered those below them, he found these extravagances did not serve the interests of the majority of people. Therefore, Master Mozi said, "Enjoying music is wrong." ("Fei Le I")

Contemporary interpretation:

When Mozi spoke out against music, he was actually condemning the nobles at the time who by indulging in music spent a lot of public money and mis-used the common man's labor. In "Fei Le I", Mozi talks about Duke Kang of Qi, who was then the ruler of the big state of Qi. Duke Kang of Qi was a corrupt ruler: he "indulged in wine and ladies, and never attended governance meetings" ("House of Tian Jingzhong" in the _Shiji_). He loved to hold night-time variety shows involving the performance of tens of thousands of singers and dancers. They were extremely lavish. In order to retain these performers for the shows, the men (most of them young) did not work in the fields and the women did not weave or make clothes. On top of this, they were obliged to maintain a healthy physique and a good appearance. This used up a lot of state treasure!

Such expense was undoubtedly a sin in Mozi's eyes in a society where people still suffered from hunger and cold, and lacked rest from working hard trying to make ends meet.

However, it is questionable that Mozi should have gone from

不聽政」（《史記·田敬仲完世家》），喜歡大型文藝晚會，常搞萬人歌舞，壯麗得一塌糊塗。要養一萬個搞音樂舞蹈的演員（大部份必須是年輕人），男的不從事耕作，女的不從事紡織，而且還要營養好，面色好，那得耗費國家多少財力呀！在墨子看來，在當時還有人饑、有人寒、有人不得休息的情況下，這無疑是一種罪過。

但墨子由非國君之樂走向了非樂本身，則是有問題的，就好比在潑洗澡水時連澡盆裏的嬰兒也一併潑出去了。其實，音樂跟奢侈是兩碼事。音樂跟勞動也可以結合的。在勞動中使用音樂，有時能促進生產，提高效率。勞動號子不就是一個例子嗎？而且音樂可以陶冶性情，增加人的靈性，使人得到休息，身心愉悅。墨子雖然勉強承認音樂也好聽，但出於實利的目的，還是嚴厲拒絕的。莊子《天下》篇就說墨子「生不歌」，想來他老人家確實跟聞韶三月不知肉味的音樂迷孔子不同，代表着像夏禹那樣為興天下利、除天下害而不知疲勞地天天奔走的那一類聖人。

criticizing the indulgence of music by the ruler to criticizing music itself. This is like throwing the baby out while getting rid of the bath water. Actually, music and extravagance are two quite different things. Music can also be combined with hard work. The use of music during work can help to enhance productivity and efficiency. Aren't labor chants an example? Besides, music can rouse the soul, nurture our character, offer a relaxing break and fill us with joy.

Even though Mozi unhesitatingly admitted that music is pleasant to our ears, he sternly rejected it for practical reasons. In "Tian Xia," Zhuangzi mentioned that Mozi "never sang in his life"; perhaps Mozi was really different from the music fan Confucius who after listening to good music, became oblivious to the taste of meat for three whole months. Mozi represents sages like Xia and Yu who made a tireless effort every day to promote the interests of the world and save mankind from calamities.

修身 *Self-edification*

一

善為君者，勞於論人，而佚於治官。

【原文】

　　子墨子言，見染絲者而歎曰：「染於蒼則蒼，染於黃則黃。所入者變，其色亦變。五入必而已，則為五色矣。故染不可不慎也。」

　　非獨染絲然也，國亦有染。……凡君之所以安者，何也？以其行理也，行理性於染當。故善為君者，勞於論人，而佚於治官。不能為君者，傷形費神，愁心勞意，然國逾危，身逾辱。……

　　非獨國有染也，士亦有染。（《所染》）

【今譯】

　　墨子說，他曾見人染絲，就感歎說：「（絲）用青色染料就變成青色，用黃色染料就變成黃

One
Good rulers painstakingly select men to work for them, so they can be at ease themselves when dealing with officials.

Translation:

Master Mozi said he once saw someone dyeing silk. He sighed and said, "What is dyed in blue becomes blue; what is dyed in yellow becomes yellow. When silk is put into a different dye, it will turn into a different color. When it is put into five dyes, it will turn into five different colors. Therefore, dyeing should be done with care."

It is not only silk that can be dyed, but a state can also be "dyed" [influenced].

What makes a ruler able to bring good order to a state? It is because he governs with good grounds, and his good grounds come from good influence. Hence, good rulers painstakingly select men to work for them, so they can be at ease themselves when dealing with officials; whereas incompetent rulers do harm to their bodies and exhaust their minds, burden their hearts and tax their wills, yet their states become increasingly endangered, and they themselves suffer more humiliation.

色。所投入的染料變了，絲的顏色也跟着變。投入五種染料後，就變為五種顏色了。所以浸染不可以不謹慎啊。」

不僅染絲如此，國家也有「染」。……大凡國君能治國安邦，是甚麼原因呢？是因為他們行事合理，而行事合理源於所染得當。所以善於做國君的，用心致力於評價選拔人才，對於管理官吏就顯得很輕鬆。不會做國君的，傷身勞神，用盡心思，國家卻更危險，自己更受屈辱。……

不單國家有染，士也有「染」。

【時析】

《所染》是墨子的名篇，屬於墨子早年跟隨儒家學習時期的作品。儒家很重視「交友」的問題，孔子認為「性相近，習相遠」，習氣決定了人成為怎樣的人，而甚麼決定習氣呢？交往的人在其中有很大的作用。孔子談論過「損友」和「益友」的分別，孔子的弟子子張和子夏在交友是應該只交比自己先進的人還是也要幫助比自己後進的人的問題上曾經產生過爭論。比墨子晚一代的

It is not only a state that can be "dyed," but an official can also be "dyed." ("Suo Ran")

Contemporary interpretation:

"Suo Ran," is a famous passage in *Mozi*, written by Mozi during his earlier years when he was a disciple of Confucianism. Confucianism takes the matter of "friendship" very seriously. Confucius believed that "by nature, men are all alike; by habit, they become different from each other." The habitual dispositions we form make us the kind of persons we are; what then, makes our habitual dispositions? The people we get along with play an important role in this. Confucius had discussions on how "maleficent friends" differ from "beneficent friends." Two disciples of Confucius, Zi Zhang and Zi Xia, debated over whether one should make friends only with those who are more advanced in learning or give a hand to those who know less. Mencius was a generation younger than Mozi and his mother had "moved three times" in search of a good learning environment for her young son, so that Mencius could learn from good "influence" ("dye"). As a result, Mencius was nurtured to develop into an outstanding person and became an excellent Confucian.

During the Enlightenment in the West, philosophers debated over whether man makes the environment, or the environment makes the man. What is undoubted is that in the shaping of a

孟子，其母親在孟子年紀小的時候為了孟子有一個好的學習環境而「孟母三遷」，讓孟子有好的「所染」，結果孟子出類拔萃，成為一個優秀的儒者。

在西方啟蒙主義時期，啟蒙哲學家們就人與環境到底誰決定誰產生過爭論。無論如何，在塑造人的品格和命運上，環境，尤其是社會環境有着非常重要的作用。我們從經驗中很容易明白這一點。墨子《所染》談的正是這個道理。

個人「所染」的結果跟國家「所染」的結果大同小異。所謂「物以類聚，人以群分」，民主國家喜歡跟民主國家相交，獨裁國家跟獨裁國家惺惺相惜，因為同類都有更多相同的價值觀，易於交流與溝通。青少年交友也不可不慎，交一個好朋友和交一個壞朋友，往往可影響一生。

二
其所循人必或作之，然則其所循皆小人道也？

man's character and his fate, the environment, especially his social environment, plays an extremely important part. Our own experience makes it easy for us to understand this. What Mozi talks about in "Suo Ran" is exactly the same.

Regarding the outcomes, "influences" on a personal level as well as on a state level are mostly the same. As the saying goes, "Similar things come together, similar people get together." Democratic countries like befriending democratic countries, while despotic countries stand up for despotic countries. This happens because similar stances share values in common, making exchanges and communication possible. Young people should be cautious in making friends, as the choice of a good friend or a bad friend can have a huge impact on one's life.

Two
What they followed must first be created. In that case, did they all follow the ways of the small-minded men?

Translation:
The Confucianists said, "A gentleman should return to the old ways in speech and in dress, then he will become benevolent."

【原文】

儒者曰：「君子必服古言然後仁。」應之曰：「所謂古之言服者，皆嘗新矣，而古人言之，服之，則非君子也。然則必服非君子之服，言非君子之言，而後仁乎？」又曰：「君子循而不作。」應之曰：「古者羿作弓，杼作甲，奚仲作車，巧垂作舟，然則今之鮑函車匠皆君子也，而羿、杼、奚仲、巧垂皆小人邪？且其所循人必或作之，然則其所循皆小人道也？」（《非儒下》）

【今譯】

儒家的人說：「君子必須說古話，穿古衣才能成仁。」回答他說：「所謂古話、古衣，都曾經在當時是新的。而古人說它穿它，就不是君子了。是不是一定要穿不是君子的衣服，說不是君子的話，才可以合乎仁義？」

儒家的人又說：「君子只遵循舊制，而不創造。」回答他說：「古時后羿造了弓，季杼造了甲，奚仲造了車，巧垂造了船。若按儒家的看法，

In answer, we said, "What are taken here as the old ways in speech and in dress were actually once new. So, when the people of the past spoke and dressed in these ways, they were not gentlemen. In this case, isn't it necessary for us to dress ungentlemanly and to speak in ungentlemanly ways, so that we can become benevolent?" And they said, "A gentleman follows but does not create." In answer, we said, "In the past, Yi created the bow, Yu created armor, Xi Zhong created the cart, Qiao Cui created the boat. Would one say, however, the tanners, armorers, cart makers and carpenters of today are all gentlemen, while Yi, Yu, Zhong Xi and Qiao Cui were small-minded men? What is more, what they followed must first be created. In that case, did they all follow the ways of the small-minded men?" ("Fei Ru II")

Contemporary interpretation:

Confucius "believed in and admired the old ways," and "retold yet did not create." Mozi intentionally struck a discordant note and emphasized the importance of "to create," that is, of invention and creation.

Most Mohists were originally craftsmen and merchants from the lower class; they wrote for practical purposes and made sure that what they wrote was easily understood. Therefore, they used the "vernacular language" time and again in their arguments. If we compare *Mozi* with the *Analects*, we may find

今天的鞋工、甲工、車工、木工，都是君子，而
后羿、季杼、奚仲、巧垂，豈不都是小人了？他
們所遵循的事物，最初都必定是人創造出來的，
這些後人都遵循的東西，難道是小人之道嗎？」

【時析】

　　孔子是「信而好古」、「述而不作」，墨子
有意唱反調，強調「作」，也就是發明創造。

　　墨家多是出身工商業者的下層賤民，他們寫
文章要求實用，讓人看得懂，因此不憚用當時的
「白話文」反復申說。如果將《墨子》與《論語》
相比，《論語》雅馴、簡潔、含蓄，不太容易看
得懂，《墨子》則顯得明白易懂，但又缺乏含蓄，
不那麼耐人尋味，可以說，這是墨子提倡用白話
文，反對「說古話」的正反兩方面的結果。

　　至於服裝，墨子大概也是從當時賤民做事的
方便出發，怎麼方便怎麼穿，反對像儒者那樣到
哪裏都高冠峨帶，束手束腳。如果看《論語》中
孔夫子針對不同場合、等級對着裝的煩瑣要求，
就能理解墨子的惱怒了。那麼墨子對時裝會是個

the *Analects* elegant, succinct and subtle, but not very easy to understand; *Mozi*, in contrast, was written in clear, simple language, but lacked subtlety and intricacy. This may well be the result of Mozi's promotion of the vernacular language in opposition to Confucius's "speaking the old language." With regard to what to wear, Mozi might also have adopted the convenient approach of the lower class, dressing casually in comfortable clothes; again in contrast to the Confucians who wore high hats and wide belts everywhere, which restrained their movement. If we look at the *Analects* and see how meticulously Confucius deliberated on his outfits with respect to different situations and ranks, we may be able to understand why Mozi was so irritated. So, what was Mozi's view on fashion? If Mozi were to see people wearing miniskirts, low-cut jeans, garments exposing the navel, and earrings, tongue rings or nose rings, would he condemn them as "bizarre outfits"? Perhaps not. As a craftsman and the leader of "advanced and innovative techniques" at the time, Mozi would be more interested in "bizarre outfits," just as he had high praise for the invention of bows, armor, carts and boats. In fact, Mozi himself was an inventor of many things! *Mozi* records many of Mozi's inventions in the areas of physics, optics, logic as well as mechanics. What is more, in "Cheng Shou," there are records of Mohist inventions of military machines and weapons, as well as original thoughts on how to protect a city from attack. While Mozi was probably

甚麼樣的態度呢？他老人家看了超短裙、低腰褲、耳環、舌環乃至鼻環，會不會指責它們是「奇裝異服」呢？恐怕不會吧。作為工匠和當時「高新技術」的領頭人，墨子對於「奇技淫巧」更有興趣，對於弓甲車船的發明都高度讚揚，墨家自己也發明了不少東西。

《墨經》中記載了墨家的不少物理、光學、邏輯發現和機械發明，《城守》篇更是記載了墨家發明使用的軍事機械和武器，以及對於守城法的各項原創性思想。看來墨子對於發明創新有一種嗜好，很可惜的是，這種對於新話語、新時裝、新技術和新時尚的愛好，後來竟飽受壓抑。

墨子指責儒家的「法古」與「泥古」是自相矛盾，因為儒家所法之古言古服，在當初也是新話語新時裝嘛！儒家所循之弓甲車船，在當初也是新鮮事物嘛！既如此，又何必跟今人過不去，非得讓他們說古話穿古衣，一成不變地遵從古人呢！

墨子重視發現、發明創造的精神，在今天尤

passionate about inventions and creativity, his enthusiasm for new language, new fashion, new techniques and new trends was later, unfortunately, very much rejected.

Mozi criticized Confucians as self-contradictory in advocating "emulate the old ways" and "guard the old ways," because these old ways of speaking and dressing they copied were once new language and fashion. The making of bows, armor, carts and boats as adopted by Confucians were once entirely new things. If so, why do we have to make life difficult for people nowadays and ask them to dress and speak in the old ways, stubbornly following what people did in the past?

Mozi valued discovery, creativity and invention. This sort of attitude is of remarkable significance for us today, where the so-called "creative industry" has seemingly linked creativity with the economy, arts and literature, and also industry. This is so much like Mozi all those centuries ago: at once a craftsman, a mechanic and a designer. As history, shows, inventions — such as the steam engine, electricity, the telephone, the motorcar, the airplane, the computer, the mobile phone and the internet — have so often facilitated a leap in the overall economic development of a region or a country, creating countless career opportunities, or even transforming lifestyles and political systems. What achievements they have enabled!

其有意義。今天所謂「創意產業」，已明顯將創造跟經濟、文藝、工業結合起來，這跟同時身為工匠和機械師、設計師的墨子是多麼相似！歷史上，類似於蒸汽機、電話、汽車、飛機、電腦、手機、互聯網這樣的發明，常常能促進一個地區、一個國家整個經濟的騰飛，創造無數的就業機會，甚至改變人們的生活方式和政治制度，功莫大焉！

三

言足以復行者，常之；不足以舉行者，勿常。不足以舉行而常之，是蕩口也。

【原文】

　　治徒娛、縣子碩問於子墨子曰：「為義孰為大務？」子墨子曰：「譬若築牆然，能築者築，能實壤者實壤，能睎者睎，然後牆成也。為義猶是也。能談辯者談辯，能說書者說書，能從事者從事，然後義事

Three

Words that can be put into practice, speak them often; those that cannot be put into practice, speak rarely. To speak often those [words] that cannot be put into practice is just pointless blather.

Translation:

Zhi Tuyu and Xian Zishuo asked Master Mozi, "What is the most important thing in practicing righteousness?"

Master Mozi said, "It is like building a wall: let those capable of laying bricks lay the bricks, let those capable of filling the earth fill the earth, let those capable of measuring measure; then the wall will be built. Practicing righteousness is the same: let those capable of debating debate, let those capable of explaining explain, let those capable of administering administer; then righteous deeds will be accomplished."

Master Mozi said, "Words that can be put into practice, speak them often; those that cannot be put into practice, speak rarely.

"To speak often those [words] that cannot be put into practice is just pointless blather." ("Geng Zhu")

成也。」

子墨子曰：「言足以復行者，常之；不足以舉行者，勿常。不足以舉行而常之，是蕩口也。」（《耕柱》）

【今譯】

治徒娛、縣子碩兩個人問墨子說：「行義，甚麼是最關緊要的事？」墨子答道：「就像築牆一樣，能築的人就築，能填土的人就填土，能測量的人就測量，這樣牆才可以築成。行義也是這樣，能演說的就演說，能講書的就講書，能做事的就做事，這樣義事才可以辦成。」

墨子說：「言論可付之實行的，就應經常講；不可以實行的，就不應經常講。不可以實行卻又天天講，那就是饒舌了。」

【時析】

孔子是個大教育家，號稱弟子三千，身通六藝者七十有二人。墨子也是大教育家，開辦私學，一生教人，弟子彌豐，來自當時各國，因此他的

Contemporary interpretation:

Confucius was a great educator who had three thousand disciples, among whom seventy-two were well versed in the six arts. Mozi was also a great educator. He ran a private school and devoted his whole life teaching countless students from all of China's states; in effect he ran an "international school."

In "Gong Shu," it was said that in order to stop Chu attacking Song, Mozi promptly mobilized three hundred combat-ready disciples to safeguard Song territory. Among Mozi's disciples, several dozen are still known by their names, while several hundred were sacrificed in different battles. From this we can conclude that the number and competency of his disciples were on a par with those of Confucius. No wonder the Mohist school became one of the most noted schools of thought.

Practicing righteousness on the whole means engaging in righteous endeavors and striving to attain ideals. Similar to the four disciplines — the practice of virtues, speech, politics and literature of the Confucian school — Mozi divided "practicing righteousness" into three disciplines and demanded there should be collaboration between the three to accomplish the great enterprise of "practicing righteousness." "Debate" refers to the skills of argument and oratory, as well as reasoning skills. The aim of having these skills was to nurture lobbyists

學校也是一間「國際學校」。

《公輸》中說，墨子止楚攻宋，一次就發動能打仗的弟子三百，去宋國守城。墨子弟子中有名可記的有數十人，歷次戰鬥中死難弟子也有幾百名，可見論弟子的數量品質，墨子都不會遜色於孔子。難怪墨家成為當時的顯學。

為義，大意是指從事正義事業，為理想而奮鬥。跟孔門有德行、言語、政事、文學四科一樣，墨子將其「為義」事業分為三科，三科要分工合作，才能把「為義」的偉大事業辦成。「談辯」，指辯論和演說技巧，當然也包括如何思考問題，培養遊說之士，主要是針對國君，使他們聽從正義的主張；「說書」指解說文化科學知識，培養學者和教師；「從事」，指學習工、商、農、兵各種實際技能，培養各種實用人才。跟孔子不耐煩「遲樊問稼」相比，墨子對於工商農業是重視的，尤其對於技術研究和創新的重視，非孔子所能及。

《墨子》中的《墨經》和《備城門》簡直就

who could persuade the rulers of states to follow their doctrines on righteousness. "Explanation" refers to explanation of cultural and scientific knowledge in order to nurture scholars and teachers. "Administration" refers to acquisition of practical skills related to craft-making, commerce, farming and the military, aimed at encouraging people to gain practical skills of all kinds. Unlike Confucius, who was somewhat annoyed when Fan Chi asked about farm work, Mozi put great emphasis on craft-making, commerce and farming, and particularly valued technical research and innovation. Such foresight never came into Confucius's thinking.

The chapters "Mo Jing" and "Bei Cheng Men" in *Mozi* were actual records of different technological experiments and practical training undertaken by Mohists. Nonetheless, since Mozi was not as experienced as Confucius in politics, he did not have as many discussions about these ideas nor did he have the sound administrative skills required for governance. This may be the result of the difference between the two in regard to their origins, the social strata they interacted with and the sources of their disciples. As Mozi was from the grassroots, his disciples were probably mostly offspring of the "lower class"; in contrast, as Confucius once held important administrative roles and was in touch with rulers of various states, his disciples were mostly officials among whom many were of noble descent.

是墨家各種科技實驗和實習的記錄。但由於墨子沒有孔子那樣的從政經驗，因此在治國觀念和具體的治理技術上就談得比孔子少。

這可能跟孔子和墨子兩人的出身、主要交遊層次及學生來源有關。墨子出身草根，身邊的弟子可能也主要是「賤民」子弟，因此和孔子曾居高位、與諸國國君長期交遊、弟子大多為士且有不少貴族子弟不同。

墨子從事教育，培養人才，是為了「為義」，為了實現天下大治，也即墨子的「兼愛」主張。為了達到這個總的目的，需要各科弟子既根據自己所長學習專門知識，有所分工，又要能積極配合，完成共同事業。

由此可以看出，墨子既有宗教徒的使命感，又有技術家的方法論。這樣的人在別的宗教傳統中也能看到。比如基督教的使徒保羅，他就要求教徒團結一心，根據各自的才能，做先知的做先知，當牧師的當牧師，說方言的說方言，要像基督的四肢一樣結成一個完整的肢體。

Mozi's engagement in education and nurturing people of talents was aimed at "practicing righteousness," and to realize good governance of the world; in other words, what Mozi claimed as the doctrine of "all-embracing love." In order to achieve this aim, he needed disciples to focus on their own professions and enhance their professional knowledge. At the same time, he needed them to collaborate actively with each other so as to accomplish the shared cause. We can see that Mozi had the dedication of a religious believer as well as the methodology of a technical expert. Similar personalities can also be found in other religious traditions. For example, Paul the Apostle from Christianity who asked fellow Christians to be united in spirit and to serve with their own talents — let prophets do their jobs, let pastors do their jobs, let people of dialects speak with their dialects; in this way, they would become the four limbs of Christ and be united as one whole body.

Mozi greatly valued "action", meaning practice. Between speech and action, he made action the criterion. This is different from Confucius. Confucius put emphasis on the teaching of ancient classics, therefore setting up a specialized study in language. When Confucius talked about "action" it was mostly used to mean "practice of virtues," that is, moral practice. Mozi, on the other hand, was an expert in advanced technology. He "worked with his hands and feet" every day

墨子非常重視「行」，也即實踐。在言與行中，他以「行」為標準。這跟孔子也有所不同。孔子所傳重在古代典籍，所以專設言語科。

孔子即使談「行」，也多指「德行」，即道德實踐。墨子卻是高科技專家，天天「動手動腳」，重視實驗和實踐，要從實踐中出真知，也要在實踐中檢驗假設，並需要實用的效果，也就是他天天掛在口上的「利」。在這點上，他有點像現代的實用主義者，以實效為行動的標準。

在科舉時代，以儒家經典為考試書目，學生以背孔孟之書為能事，哪裏有墨子「動手動腳」的實驗精神。

即使在今天的中國，重孔忽墨的教育後果仍舊可見一斑，應試教育使學生記憶力強而動手做實驗、從事社會實踐的能力弱。

像德國那樣的技工學校和日本那樣的工匠培養法，在中國很少受重視。而這種動手的能力恰恰是當前作為「世界工廠」的中國最需要的。

doing experiments and valuing practice. He wanted to find the truth from practice, to test hypotheses from practice and also needed to see the effects from practice — which was what he often talked about and meant by "the benefits." In this respect, he was a bit like the modern pragmatist who sees practical outcomes as the standard for actions. During the imperial examination period when Confucian classics were listed as examination pieces, students had to be good at reciting the books of Confucius and Mencius. Thus Mozi's "hands on" experimental spirit was rarely encouraged. Even in today's China, we can still see traces of how schooling has prioritized Confucianism over Mohism. Our examination-oriented education system has strengthened students' memory skills but left their hands-on experimentation and social engagement abilities undeveloped. Technical training in China is not given as much attention as it is by technical schools in Germany or the nurturing of craftsmen as it is in Japan. Hands-on ability, however, is most needed for China in order to fulfill its current role as "the world's factory."

If we compare the organization of the Mohist school with the Confucian, the Confucian school had a looser teacher-student relationship whereas the teacher-student relationship among Mohists was close-knit. Mohists came together and formed an organization for "practicing righteousness," somewhat similar to a semi-religious, semi-military organization. When

　　這裏要說一說墨家的組織。跟孔子師生關係比較鬆散不同，墨子師生關係比較緊密，他們結成為一個「為義」團體，有點類似於半宗教半軍事性的組織。墨子的弟子學成後，會被推薦到各國做官，或做各項專業，或留在墨家團體中。

　　墨子的大弟子禽滑厘充當墨子助手，協理全面工作，而耕柱子、高石子、勝綽、公尚過這些弟子則被派往楚、衛、越等國從政從軍。他們中若有人表現不好，違背墨子的主張，就會被召回，重新接受教育。

　　如勝綽被派去做齊將項子牛的侍從，但他多次助項子牛侵略魯國，違背了墨子「非攻」、「兼愛」的原則，因此被墨子召回教育。

　　墨家要求團體成員有財分享，起碼要拿出一部份給首領，以做團體繼續發展之用。比如耕柱子被推薦到楚國當官，幾個老同學到楚國出差找耕柱子，招待得不好，他們回來後向墨子發牢騷，說耕柱子混得太差，待他們很小氣，把他調回來吧！墨子不相信耕柱子是個小氣人。果然，沒多

the disciples of Mozi graduated from their studies, they would be recommended to the states to become officials, or would specialize in different professions, or would stay and work for the Mohist organization. The most senior of Mozi's disciples, Qin Huali, became Mozi's assistant and coordinated the overall running of the organization. Others such as Geng Zhuzi, Gao Shizi, Sheng Zhuo and Gong Shangguo were dispatched to the states of Chu, Wei or Yue to work for the government or the military. Any who did not perform well or betrayed Mozi's principles would be called back and re-educated. For instance, Sheng Zhuo was assigned to serve Xiang Ziniu, a general of Qi, but he assisted many times in Xiang's attack of Lu, which betrayed Mozi's principles of "anti-aggression" and "all-embracing love," so he was called back by Mozi for re-education.

Also, the Mohist school required its members to share their wealth and donate a part of it to the leader to fund the organization's development. An example, of this is seen in Geng Zhuzi. He had been recommended to Chu to serve as an official and was visited by a few alumni on business. They did not receive the hospitality from Geng Zhuzi they were expecting and complained to Mozi about him, saying that he did not give his best to his job and had been mean to them during their stay. They suggested Geng Zhuzi should be called back. Mozi, however, did not believe him to be ungenerous.

久，耕柱子攢夠了二百金，恭恭敬敬把它奉獻給了墨子。墨子高興地表揚了耕柱子。

墨家團體還能通過教育改造人，把各種有缺點的人改造成「為義」之士。高何、縣子碩、索盧原都是暴徒、潑皮無賴，成為墨子和禽滑厘的學生後，不僅「免於刑戮之辱」，而且成為「天下名士顯人，以終其壽，王公大人從而禮之」（《呂氏春秋・尊師》）。

墨家組織嚴密，要求嚴格，墨子要求墨者只穿粗布衣，腳登木麻鞋，「日夜不休，以自苦為極」。他們不僅要學會各種專業技能，還要接受軍事訓練，隨時準備幫助被侵略的弱國打守城戰，為正義戰爭而犧牲。

可以說，墨家團體是中國最早的非政府組織，它的首領被稱為「鉅子」，它的組織嚴密，有嚴格的紀律（「墨者之法」），鉅子一聲令下，墨者就可以赴火蹈刃，死不旋踵。墨家團體是墨子的「兼相愛、交相利」社會理想的試驗田，它的內部有財產公有制的苗頭。

Just as he thought, a short while later Geng Zhuzi respectfully offered everything he'd saved to Mozi: two hundred pieces of gold. Mozi gladly commended Geng Zhuzi for this action.

The Mohist organization also undertook the reshaping of people through education, so that men with weaknesses could be reformed into upright citizens "practicing righteousness." Gao He, Xian Zishuo and Suo Luyuan had been violent and despicable men, yet after studying under Mozi and Qin Huali, not only could they "avoid the shame of punishment and murder," but became "world-renowned notable people treated with due respect by nobles and high-ranking people until their deaths." ("Zun Shi", _Lushi Chunqiu_)

The Mohist school was a cohesive organization with stringent requirements. Mozi asked Mohists to wear only rough woven clothes and shoes made from hemp, "taking no rest day and night, regarding the ascetic as the highest form of life." Apart from acquiring professional skills in various fields, they were required to receive military training to be prepared to fight in defense of weak states under attack, ready to sacrifice themselves for the righteous call. It can be said that the Mohist group was China's earliest non-governmental organization. Its leader was called "the mogul," its organization was tight-knit and its discipline strict ("The law of the Mohist"). Once the mogul gave an order, the Mohists would tread on fire and

四

言足以遷行者，常之；不足以遷
行者，勿常。

【原文】

　　子墨子曰：「凡言凡動，利於天鬼百
姓者為之；凡言凡動，害於天鬼百姓者舍
之；凡言凡動，合於三代聖王堯舜禹湯文
武者為之；凡言凡動，合於三代暴王桀紂
幽厲者舍之。」

　　子墨子曰：「言足以遷行者，常之；
不足以遷行者，勿常。不足以遷行而常之，
是蕩口也。」

　　子墨子曰：「必去六辟。嘿則思，言
則誨，動則事，使三者代御，必為聖人。
必去喜，去怒，去樂，去悲，去愛，而用
仁義。手足口鼻耳，從事於義，必為聖
人。」

　　子墨子謂二三子曰：「為義而不能，

blades, willing to sacrifice themselves without regret. The Mohist group was the testing ground for Mozi's social ideal of "all-embracing mutual love and mutually beneficial acts," and its internal structure showed the early signs of common ownership of assets.

Four
Words that can improve practice, speak them often; those that cannot improve practice, speak them rarely.

Translation:

Master Mozi said, "Any words or any actions that are beneficial to heaven, spirits and the people should be taken. Any words or any actions that are harmful to heaven, spirits and the people should be forsaken. Any words or any actions that are in accordance with the sage kings of the Three Dynasties — Yao, Shun, Yu, Tang, Wen and Wu — should be taken. Any words or actions that are in accordance with the tyrants of the Three Dynasties — Jie, Zhou, You and Li — should be forsaken."

Master Mozi said, "Words that can improve practice, speak

必無排其道。譬若匠人之斲而不能，無排
其繩。」（《貴義》）

【今譯】

墨子說：「一切言行，有利於天、鬼神、百
姓的，就去做；一切言行，有害於天、鬼神、百
姓的，就捨棄。一切言行，符合三代聖王堯、舜、
禹、商湯、文王、武王的，就去做；若與三代暴
君夏桀、商紂、周幽王、周厲王相同的，就捨
棄。」

墨子說：「言論足以改善行為的，就經常
講；不足以改善行為的，就不要天天提。不
足以改善行為，卻要天天提，就是繞舌的空話
了。」

墨子說：「一定要去掉六種邪僻，沉默時能
思索，出言能教導人，行動能從事義。使這三者
交替進行，定能成為聖人。一定要去掉喜，去掉
怒，去掉樂，去掉悲，去掉愛，以仁義作為一切
言行的準則。手、腳、口、鼻、耳，都用來從事
義，這樣的人定能成為聖人。」

them often; those that cannot improve practice, speak them rarely. To speak often those [words] that cannot improve practice is just pointless blather."

Master Mozi said, "One must do away with the six partialities. When silent, think; when speaking, counsel; when in action, engage in righteousness; practice these three in turn and one will certainly become a sage. One must do away with pleasure, do away with anger, do away with joy, do away with sadness, do away with love; instead, make use of benevolence and righteousness. When one uses his hands, feet, mouth, nose and ears to engage in righteousness, he will become a sage."

Master Mozi then spoke to a few disciples, "When one fails at practicing righteousness, one must not give up the way. It is like when a carpenter fails to carve, he must not give up the measuring line." ("Gui Yi")

Contemporary interpretation:

Mozi argued for "promoting the interests of the world, saving the world from calamities." At the same time, he stressed that we should not only care about the interests of human beings, but also about the interests of heaven and the gods, in other words, "the three interests." To rephrase them in modern terms: state policies should adhere to the way of heaven, the way of the earth, as well as the way of humanity.

墨子對幾個弟子說：「行義而不能勝任，一定不可放棄道理。好像木匠不能劈好木材，也不可放棄墨線一樣。」

【時析】

墨子主張「興天下之利，除天下之害」，同時他還主張不只單純興人間之利，還要關注天神的利益，即「三利」。若用今天的話來說，就是國家政策要符合天道、地道、人道。換了基督教福音派的語言，就是既要符合人道，也要符合上帝之言。因此，若墨子看到當代的民主政治，會認為它符合人民一時的利益，但不是完美無缺。

基於一時民意的決策，從長遠眼光來看不一定有好後果（比如，破壞生態環境、賞懶罰勤）。在墨子看來，做到了「三利」的榜樣是三代聖王，違反「三利」，搞「三不利」的壞榜樣是三代暴君。

墨子是個實踐家，重視「行」或實踐的效果，不喜歡空談沒有效果的話。這對現代崇尚空談的人不失為一個忠告。

In evangelical Christian concepts, the policies should be humane and obey the words of God. If Mozi had the chance to look at today's democratic politics, he would not think them perfect and flawless as they only consider people's short-term interests. Decisions based on public opinion at any one time may not bring good in the long-term, such as damaging the ecological environment, rewarding the lazy and punishing the hardworking. The figures whom Mozi saw as exemplary and acting in the "three interests" were the sage kings of the Three Dynasties. Those who represented the betrayal of the "three interests" and caused the "three harms" were the tyrants of the Three Dynasties.

Mozi, being a pragmatist, valued "action," or effective practice, and disliked empty talk that got nowhere. This still serves as good advice today to discourage people indulging in rhetoric.

Mozi's thought on practicing benevolence and righteousness is different from that of Confucianism. Laozi, in his book, believed to be published later than Mozi's, states, "Heaven and earth are impartial, treating all things as straw dogs," emphasizing the impartiality of heaven and the fairness of the sage, since they treat everything — be it a man or a thing — equally, without discrimination. Daoists argued against having strong emotions (love or hatred) about things, including moral behavior. German philosopher Kant believed that we carry

　　對於仁義的踐行，墨子與儒家不同。一般認為比《墨子》要晚出的《老子》說，「天地不仁，以萬物為芻狗」，強調天無偏私，聖人也沒有偏愛，對任何人、物都一視同仁，沒有分別心。道家不主張對事物有強烈的愛憎，包括道德行為。德國哲學家康德認為，我們履行道德義務是一種絕對命令，不能受情感的支配，因此，康德式的君子即使是孝敬父母，也能做到表情漠然，不帶私愛。

　　這跟孔子講究對父母的孝要帶有「敬」不同，而跟這裏墨子所主張的「去喜、去怒、去樂、去悲、去愛」，即去掉這些自然情感，專注地執行仁義的事業相當一致。佛教主張「泛愛」，反對私愛或偏愛，也反對因私愛而起的七情六欲（怨憎等），因此與墨子這裏所說亦有近似之處。由此可見墨子思想的深刻性，可擴闊人們對仁義的踐行的看法。

　　墨子認為即使做不到道理要求我們去做的，也不能因為自己做不到，就放棄道理本身。生活中常常有「因人廢言」的現象，他人說的話

out moral obligations from a kind of categorical imperative, which must not be dictated by emotions. Therefore, a Kantian gentleman can honor his parents in his filial act and yet not show any emotion, because he does so without partial love. Such a view is different from that of Confucius who considers "respect" as essential to one's filial piety, but is more in line with that of Mozi who urges people to "do away with pleasure, do away with anger, do away with joy, do away with sadness, do away with love." Meaning, to do away with all these natural emotions so that people can focus on carrying out benevolence and righteousness. Buddhism advocates "compassion" and opposes partial love or favoritism; it also opposes the variety of emotions and desires (such as resentment or hatred) that are aroused by partial love. Here we can see similarities between Buddhism and Mozi's claims.

The profundity of Mozi's thought can help broaden people's view on practicing benevolence and righteousness.

Mozi contended that even though we may not be able to achieve what reason obliges us to do, we should not give up the attempt just because we fail to achieve it. In daily life, we often judge the words of others because of their perceived character. However, what others have to say may be reasonable even though their characters are in doubt, or they fail to do what they have said. It is wrong to ignore the

雖然有道理，但由於他們品格不好，或者做不到所說的，我們就因此否定他們所說的話的道理 —— 這是不對的。有時還真需要把言和行分開，言本身的真理性並不因某個人的行為而受到損害。

五

今若過之心者，數逆於精微，同歸之物，既已知其要矣，是以不教以書也。

【原文】

　　子墨子南遊使衛，關中載書甚多，弦唐子見而怪之，曰：「吾夫子教公尚過曰：『揣曲直而已。』今夫子載書甚多，何有也？」子墨子曰：「昔者周公旦朝讀書百篇，夕見漆十士。故周公旦佐相天子，其脩至於今。翟上無君上之事，下無耕農之難，吾安敢廢此？翟聞之：『同歸之物，信有誤者。』然而民聽不鈞，是以書多也。

merit of others' words because of their conduct. Sometimes we really need to separate words from deeds because the truth in people's words will not be undermined by what they do.

Five
Now, for those who have a heart like Gong Shangguo, who can think deeply and attend to detail, they already know the essentials of how different things in the world head towards the same end. It is therefore unnecessary to teach them with books.

Translation:
Master Mozi traveled south to Wei as an envoy. There were many books in the cart that he took with him. Xian Dangzi was astonished by what he saw, and he said, "Master, you once taught Gong Shangguo and said, '[Books are] used just for judging what is right and what is wrong.' Now Master you take so many books with you, what is the point?"

Master Mozi said, "In the past, Duke Dan of Zhou read a hundred articles every morning and met with seventy scholars

今若過之心者，數逆於精微，同歸之物，既已知其要矣，是以不教以書也。而子何怪焉？」（《貴義》）

【今譯】

　　墨子南遊到衛國去，車中裝載的書很多。弦唐子見了很奇怪，就問：「老師您曾教導公尚過說：『書不過是用來衡量是非曲直罷了。』現在您裝載這麼多書，有甚麼用處呢？」墨子說：「過去周公旦早晨讀一百篇文章，晚上見七十士。所以周公旦輔助天子，他的美善傳到了今天。我墨翟上沒有承擔國君授予的職事，下沒有耕種的艱難，如何敢拋棄這些書呢！我聽說過：『天下萬事萬物殊途同歸，流傳時確實會有差錯。』但是由於人們聽到的不一致，書就多起來了。現在像公尚過那樣的人，其心對於事理已能洞察入微，對於殊途同歸的天下事，也已知道切要之處，因此就不必拿書來教育他了。你為甚麼要奇怪呢？」

【時析】

　　墨子跟孔子一樣，也是因材施教，針對不同

in the evenings. Thus, Duke Dan of Zhou assisted the Son of Heaven in his governance, and his achievements have lasted until today. As I do not have any duties serving the ruler above and I do not need to bear the hardship of growing crops, how dare I give up the books? I have heard that 'Even though different things in the world head towards the same end, mistaken messages might be circulated.' Since people heard different stories, the number of books increased. Now, for those who have a heart like Gong Shangguo, who can think deeply and attend to detail, they already know the essentials of how different things in the world head towards the same end. It is therefore unnecessary to teach them with books. How come you are astonished?" ("Gui Yi")

Contemporary interpretation:

Like Confucius, Mozi was able to align his teaching with his students' abilities; he gave different answers to different students in response to their questions. For example, his disciple Gong Shangguo was an intelligent man who had already grasped the great principles, and Mozi considered that he no longer needed to read. All he needed was to practice. For other disciples, however, Mozi might still ask them to continue with their books.

Mozi's love of learning was comparable to Confucius's. So, in his trip to the state of Wei, he took with him a cart full of

的學生的問題予以不同的回答。他的學生公尚過是個聰明人，已了悟大道理，墨子認為他不必再多讀書，多去實踐就行了。對別的學生，墨子卻可能是要求他們多讀書的。

墨子自己則跟孔子一樣，好學不倦。這次外出衛國，也隨身帶了一車的書（那時書都是木牘竹簡，佔面積很大），真是走到哪學到哪。墨子的知識結構如何？他對於古代典籍如《尚書》、《詩經》、各國《春秋》非常熟悉（這些《春秋》有些可能連孔子也沒讀過），經常引用。

他還有廣泛的科技和軍事方面的知識，《墨經》和《備城門》顯示了這點，在這些範疇連孔子也望塵莫及。當然，跟以人文知識見長的孔子這樣的「博雅君子」相比，墨子可能更像今天的社會科學家和自然科學家。他們的知識結構雖然有交叉的地方，但差異也是很明顯的。

六
士之計利不若商人之察也。

books (at the time books were made with wooden tablets and bamboo slips, so they took up much space). He was truly a person who kept studying wherever he went.

How did Mozi build up his knowledge system?

He was well read in the classics like _Shang Shu, Shi Jing_ and the Spring and Autumn annals from different states (probably even Confucius had not read these Springs and Autumns) and he referred to them often in his own writings. He also acquired a wide range of scientific, technological as well as military knowledge, which is found in "Mo Jing" and "Bei Cheng Men" — in these fields, even Confucius was way behind. Of course, in comparison with Confucius, who was famous for his knowledge of the humanities, Mozi may well have been more like a social or natural scientist of today's world. Even though there are areas in the knowledge systems of each that overlap, their differences are also evident.

Six
Scholars are not as discerning as the merchants when it comes to calculation of interests.

【原文】

子墨子曰:「商人之四方,市賈信徙,雖有關梁之難,盜賊之危,必為之。今士坐而言義,無關梁之難,盜賊之危,此為信徙,不可勝計,然而不為。則士之計利不若商人之察也。」(《貴義》)

【今譯】

墨子說:「商人到四方去,買賣的價錢相差一倍或數倍,即使有通過關卡那種艱難,碰見盜賊那種危險,也一定去做。現在士只要坐着說說義,沒有關卡的艱難,沒有盜賊的危險,這樣做所取得的利益,倍數多得沒法計算,卻還是不去實行。可見士人計算利益,不如商人精明。」

【時析】

墨子熟悉工商業者,尊重他們的勞動和價值;他自己也不恥於談「利」,還將「利」與「義」等同起來。孔子尚且說「沽之哉,沽之哉」,要為自己的知識和思想找到好買主。等同義利的墨子當然鼓勵士子像商人那樣精明冒險,出售關於「義」的知識,可是他發現他們很蠢,即使唾手

Translation:

Master Mozi said, "Merchants travel everywhere to do business and gain from differences in doubling or multiplying prices. Even though it is hard passing through gates and bridges, and there are dangers bumping into thieves and robbers, they still do it. Now scholars just sit there and talk about righteousness, face no hardships from gates and bridges and no dangers from thieves and robbers. Their gain from it will double or multiply and become incalculable, yet they still do not do it. It is clear that scholars are not as discerning as the merchants when it comes to the calculation of interests." ("Gui Yi")

Contemporary interpretation:

Mozi was well-acquainted with a lot of craftsmen and merchants, and he had a high regard for their labor and contribution. He himself was not ashamed of talking about "interests," and placed "interests" on a par with "righteousness." Even Confucius once said ,"Let's sell it, let's sell it," and was eager to find a good buyer for his knowledge and ideas. Mozi, who placed interests on a par with righteousness, would certainly encourage scholars to be as smart and adventurous as the merchants when it came to selling their knowledge of "righteousness." Yet he discovered they were really incompetent at grasping chances close at hand to sell "righteousness" in order to gain "interests."

可售「義」得「利」，卻連這個都算不好。

在墨子看來，讓天下得到了利，就是使天下得到了義。因此，他才會像商人計算利潤一樣計算「義」的利潤。他是具有類似功利主義思想的大思想家。

七
告子言談甚辯，言仁義而不吾毀，告子毀，猶愈亡也。

【原文】

二三子復於子墨子曰：「告子曰：『言義而行甚惡。』請棄之。」子墨子曰：「不可，稱我言以毀我行，愈於亡。有人於此，翟甚不仁，尊天、事鬼、愛人，甚不仁，猶愈於亡也。今告子言談甚辯，言仁義而不吾毀，告子毀，猶愈亡也。」（《公孟》）

【今譯】

有幾個弟子告訴墨子說：「告子說：『墨子

Mozi thought that by allowing the world to gain interests, the world would achieve righteousness. That is why he calculated the benefits of "righteousness" in the same way as the merchants calculated profit. He was a great thinker whose moral principles were similar to those of Utilitarianism.

Seven

Now, even though Gaozi's arguments are misleading, he did not criticize me for advocating benevolence and righteousness. It is better for him to have criticized me than to remain indifferent.

Translation:

A few of Master Mozi's disciples reported Gaozi to him, saying: "Gaozi said, 'Mozi talks about righteousness, but his conduct is bad.' Please ignore him."

Master Mozi replied, "No, I can't. It is better for him to praise my words and criticize my conduct than to be indifferent. Suppose someone comes up and says, 'Mo Di is very malevolent. He respects heaven, serves the spirits and loves people; he is very malevolent.' This is still better

口言仁義而行為很壞。』請您棄之不理。」墨子說：「不可以。他稱讚我的言論卻誹謗我的行為，總要比沒有批評好。假如現在這裏有人說：『墨翟很不仁義，尊重上天、侍奉鬼神、愛護百姓，很不仁義。』這還是勝過沒有批評。現在告子講話非常強詞奪理，但不批評我講仁義，告子的批評仍然勝過沒有批評。」

【時析】

墨子對於批評持歡迎的態度，而不是掩耳盜鈴地裝着聽不見，更不會讓人收聲，營造出形勢一片大好的局面。墨子對告子批評的內容也能分析地看。他認為，告子批評他（墨子）沒有照着他（墨子）所提倡的仁義去做，儘管不正確（墨子認為自己是在身體力行仁義），但告子也認同墨子所提倡的仁義，對此墨子是欣賞的。何況告子對墨子提出批評，也是出於興趣和關注，這跟完全忽視墨子不同。

換在資訊時代的今天，批評更加重要，批評使人關注，引發人們的興趣，也能引起深入的討論。

than indifference. Now even though Gaozi's arguments are misleading, he did not criticize me for advocating benevolence and righteousness. It is better for him to have criticized me than to remain indifferent." ("Gong Meng")

Contemporary interpretation:
Mozi always welcomed criticism. He would not bury his head and pretend not to have heard what had been said; nor would he silence such voices in order to make the situation look more personally favorable.

In this passage, Mozi was able to look at Gaozi's criticism. When Gaozi wrongly criticized Mozi for not practicing benevolence and righteousness, despite the fact that he (Mozi) considered himself to be truly practicing benevolence and righteousness, Mozi appreciated Gaozi's endorsement of his advocacy on benevolence and righteousness. What is more, in being critical of him, Gaozi showed his interest in and awareness of Mozi's claims.

This shows an attitude that is quite different from total indifference.

In the information age of today, criticism is even more important because it stimulates people's awareness, invokes their interest and initiates deep discussions.

八

釣者之恭，非為魚賜也；餌鼠以蟲，非愛之也。

【原文】

魯君謂子墨子曰：「我有二子，一人者好學，一人者好分人財，孰以為太子而可？」子墨子曰：「未可知也，或所為賞與為是也。釣者之恭，非為魚賜也；餌鼠以蟲，非愛之也。吾願主君之合其志功而觀焉。」（《魯問》）

【今譯】

魯國國君對墨子說：「我有兩個兒子，一個愛好學習，一個喜歡將財物分給別人，誰可以立為太子？」墨子答道：「這還不能知道。二子也許是為着賞賜和名譽而這樣做的。釣魚人躬着身子，並非為了給魚以恩賜；用蟲子作為捕鼠的誘餌，並不是因為喜歡老鼠。我希望主君把他們的動機和效果結合起來進行觀察。」

Eight

The fisherman bows not because he wants to feed the fish; a man lures a mouse with worms not because he loves it.

Translation:

The ruler of Lu said to Master Mozi, "I have two sons: one likes learning and the other likes sharing his wealth with others. Which one should be crowned prince?"

Master Mozi said, "As yet, it is not sure. What they do may be driven by reward and praise. The fisherman bows not because he wants to feed the fish; a man lures a mouse with worms not because he loves it. I wish Your Majesty to observe both their intentions and their achievements." ("Lu Wen")

Contemporary interpretation:

Which of the two sons of the ruler of Lu should become the successor? Mozi thought it important to take note of their words as well as their behavior in order to reach a full assessment of their intentions and the consequences. This was the only way not be misled by appearance. Mozi objected to both deontology (the study of the nature of duty) and consequentialism (where the morality of an action is judged by

【時析】

魯君的兩個兒子到底哪個適合繼位？墨子認為應該聽其言，觀其行，把他們的行動動機和效果結合起來考察，這樣才能不被外表迷惑。墨子一方面反對唯動機論，另一方面也反對唯效果論，看來是一個穩妥的辦法。

但在真實的政治世界中，動機很難揣測，常常只能從效果來逆推動機的好壞。好的動機辦了壞事，壞的動機卻客觀上促成了好事，都不乏這樣的例子。下面舉一個隱藏動機的例子。

在 1960 年代的非洲獨立運動中，馬西埃·恩圭馬在西班牙統治時期從政，逐步高升；他表面上對西班牙人很忠誠，因此西班牙人在迫於當時世界大勢不得不從赤道幾內亞撤出時，幫助他贏得了大選。但是馬西埃在取得政權後，就驅逐西班牙人，沒收其財產，又在全國搞大清洗運動，把政府裏的 12 個部長殺掉 10 個，全部換上自己的家人。

馬西埃建立特務機構，宣稱自己是神，大搞

its consequences only, not the circumstances or the nature of the act), which sounds a sensible choice to make.

However, in real politics, intentions are difficult to figure out, and most of the time we can only surmise that the intentions are good or not from the consequences. It is often the case that good intentions end up with bad results, and bad intentions end up having good results. Here is an example of how one's intentions can be concealed. During the African independence movements of the 1960s, Macías Nguema started his political career under Spanish colonial rule and rose to power gradually. When global pressure eventually forced the Spanish to withdraw from Equatorial Guinea, Nguema won the support of the Spanish in the country's presidential election by outwardly showing loyalty to them.

However, once he had control of the government, he expelled the Spanish from the country and confiscated their properties. He also undertook ethnic cleansing of the country, killing ten of the twelve government ministers and replacing them with his own family members. He set up intelligence agencies, declared himself God and promoted a personality cult. His hatred of intellectuals was so intense that he had most of them slaughtered. By the late 1970s, he had had nearly half of the country's population exterminated. No intellectuals survived, and the most educated people were the dozen or

個人崇拜，對知識份子極端仇恨，大肆屠殺。到1970年代晚期，全國的人口被他消滅了一半，國內沒有一個知識份子，文化程度最高的只有十來個技工。1979年，他的侄子發動政變把他推翻，國家才逐漸恢復正常。

九

擇務而從事。

【原文】

　　子墨子遊，魏越曰：「既得見四方之君子，則將先語？」子墨子曰：「凡入國，必擇務而從事焉。國家昏亂，則語之尚賢、尚同；國家貧，則語之節用、節葬；國家憙音湛湎，則語之非樂、非命；國家遙僻無禮，則語之尊天、事鬼；國家務奪侵凌，即語之兼愛、非攻，故曰擇務而從事焉。」（《魯問》）

【今譯】

　　墨子出外遊歷，魏越問他：「如果能見各地

so skilled workers. In 1979, his nephew mounted a coup and overthrew him; since then the country has gradually returned to normalcy.

Nine
Pick the important tasks to undertake.

Translation:
As Master Mozi was about set off to travel, Wei Yue asked, "When you meet with the rulers of different states, what will you say?"

Mozi said, "Whenever someone visits a state, he must pick the important tasks to undertake. If the state is in chaos, then tell the ruler about the worthiness of virtue and unity; if the state is poor, then tell him about the principles of frugality and simple funerals; if the state indulges in music and alcohol, then tell him about the demerits of music and the falsehood of fatalism; if the state is outlandish and indecent, then tell him about honoring heaven and serving the spirits; if the state takes other states by force and oppression, then tell him about the worthiness of all-embracing mutual love and the falsehood of aggression. This is what I mean by picking the important tasks to undertake." ("Lu Wen")

的諸侯,您將說甚麼呢?」墨子說:「凡到一個
國家,一定要選緊要的事去做。假如國家昏亂,
就告訴他們尚賢、尚同的道理;假如國家貧窮,
就告訴他們節用、節葬的道理;假如國家喜好聲
樂、沉迷於酒,就告訴他們非命、非樂的道理;
假如國家荒淫怪僻、不講究禮節,就告訴他們尊
天、事鬼的道理;假如國家專門掠奪侵略別國,
就告訴他們兼愛、非攻的道理。所以說要選擇緊
要的事去做。」

【時析】

　　有人認為這段話是墨子學說的總綱,關鍵在
「擇務從事」。其實,這不過是墨子見機行事,
針對不同國家的「病情」對症下藥而已,但也確
實是對墨子政治思想不同側面的一個綜覽。至於
其背後的總體精神,有人認為是「興天下之利,
除天下之害」,有人認為是「天志」,有人認為
是「兼相愛、交相利」,其實都一樣,那就是天
既兼愛,人也要兼愛,由是而有對上的尊天事鬼,
對鄰人的非攻兼愛,內政要尚賢尚同,生活上要
節用節葬、非樂非命,如此才能真正做到人與人
的兼愛。這精神可總結為一個現代詞──博愛。

Contemporary interpretation:

Some people think that this passage contains the essence of Mozi's thought, and "picking the important tasks to undertake" is its key feature. In fact, the passage just shows that Mozi's actions depended on circumstance; he'd offer appropriate remedial proposals for countries with different "illnesses." However, it does give a general summary of the different facets of Mozi's political thought. As for the underlying overall spirit, some people think it is "promote the interests of the world, save the world from calamities"; others think it is "heaven's will"; yet others think it is "all-embracing mutual love and mutually beneficial acts." In fact, they are all the same. In other words, heaven should love all-embracingly; and people should love all-embracingly. Thus, we come to honor heaven and serve the spirits above; we treat neighbors with tolerance and all-embracing love; we value virtue and unity in domestic governance; we cut costs, practice simple funerals, stop indulgence in music and condemn fatalism in daily life. This is the only way to realize all-embracing mutual love among people.

The general spirit of this can be summed up in the modern expression "universal love."

治學做人 On Conduct

一

言必有三表。

【原文】

子墨子言曰：「執有命者以襍於民間者眾。執有命者之言曰：『命富則富，命貧則貧；命眾則眾，命寡則寡；命治則治，命亂則亂；命壽則壽，命夭則夭；命雖強勁，何益哉？』上以說王公大人，下以駔百姓之從事，故執有命者不仁。故當執有命者之言，不可不明辨。」

然則明辨此之說將奈何哉？子墨子言曰：「必立儀，言而毋儀，譬猶運鈞之上而立朝夕者也，是非利害之辨，不可得而明也。故言必有三表。」何謂三表？子墨子言曰：「有本之者，有原之者，有用之者。於何本之？上本之於古者聖王之事。於何原之？下原察百姓耳目之實。於何用之？廢以為刑政，觀其中國家百姓人民之利。此所謂言有三表也。」（《非命上》）

One

For any opinion there are three criteria.

Translation:

Master Mozi said, "There are many fatalists among the masses. Those who believe in fatalism say, 'One who is rich is fated to be rich, one who is poor is fated to be poor; when it is fated to have many people there will be many people, when it is fated to have few people there will be few people; when it is fated to have order there will be order, when it is fated to have disorder there will be disorder; one who lives long is fated to live long, one who dies early is fated to die early. Even if one exerts all one's strength, what is the point?' They try to persuade the nobles and the high-ranking people above with these words, and to discourage the common people below from their work. That is why the fatalists are malevolent. Therefore, we must examine carefully what the fatalists claim. Yet how should we examine their claims?" Master Mozi then said, "We should set up some standards. If one speaks without standards, it is like putting a time-measuring device on a revolving potter's wheel, and judgments of right or wrong as well as beneficial or harmful can hardly be made clear. Hence, for any opinion there are three criteria."

What are the three criteria?

【今譯】

墨子說：「主張有命的人，雜處於民間太多了。主張有命的人說：『命裏富裕則富裕，命裏貧困則貧困；命裏人口眾多則人口眾多，命裏人口少則人口少；命裏治理得好則治理得好，命裏混亂則混亂；命裏長壽則長壽，命裏短命則短命。你雖然使出強大的力量，又有甚麼用呢？』用這話對上遊說王公大人，對下阻礙百姓生產。所以主張有命的人是不仁義的。對主張有命的人的話，不能不明加辨析。」

可是如何去明辨這些話呢？墨子說：「必須訂立準則。說話沒有準則，好比在陶輪之上，放立測量時間的儀器，這麼搞，是非利害之分是不可能搞明白的。所以言論必須有三條標準。」

是哪三條標準呢？墨子說：「有考察本原的，有推究原因的，有用於實踐的。怎麼考察本原？要向上溯源於古時聖王的事跡。怎麼推究原因？要向下考察百姓耳目所見的事實。怎麼用於實踐？把它用作刑法政令，看看它是否符合國家百姓人民的利益。這就叫言論三標準。」

Master Mozi said, "There is the foundation, there is the evidence, there is the usefulness. Where comes the foundation? One looks upon the deeds of the sage kings of the past for the foundation. Where comes the evidence? One looks for the evidence through the ears and eyes of the common people below. Where comes usefulness? Apply it to the law and governance and observe how it can serve the interests of the common people and the state. This is what we call the three criteria of opinions." ("Fei Ming I")

Contemporary interpretation:

In this passage, Mozi put forward his famous "three criteria method," that is, the three criteria for judging whether an opinion is right or wrong, beneficial or harmful. The first criterion rests on indirect experience — the experience of the sage kings of the past; the second criterion also rests on indirect experience — the experience of the common people; the third criterion seeks to verify the truth and merits of policies with their effects. We can see from these three criteria that Mozi was an empiricist in an "inductive" sense. Mozi did not like empty talk or abstract arguments (here he differed from Laozi and Zhuangzi), but valued learning from experience and practical results. This is on the one hand a merit of his thought, yet on the other one of his shortcomings. For example, Mozi applied this "three criteria method" to his arguments for the existence of spirits and gods. Deeds of spirits and gods were recorded

【時析】

墨子在這裏提出了他著名的「三表法」，即確定言論的是非利害的三條標準。第一條是間接經驗，古代聖王的經驗；第二條也是間接經驗，老百姓的經驗；第三條是用效果來檢驗政策的成敗優劣。由此三條標準可以看出墨子是個經驗主義者，而且是個「歸納」意義上的經驗主義者。墨子不尚虛談和抽象的思辨（跟老莊不同），他重視的是經驗總結和實際效果，這一方面是其思想的優點，另一方面卻也構成其缺陷。

比如，墨子用這個「三表法」論證鬼神的存在，因為古書記載了鬼神的事跡，百姓也口耳相傳有鬼神出沒，鬼神在政治上亦起到賞善罰惡，警醒人心，使人不敢犯罪的良好作用。顯然，墨子的這種經驗主義由簡單的歸納而來，其效果也只是考慮到利害而跟「真理」沒有多少關係。而且，墨子似乎沒有意識到「利害」（效果）與「是非」（真假）之間常常是有矛盾的，有好處的言論並不總是真的，比如「善意的謊言」、「高貴的謊言」就是能夠取得好的效果，但終究是假話。在政治設計上，無論中西，都有些思想家認為應

in the ancient documents, and sights of spirits and gods were also widely talked about by the common people. This aside, spirits and gods in the political realm served to remind people that good would be rewarded and bad would be punished, so that they were careful about not committing crimes.

It seems that Mozi's adopted empiricism was grounded in simple inductive thinking, and the underlying consequentialism only considered the benefits and harms, regarding "truth" as rather irrelevant. What is more, Mozi seemed unaware of the contradiction that often happens between "benefit and harm" (effects) and "right and wrong" (truth and falsehood), since advantageous opinions might not always be true. For example, "white lies" and "graceful lies" can have beneficial consequences, and yet they are still untruths. Regarding political designs, be they in China or in the West, there are thinkers who support "Teaching in the name of God or the Dao" — even if they do not believe in the existence of spirits and gods, they still think that a faith in spirits and gods among common people is useful for governance. They therefore encourage and promote the practice of faith among common people (most often resulting in them becoming superstitious).

Nonetheless, Mozi's "three criteria method" as a kind of empiricism is still worth studying. Its last criterion is similar to

該「神道設教」，他們自己明明不相信鬼神的存在，卻認為讓老百姓相信鬼神存在有助於治理，因此慫恿和助長老百姓的信仰習慣（大多數時候是迷信）。

雖然如此，墨子的「三表法」作為一種經驗主義，還是有值得參考的地方。三表法中的最後一條，跟今天的「社會實驗」（試錯法、試點）有點相似。再比如馬克思主義哲學，也很符合「三表法」：第一，強調學習歷史經驗（如黨史），相當於墨子的「上本之於古者聖王之事」；第二，「從群眾中來到群眾中去」，相當於「下原察百姓耳目之實」；第三，「試點法」，相當於「廢以為刑政，觀其中國家百姓人民之利」。可見，即使在今天，「三表法」也在被人們自覺不自覺地運用着。

二
足敝下光，故成景於上。首敝上光，故成景於下。

"social experiment" (the trial-and-error, or try-out method). In addition, Marxist philosophy also matches well with the "three criteria method." First, it stresses learning from historical experience (e.g., the history of the Communist Party), which is equivalent to "one looks upon the deeds of the sage kings of the past for the foundation" in *Mozi*; second, "one comes from the people and returns to the people" is equivalent to "one looks for the evidence through the ears and eyes of the common people from below"; third, the "try-out method" is equivalent to "apply it to the law and governance and observe how it can serve the interests of the common people and the state." It can be seen that, even nowadays the "three criteria method" is employed by people, whether they are aware of it or not.

Two

The foot shields the light coming from below, so the image forms at the top. The head shields the light coming from above, so the image forms at the bottom.

Translation:

("Jing Xia") An inverted image [jing dao] forms when the light

【原文】

（經下）景到，在午有端與景長，說在端。

（經說下）景：光之人煦若射。下者之人也高，高者之人也下。足敝下光，故成景於上。首敝上光，故成景於下。在遠近有端，與於光，故景庫內也。（《經下》、《經說下》）

【今譯】

（經下）形成倒影的條件，在於光線交錯、有一個小孔並且有一定長度的影子，論證的關鍵在於小孔的存在。

（經說下）光線到達人的身上，光線的照射就像箭一樣是直的。光線照到人身上，人下處的影子形成於高處，人高處的影子形成於下處。因為人的腳部遮蔽從下邊照來的光線，所以形成的影子在上邊。人的頭部遮蔽從上邊照來的光線，所以形成的影子在下邊。因為人站在離牆有一定遠近的地方，牆上有一個小孔，並且被光線照射，

rays intersect [wu] at a small hole [duan] and the image is at a certain distance; the justification rests on the small hole.

("Jing Shuo Xia") The image: The light shines on [xu] the person directly like a shooting arrow. When the light reaches the bottom of the person, the image forms at the top; when the light reaches the top of the person, the image forms at the bottom. The foot shields the light coming from below, so the image forms at the top. The head shields the light coming from above, so the image forms at the bottom. When the person stands at a certain distance from a wall with a small hole in it, and there is light shining on it [yu], the image will form inside the chamber [ku]. ("Jing Xia," "Jing Shuo Xia")

Contemporary interpretation:

This passage talks about the principle of "pinhole imaging." Early cameras made use of this principle. Although the camera is a modern European invention, it remains remarkable that Mohists, more than two thousand years ago, had already discovered the principle upon which it worked.

The ancient character "dao" also stands for "inverted," meaning upside down. "Wu" refers to the intersecting of two light rays. "Duan" in ancient Han language signifies "extremity," a "tiny point". So, when the passage says "the light rays intersect [wu] at a small hole [duan]" it is referring

所以倒影在室內形成。

【時析】

這裏說的就是「小孔成像」的原理。近代歐洲發明的照相機，就是運用了這一原理。當然，歐洲人是獨立發明相機的，但是遠在二千多年前，墨家就發現了「小孔成像」原理，不能不說是一個奇跡。

這裏的「到」古文通「倒」，即倒立的意思。「午」指兩束光線正中交叉的意思。「端」在古漢語中有「終極」，「微點」的意思。「在午有端」指光線的交叉點， 即針孔。物體的投影之所以會出現倒像，是因為光線為直線傳播，在針孔的地方，不同方向射來的光束互相交叉而形成倒影。「與」指針孔的位置與投影大小的關係而言。

「光之人煦若射」是一句很形象的比喻。「煦」即照射，照射在人身上的光線，就像射箭一樣。「下者之人也高，高者之人也下」是說照射在人上部的光線，則成像於下部；而照射在人下部的光線，則成像於上部。於是，直立的人通

to the pinhole. For any projected object, an inverted image will be formed because light travels in a straight line through the pinhole, and light rays coming from the top and the bottom of the object intersect at the pinhole and progress in a linear manner beyond it (presenting an upside-down image). "Yu" refers to the relationship between the location of the pinhole and the size of the projected image. "The light shines on the person directly like the shooting arrow" offers a vivid analogy. "Xu" means "shine on" — the light shining on the person is like the shooting of an arrow. "When the light reaches the bottom of the person, the image forms at the top; when the light reaches the top of the person, the image forms at the bottom" means the light that shines on the upper body will form an image at the bottom, and the light that shines on the lower body will form an image at the top. In other words, when a person is standing upright, his image formed through the pinhole is projected upside down. "Ku" means the inside of the dark box. The part that "the person stands at a certain distance from a wall with a small hole in it, and there is light shining on it" refers to the relationship between the light rays reflected from the object, the size of the image and the distance between the image and the pinhole: the farther the object is from the pinhole, the smaller the image; the closer the object, the bigger the image.

The description about pinhole imaging in "Mo Jing" matches

過針孔成像，投影便成為倒立的。「庫」指暗盒內部而言。「遠近有端，與於光」，指出物體反射的光與影像的大小同針孔距離的關係：物距越遠，像越小；物距越近，像越大。

《墨經》關於針孔成像的描述與今天的照相光學所講是完全吻合的。這是對光直線傳播的第一次科學解釋。

墨家還利用光的這一特性，解釋了物和影的關係。飛翔着的鳥兒，牠的影也彷彿在飛動着。墨家分析了光、鳥、影的關係，揭開了影子自身並不直接參加運動的秘密。墨家指出鳥影是由於直線行進的光線照在鳥身上被鳥遮住而形成的。

當鳥在飛動中，前一瞬間光被遮住出現影子的地方，後一瞬間就被光所照射，影子便消失了；新出現的影子是後一瞬間光被遮住而形成的，已經不是前一瞬間的影子。因此，墨家得到了「景不徙」的結論，「景」通「影」，就是說，影子不直接參加運動。

with modern optical theories in photography. This is the first scientific explanation of how light travels in a straight line.

Mohists also made use of this feature of light to account for the relationship between objects and shadows. When a bird flies, it seems that its shadow also flies. Mohists investigated the relationship between light, the bird and the shadow, revealing the secret of the shadow not being directly involved in the movement. Mohists pointed out that the shadow of the bird is formed by the light rays shining in a straight line onto the bird and then being shielded by it. When the bird is flying, a shadow will form at the moment when the light is shielded by the bird. But the shadow will disappear in the next moment as the light rays shine on it again. The shadow that next appears is formed by the next beam of light that is shielded by the bird, and should not be counted as the shadow of the former moment. Mohists thus concluded that "images don't move." "Jing"("image") also stands for "ying" ("shadow").

They correctly recognized that the shadow does not participate directly in the movement. Then why does the shadow appear to be moving? This happens because when a bird is flying, the shadow of its every moment of progression is updated continuously. As the bird moves forward and its position changes, so does its shadow such that it looks as though it is flying together with the bird.

那麼為甚麼影子看起來是活動的呢？這是因為鳥飛動的時候，前後瞬間影子是連續不斷地更新着，並且變動着位置，看起來就覺得影是隨着鳥在飛動一樣。

《墨經》中小孔成像的發現並非後繼乏人。到了十四世紀中葉，元代天文數學家趙友欽在他所著的《革象新書》中記載了對日光通過牆上孔隙所形成的像和孔隙之間關係的詳細考察。

他通過實驗表明，小孔的像和光源的形狀相同、大孔的像和孔的形狀相同的結論，並指出這個結論是「斷乎無可疑者」。趙友欽的實驗證明了光的直線傳播，闡明小孔成像的原理。

現在的一些照相機就是利用了小孔成像的原理 —— 鏡頭是小孔（大多數為凸透鏡以保證光線成像距離），景物通過小孔進入暗室，像被一些特殊的化學物質（如顯影劑等）留在膠片上（數碼相機、攝影機等則是把像通過一些感光元件存儲在存儲卡內）。（本節參考了《百度百科》「小孔成像」條。）

The investigation of pinhole imaging discussed in "Mo Jing" was pursued in later generations. In the mid-fourteenth century in the Yuan dynasty, an astrologist-cum-mathematician Zhao Youqin made a detailed study of the relationship between the image formed by the sunlight passing through a hole in the wall and the hole itself and had it recorded in his book, *Ge Xian Sin Shu*. Through experiments, he demonstrated that the image of a small hole and the shape of the light source is the same, and the image of a big hole and the shape of the hole is the same. He said that this conclusion "is absolutely beyond doubt."

Zhao Youqin's experiments proved that light travels in a straight line and explained the principle behind pinhole imaging.

Nowadays some cameras still employ the principle of pinhole imaging: the lens is like the small hole (mostly they are convex lenses to keep enough distance for the image to form); when the subject enters the dark box through the small hole, its image will be imprinted onto the film (digital cameras and video-cameras have built-in light-sensitive sensors to convert and save the image into a memory card) with the application of special chemicals (such as contrast media, etc.).

(Acknowledgment is made here to "pinhole imaging" in Baidu Baike.)

三

之入之言可,是不誖,則是有可也。

【原文】

(經下)以言為盡誖,誖。說在其言。

(經說下)以:誖,不可也。之入之言可,是不誖,則是有可也。之人之言不可,以當必不審。(《經下》、《經說下》)

【今譯】

(經下)認為「所有的言論都是虛假的」,是自相矛盾的,論證的理由在於分析「所有的言論都是虛假的」這句話本身。

(經說下)所謂虛假,就是不正確。這個人的這句話如果正確,這就是有不虛假的言論,則是有正確的言論。這個人的這句話如果不正確,那麼認為它恰當,就必然不恰當。

【時析】

《墨經》揭示了不少邏輯現象,這裏所揭示

Three
If a statement is correct, then it is not erroneous; hence there exists a correct statement.

Translation:
("Jing Xia") To think that "all statements are erroneous" is erroneous. The justification rests on [an analysis of] the statement itself.

("Jing Shuo Xia") To be erroneous is to be incorrect. If an asserted statement is correct, then it is not erroneous; hence there exists a correct statement. If an asserted statement is incorrect, then it is necessarily unsound for one to take it as sound. ("Jing Xia," "Jing Shuo Xia")

Contemporary interpretation:
"Mo Jin" covers quite a few logical issues. The one discussed here amounts to "the liar's paradox" of the West.

When someone says, "I am lying," what do we understand? Is the statement true or false?

If the person is really lying, by saying "I am lying," he is telling

的相當於西方所說的「說謊者悖論」。

如果有人說「我在說謊」，那麼，他這句話到底是真的還是假的？如果他確實在說謊，那麼「我在說謊」就是真話；如果他確實在說真話，那麼「我在說謊」就是謊話。矛盾不可避免。它的一個版本是：「這句話是錯的。」

這類悖論的一個標準形式是：如果事件 A 發生，則推導出非 A，非 A 發生則推導出 A，這是一個自相矛盾的無限邏輯循環。「說謊者悖論」違反了人類思維規律，即矛盾律和排中律。

1903 年，英國哲學家羅素發現了著名的「羅素悖論」，他形象化地將它表達如下：

在某個城市中有一位理髮師，他的廣告詞是這樣寫的：「本人的理髮技藝十分高超，譽滿全城。我將為本城所有不給自己刮臉的人刮臉，我也只給這些人刮臉。我對各位表示熱誠歡迎！」

來找他刮臉的人絡繹不絕，自然都是那些不

the truth. If he is really telling the truth, while saying "I am lying," he is telling a lie. Contradiction is unavoidable.

Another version of it is: "This statement is false."

The standard pattern of paradoxes like these is this: If a state of affairs A occurs, then a state of affairs non-A logically follows; if non-A occurs, then A logically follows. It involves infinite logical loops of self-contradiction.

The liar's paradox defies principles of human thinking, namely, the law of contradiction and the law of excluded middle.

In 1903, the British philosopher Bertrand Russell published his famous mathematical "Russell's paradox." He subsequently illustrated it with an interesting scenario:

In a city there lived a barber, on whose billboard was written, "I have mastered outstanding hairdressing skills and am famous around the world. I will shave those who never shave themselves, and I will shave only these people. You are all warmly welcomed!"

Endless people came to be shaved by him, and for sure all were people who never shaved themselves. However, one

給自己刮臉的人。可是，有一天，這位理髮師從鏡子裏看見自己的鬍子長了，他本能地抓起了剃刀……這裏的問題是，他能不能給他自己刮臉呢？如果他不給自己刮臉，他就屬於「不給自己刮臉的人」，他就要給自己刮臉；如果他給自己刮臉呢？他又屬於「給自己刮臉的人」，他就不該給自己刮臉。

羅素通過這個悖論，打破了當時數學家們試圖利用康托爾的集合論建立邏輯嚴密的數學大廈的努力，造成了「第三次數學危機」，促進了現代數學的發展。

《墨經》中有關「說謊者悖論」提出的知識背景，我們今天已不能瞭解，因此很難評估它在中國邏輯史上的作用。《墨經》及整本《墨子》頻繁地使用了悖論、歸謬等方法來進行論辯，如上文談及，墨子在反駁儒家「述而不作」的守舊觀點時，就指出了儒家的自相矛盾（儒家所法之古服、古言、古器在最初時都是創造和發明）。可以說，墨子常用的悖論、歸謬法對後來的名家有很直接的影響。

day, when the barber looked at himself in the mirror and found that his beard had grown long, he instinctually picked up the razor… The question here is, does the barber shave himself? If he does not shave himself, he belongs to "those who never shave themselves." It then follows that he should shave himself. Yet, if he shaves himself, he then belongs to "those who shave themselves," and it follows that he should not shave himself.

In putting forward this paradox, Russell refuted the possibility of establishing a strictly logical mathematical system by utilizing Cantor's set theory, an endeavor being attempted by his contemporary mathematicians. As a result, he brought forth "the third crisis in Mathematics," which fostered the development of modern Mathematics.

Today we are not familiar with the epistemological background of "the liar's paradox" uncovered in "Mo Jing," it is therefore rather difficult to evaluate its role in the development of Chinese logical theories. In "Mo Jing," and in fact throughout *Mozi*, there is frequent use of paradox and reductio ad absurdum in arguments, such as the one quoted above — when arguing against the conservative view of "to tell but not to create" held by the Confucians, Mozi pointed to the self-contradictions made by Confucians (the old styles of dressing, speech and artefacts they emulated had originated

四

有諸己不非諸人，無諸己不求諸人。

【原文】

夫辯者，將以明是非之分，審治亂之紀，明同異之處，察名實之理，處利害，決嫌疑。焉摹略萬物之然，論求群言之比。以名舉實，以辭抒意，以說出故，以類取，以類予。有諸己不非諸人，無諸己不求諸人。或也者，不盡也。假者，今不然也。效者，為之法也，所效者，所以為之法也。故中效，則是也；不中效，則非也，此效也。辟也者，舉也物而以明之也。侔也者，比辭而俱行也。援也者，曰「子然，我奚獨不可以然也」？推也者，以其所不取之同於其所取者，予之也。是猶謂「也者同」也，吾豈謂「也者異」也。（《小取》）

【今譯】

辯論的目的，是要分清是非的區別，審察治亂的規律，搞清同異的地方，考察名實的道理，

as creations and inventions in the very beginning). We can say Mozi's uses of paradox and reductio ad absurdum directly influenced the later School of Names.

Four

If one endorses an opinion, he should not repudiate others for endorsing it; if one rejects an opinion, he should not urge others to endorse it.

Translation:

The purpose of debate is to distinguish right from wrong, to investigate the rules of order and disorder, to clarify similarities and differences, to examine the principles of names and reality, to determine benefits and harms, and to resolve doubts and uncertainties. Hence, the truth of all things is sought after, and the merits of various opinions are examined. Reality is revealed in names, thoughts are expressed through words, causes are uncovered in arguments. Any proof is offered with illustrations according to its kind; any disproof is offered with illustrations according to its kind. If one endorses an opinion, he should not repudiate others for endorsing it; if one rejects an opinion, he should not urge

斷決利害，解決疑惑，於是要探求萬事萬物本來的樣子，探求各種不同的言論利弊。用名稱反映事實，用言詞表達思想，用推論揭示原因。按類別取例證明，按類別予以反駁。自己所贊同的論點不能反對別人贊同，自己不贊同的觀點也不能要求別人贊同。

「或」，是表示並不都如此。「假」，是表示現在不如此。「效」，是為事物立個標準，用它來作為評判是非的標準。符合標準，就是對的；不符合標準，就是錯的。這就是「效」。「辟」，是列舉別的事物來說明這一事物。「侔」，是比較同類的詞句來說明它們都是行得通的。「援」，是說「你可以這樣，我為甚麼偏不可以這樣呢」？「推」，是我擺出一個證明給對方來反駁他，我這個證明是說明，對方所不贊成的與對方所贊成的本是同類。「是猶謂」（這就好比說）指含義相同，前後兩種議論相同。「吾豈謂」（我難道說），指含義不相同，前後兩種議論不同類。

【時析】

論者普遍認為先秦諸子百家一般缺乏對邏輯

others to endorse it. "Or" (　或　) means it can be otherwise. "Untrue" (　假　) means it is not so now. "Modeling" (　效　) means setting a standard, and using it to make judgment. So, if the model is followed, it is right; if the model is not followed, it is wrong. This is what "model" stands for. "Analogy" (辟) means offering an explanation on one thing by drawing on another thing. "Likening" (　侔　) means putting side by side things of the same sort to show that both are plausible. "To cite" (　援　) is like saying "If you can take it as true, why is it only me who cannot take it so?" "To infer" (　推　) means, when making a rebuttal, show that what the other opposes is actually identical to what he endorses. "It is like what is said" (是猶謂) means equivalence in meanings, and both opinions are the same; "How could it be me to say so" (吾豈謂) means discrepancy in meanings, and the two opinions are of different kinds. ("Xiao Qu")

Contemporary interpretation:

It has been a widely held view that pre-Qin schools of thought generally lacked deep exploration of logic. Mohism is an exception. Mohists made elaborate classifications of the logical rules of the Chinese language. The passage here taken from "Xiao Qu" represents just a small part of their work. If we put it together with the other passages in *Mozi*, we can see that as early as two thousand, four hundred years ago, Mohists were already very concerned with logical problems and formulated

的深入探究，墨家則是個例外。《墨子》對語言中的邏輯規則作了頗詳細的分類，這裏所引用的《小取》的段落只是一部份而已。結合《墨子》別的章節，我們可以發現，早在二千四百年前，墨家就已經十分關注邏輯問題，並總結其規律。在古希臘，是到亞里斯多德才系統地總結邏輯規律。

墨子對邏輯問題的關注，對後來的名家有直接影響，墨子的後學跟公孫龍、惠施這些辯論家和名家亦有互動。甚至後來超然世外的莊子，也要在著述中頻頻地涉及「儒墨之辯」，受他的老友兼同鄉惠施影響，來一個「道家之辯」，興致來了也談一下墨家早已談過的「鳥影不動」的悖論。但墨家對邏輯的興趣沒有形成中國文化對此領域重視的傳統，倒是歷史事實。

五
夫知者必量亓力所能至而從事焉。

their own rules. In ancient Greece, it was not until Aristotle that a systematic account of logical rules was accomplished.

Mozi's interest in logical problems had a direct influence on the later School of Names; his followers had interactions with orators from the School of Names like Gongsun Long and Hui Shi. Even the unworldly philosopher Zhuangzi later made frequent references to "the Confucian-Mohist debate"; under the influence of his good friend and fellow countryman Hui Shi, he took up a "Daoist debate" and enthusiastically talked about "the immobility of the shadow of the bird" paradox discussed by Mohists. Nevertheless, that Mohists' interest in logic had not established in Chinese culture a tradition of attaching importance to the topic is historical fact.

Five
A wise person must assess his capability and act accordingly.

Translation:
A few disciples told Master Mozi that they wanted to learn archery. Master Mozi said, "It is not possible. A wise person must assess his capability and act accordingly. Even an outstanding person of the state cannot handle fighting

【原文】

二三子有復於子墨子學射者，子墨子曰：「不可，夫知者必量亓力所能至而從事焉，國士戰且扶人，猶不可及也。今子非國士也，豈能成學又成射哉？」（《公孟》）

【今譯】

有幾個弟子告訴墨子，他們還想要學射箭。墨子說：「不可以。聰明的人一定要衡量自己的力氣所能達到的地方，然後再進行實踐。國中最傑出的人物一邊作戰一邊去扶人，尚且顧不過來。何況你們並非國士，怎麼能夠既學好文化，又學好射箭呢？」

【時析】

看來墨子跟孔子一樣，也是精通「六藝」之全才。

墨子因材施教，這幾個弟子大概是 freshmen，基本功課還沒學紮實，就要貪多圖全，想再學射箭，文理兼修。墨子考慮到他們的

and helping people at the same time; now you are not an outstanding person of the state, how can you be accomplished in your study and in archery at the same time?" ("Gong Meng")

Contemporary interpretation:

It appears that Mozi, like Confucius, was an all-round master in "the six arts."

Mozi taught according to individual students' abilities. The few disciples here probably were freshmen who although they had not even mastered the basics of their study were eager to learn both the arts and the science (expressing their ambitions in their wish to learn archery). Mozi considered their capability and strength and suggested that they should act within their own limits: they should first learn well in their cultural studies; if they wished to take up archery, it should not be done in a hurry and could be learned later. In Mozi's time, the disciplines were not highly specialized; if a person learned one step at a time, he should be able to master the six arts. This contrasts with today's attitude to learning. Take for example a student of fine arts or music who does not exert himself to the full in his study. How then is it possible for him to enter the academy of fine arts or music? One has to lower the expectations for such a student's learning in cultural studies. As for those children in mainland China or Hong

能力和精力，建議他們量力而為，先學好文化課，至於射箭嘛，不着急，慢慢來。

墨子時代學科分類尚未精細，一個人按步驟去學，還是有可能做到通六藝的。今天就不同了，考美術、音樂的學生若不盡全力在專業上，哪裏考得上美術學院、音樂學院？因此對他們的文化課要求，就只能降低一等了。至於中國內地、香港有些仍讀幼稚園的小朋友，被父母望子成龍心切地灌輸以高等數理、七八門特長，那就是「催谷」了。

不過，能否「一心多用」？看來人類也在「與時俱進」。譬如電腦發明之後，現在的「80後」「90後」及「00後」新新人類，早已進化出一邊上網聊天聽音樂，一邊抽空拼貼網文寫作文的「一心可多用」的「多元智慧」了。

六
天下匹夫徒步之士少知義，而教天下以義者，功亦多。

Kong now who are only in kindergarten but have already been coached in advanced arithmetic and a variety of other skills to fulfill the high hopes of their parents, we may call it "hastened ripening of crops."

Nonetheless, is "multi-tasking" possible? It seems that human beings are "evolving in a timely manner." For example, after the computer was invented, the Millennials, born in the eighties and nineties, and then later Generation Z, have long since evolved with "multi-tasking" "multiple intelligences" that enable them to simultaneously chat online, listen to streaming music while copying-and-pasting internet articles into their assignments.

Six
The commoners and grassroots people do not know much about righteousness, so those who teach the world about righteousness are making a great contribution.

Translation:
There was a rustic in the south of Lu by the name of Wu Lu. He made pottery in the winter and farmed in the summer and

【原文】

魯之南鄙人，有吳慮者，冬陶夏耕，自比於舜。子墨子聞而見之。吳慮謂子墨子：「義耳義耳，焉用言之哉？」子墨子曰：「子之所謂義者，亦有力以勞人，有財以分人乎？」吳慮曰：「有。」子墨子曰：「翟嘗計之矣。翟慮耕而食天下之人矣，盛，然後當一農之耕，分諸天下，不能人得一升粟。籍而以為得一升粟，其不能飽天下之飢者，既可睹矣。翟慮織而衣天下之人矣，盛，然後當一婦人之織，分諸天下，不能人得尺布。籍而以為得尺布，其不能煖天下之寒者，既可睹矣。翟慮被堅執銳救諸侯之患，盛，然後當一夫之戰，一夫之戰其不禦三軍，既可睹矣。翟以為不若誦先王之道，而求其說，通聖人之言，而察其辭，上說王公大人，次匹夫徒步之士。王公大人用吾言，國必治；匹夫徒步之士用吾言，行必脩。故翟以為雖不耕而食飢，不織而衣寒，功賢於耕而食之、織而衣之者也。故翟以為雖不耕織乎，而功賢於耕織也。」吳慮謂子墨子曰：「義耳

compared himself to Shun. Master Mozi heard of him and went to see him.

Wu Lu said to Master Mozi, "Ah righteousness, righteousness, what is the point of talking about it?"

Master Mozi said, "Does what you call righteousness involve those mighty ones serving people with their strength, and those wealthy ones sharing their wealth with people?"

Wu Lu said, "Yes."

Master Mozi said, "I did ponder on it. I considered becoming a farmer so that I could feed the people of the world. Yet at best I can produce as much as one farmer can produce; if I share my crops among the people of the world, each of them would get not even one sheng of grain. Even if each of them can get one sheng of grain, obviously it would not be enough to feed all the hungry people in the world. I considered becoming a weaver so that I could clothe the people of the world. Yet at best I can weave as much as one woman can weave; if I share my garments with the people of the world, each of them would get not even a foot of garment. Even if each of them can get one *chi* [1/3 meter] of garment, obviously it would not be enough to give warmth to all the people against the cold. I considered putting on armor and taking up weapons so that

義耳，焉用言之哉？」子墨子曰：「籍設而天下不知耕，教人耕，與不教人耕而獨耕者，其功孰多？」吳慮曰：「教人耕者其功多。」子墨子曰：「籍設而攻不義之國，鼓而使眾進戰，與不鼓而使眾進戰，而獨進戰者，其功孰多？」吳慮曰：「鼓而進眾者其功多。」子墨子曰：「天下匹夫徒步之士少知義，而教天下以義者，功亦多，何故弗言也？若得鼓而進於義，則吾義豈不益進哉？」（《魯問》）

【今譯】

　　魯國南郊有一叫吳慮的人，冬天製陶夏天耕作，以舜自比。墨子聽說了，就去見他。吳慮對墨子說：「義啊義啊，貴在切實之行，何必空言！」墨子說：「你所謂的義，包括有力者為別人操勞，有財者把財物施給別人嗎？」吳慮回答：「有。」墨子說：「我曾經計算過，我想自己耕作給天下人飯吃，充其量才相當於一個農民的勞動，把所得的收穫分配給天下人，每一個人得不到一升粟。就算一個人能分到一升粟，也不足以餵飽天下饑餓的人，這是顯而易見的。我想

I can rescue the vassal lords from their troubles. Yet at best I can fight as much as one soldier can fight, and obviously one soldier would not guard against the attack of three armies. In my opinion, it is better to study the way of the former kings and learn their principles, to understand the words of the sages and examine their meanings, to try to convince the nobles and the high-ranking people from above, and then the commoners and the grassroots people from below. If the nobles and the high-ranking people take my word, the state will be in good order; if the commoners and the grassroots people take my word, they will behave better. Therefore, in my opinion, even if I do not plough, I can feed the hungry; even if I do not weave, I can clothe people against cold. Therefore, in my opinion, even though I do neither ploughing nor weaving, my contribution is better than those who plough or weave."

Wu Lu said to Master Mozi, "Ah righteousness, righteousness, what is the point of talking about it?"

Master Mozi said, "Suppose the people of the world do not know anything about farming, there are people who teach others farming and there are people who do not teach others farming and choose instead to work in their fields alone. Between them, who contributes the more?"

Wu Lu said, "Those who teach farming contribute more."

自己紡織給天下的人衣服穿，充其量才頂得上一名婦人的紡織，把布匹分配給天下人，每個人得不到一尺布。就算一個人能得一尺布，還是不足以溫暖天下受凍的人，這是顯而易見的。我想身披堅固的鎧甲，手執銳利的武器，解救諸侯的患難，充其量才頂得上一名戰士作戰。一個戰士打仗，不能抵擋三軍的進攻，這是顯而易見的。我認為不如學習先王之道，研究他的學說，搞懂聖人的話，在上勸說王公大人，在下勸說平民百姓。王公大人採用了我的學說，國家一定能得到治理；平民百姓採用了我的學說，品行必定會有修養。所以我認為即使不耕作，也可以給饑餓的人飯吃，不紡織也可以給寒冷的人衣服穿，效果勝過自己耕作給人飯吃、自己紡織給人衣穿的人。所以，我認為即使不耕不織，效果也勝過耕田織布。」吳慮對墨子說：「義啊義啊，貴在切實之行，何必空言！」墨子問道：「假設天下的人不知道耕作，教人耕作的人，與不教人耕作而自顧自耕作的人，哪個的功勞大？」吳慮答道：「教人耕作的人功勞大。」墨子又問：「假設進攻不義的國家，擊鼓使大家作戰的人，與不擊鼓使大家作戰卻只是獨自作戰的人，兩者的功勞誰

Master Mozi said, "Suppose an attack against an unrighteous state is necessary, there are people who beat the drums and rally others to fight and there are people who do not beat the drums and rally people to fight and choose instead to fight alone, between them who contributes more?"

Wu Lu said, "Those who beat the drums and rally others to fight contribute more."

Master Mozi said, "The commoners and the grassroots people do not know much about righteousness, so those who teach the world about righteousness are making a great contribution. Why do we not talk about righteousness? If, like the drummers, I can motivate people to achieve righteousness, doesn't it also help to promote my righteousness? ("Lu Wen")

Contemporary interpretation:

This "worry-free" guy, Wu Lu, demonstrated the characteristic of Daoist and Agriculturalist outlooks: he fed himself by working in the fields, helped himself and sustained himself, and cherished the ideal of "How free I am from the power of the ruler!"

In the Spring and Autumn period, quite a few people led a life like this. When Confucius bustled around like a homeless dog, he once ran into a "Daoist before Daoism" or "hermit" like this

的大？」吳慮答道：「擊鼓使大家作戰的人功勞
大。」墨子說：「天下平民百姓少有人知道仁義，
因而用仁義教導天下的人，其功勞也大。為甚麼
不努力宣傳仁義呢？假若我能像擊鼓一樣鼓動大
家達到仁義，那麼，我的仁義豈不是更加發揚光
大了嗎？」

【時析】

　　這個「無慮」（吳慮）頗有道家和農家的風
範：自耕自食，自救自得，懷抱「帝力於我何有
哉」的理想。在春秋時代，頗有這樣的一些人。
孔子如喪家之犬到處奔走時，就曾碰到過這樣的
「道家前的道家」或「隱士」。如果說孔子和墨
子這樣的「有為士」，面對當時天下「禮崩樂
壞」，「知其不可而為之」，那麼這些隱士就是
認為天下已無藥可救，救也白救，不如退居一隅，
過自給自足的生活，「救人先救己」嘛！西方也
有兩類人可以用來作比較。在十九世紀末、二十
世紀初，西方基督教興起了「社會福音」「福音
派」，認為基督徒就是要面對和介入社會問題，
努力解決問題，提高社會福利。另一派「基要派」
則認為世界無藥可救，況且如果你自己都充滿罪

guy. If we take Confucius and Mozi as "activists" who "strived against all odds" to rescue the world from "failing rites and foundering music," then these hermits would be the ones who considered the world as beyond remedy — so hopeless that any attempt at remedy would be in vain. They therefore chose to withdraw themselves to a distant spot and led a self-sufficient life: "One has to save oneself before saving others"!

There are two types of character in the West comparable to these people. In late nineteenth century and early twentieth century, with the rise of "Social Gospel" in Christianity in the West, some Christians took it as their responsibility to make great effort to tackle social problems and to promote social welfare. At the same time, there were the "fundamentalists" who thought that the world was beyond remedy: if a man was sinful himself, how could he save others? All outward achievements were considered insignificant; a man should focus on saving his own soul instead. If we compare Confucianism and Mohism with Daoism, the former two are equivalent to Mahayana Buddhism or "the way of the bodhisattva" in the Buddhist tradition, which aims at saving the world. In contrast, Hinayana Buddhism or "arhat-phala," "the self-enlightened mind" aims at saving one's self. According to Hinayana or fundamentalist beliefs, if everyone in the world manages himself well, then the world will be free of any troubles. According to Mahayana or evangelical beliefs,

惡，如何能救別人？一切外在的事物都是皮毛，先救自己的靈魂才是正道。孔墨與道家的比較，也相當於佛教之中的大乘之道或「菩薩道」，以救世為目標，小乘或「羅漢果」、「自了漢」則以自救為目標。按小乘、基要派的主張，如果天下人都管好自己，天下自然也就無事了。按大乘、福音派的主張，世界上總是有智愚、先進後進、聖人不肖之別，一些人有責任救另一些人，如此世界才會逐漸平安和諧。

「無慮」看不起墨子到處奔走宣傳自己的主張，認為他不切實際，說空話，行為虛妄，如果天下人人都像他「無慮」那樣，自耕自種，帝力於我何加焉，天下自然也就太平。墨子只好從救世功效的大小的角度為自己辯護，他到處奔走勸說、教育王公大人與平民百姓奉行墨家主張，遠比他自耕自織的功效要大得多。墨子重視教育，作為當時的大教育家，他強調教育的作用，教育一群人遠比只是自己掌握一些技能要有功績。墨子反對道家和農家的自耕農式的「簡樸」生活，主張最大範圍地使社會趨向正義，這就需要墨家式的教師和遊說之士，宣傳正義學說並使政治家

however, there is always a gap between the wise and the unwise, the early and the late awakened ones, as well as the sage and the fool. Consequently, some people are responsible for saving other people so that the world can gradually become a peaceful and harmonious place.

Mr "Worry-free" scorned Mozi bustling around to advocate his doctrines; he thought Mozi was unrealistic, empty in words and presumptuous in behavior. He thought that if everyone could be as worry-free as him and become self-sufficient by farming, then one could be free from the power of the ruler, and as a result the world would be in good order!

In defense, Mozi argued that one's contribution to saving the world should be judged by the outcome: by running around to persuade and educate the nobles, the high-ranking people, the commoners and the grassroots people to adopt Mohist principles is way more significant than farming and weaving in solitude. Mozi valued education. As a great educator of his time, he emphasized the impact of education: that educating people serves a far greater purpose than acquiring skills for oneself. Mozi opposed the "simplistic" self-sufficient farming lifestyle advocated by Daoists and Agriculturalists and argued for promoting righteousness in society to the largest extent possible. In order to achieve this, Mohist teachers and lobbyists were needed to promote the theory of righteousness

在全社會推行正義學說。

　　看來，「無慮」式的人物以農為本，強調自食其力，反對當時一些到處做說客的知識份子。後來，孟子也面對這樣的問題。孟子用「勞心者治人，勞力者治於人」作了回答，從社會分工和社會管理的角度對體力勞動和腦力勞動作出分別，強調了腦力勞動的貢獻。可以說，在反對簡單地將「勞動」等同於體力勞動，強調社會整體的發展需要知識份子的參與上，墨子和孟子是一致的。

七
治於神者，眾人不知其功，爭於明者，眾人知之。

【原文】

　　公輸盤為楚造雲梯之械，成，將以攻宋。子墨子聞之，起於齊，行十日十夜而至於郢，見公輸盤。公輸盤曰：「夫子何

and persuade politicians to adopt comprehensively the theory of righteousness in their governance.

Apparently, the "worry-free" people who earned their living by farming and promoted self-reliance were against their intellectual contemporaries who bustled around lobbying for support. Later, when Mencius was faced with a similar challenge, he responded, "Those who work with the mind govern people, those who work with their strength are the subjects of governance." Viewing the situation from a perspective of social division of labor and social management, Mencius distinguished physical labor from mental labor and emphasized the contribution of mental labor. We can say that Mozi and Mencius shared the same opinion in their opposition to the simplistic identification of "labor" as physical labor: both emphasized the important contribution of intellectuals in the overall development of society.

Seven
For those who manage with wonderful foresight, people do not know their contribution; for those who argue endlessly in public, people are familiar with them.

命焉為？」子墨子曰：「北方有侮臣者，
願藉子殺之。」公輸盤不說。子墨子曰：
「請獻十金。」公輸盤曰：「吾義固不殺
人。」子墨子起，再拜曰：「請說之。吾
從北方，聞子為梯，將以攻宋。宋何罪之
有？荊國有餘於地，而不足於民，殺所不
足，而爭所有餘，不可謂智。宋無罪而攻
之，不可謂仁。知而不爭，不可謂忠。爭
而不得，不可謂強。義不殺少而殺眾，不
可謂知類。」公輸盤服。子墨子曰：「然，
乎不已乎？」公輸盤曰：「不可。吾既
已言之王矣。」子墨子曰：「胡不見我於
王？」公輸盤曰：「諾」。子墨子見王，曰：
「今有人於此，舍其文軒，鄰有敝轝，而
欲竊之；舍其錦繡，鄰有短褐，而欲竊之；
舍其粱肉，鄰有糠糟，而欲竊之。此為何
若人？」王曰：「必為竊疾矣。」子墨子曰：
「荊之地，方五千里，宋之地，方五百里，
此猶文軒之與敝轝也；荊有雲夢，犀兕麋
鹿滿之，江漢之魚鱉黿鼉為天下富，宋所
為無雉兔狐貍者也，此猶粱肉之與糠糟
也；荊有長松、文梓、梗柟、豫章，宋無

Translation:

Gongshu Pan was to build a scaling ladder for Chu, and when it was completed it would be used to attack Song. When Master Mozi heard of it, he set out from Qi and traveled for ten days and ten nights to reach Ying [the capital of Chu], and went to see Gongshu Pan.

Gongshu Pan said, "Master, how can I help you?"

Mozi said, "Someone in the north humiliated me, I want you to kill him for me."

Gongshu Pan was not pleased.

Master Mozi said, "I can offer you ten pieces of gold."

Gongshu Pan said, "I uphold righteousness and am determined not to kill anyone."

Master Mozi stood up, bowed to him and said, "Please listen to me. While I was in the north, I heard that you have built a ladder that will be used to attack Song. What is Song guilty of? The state of Chu (Jing) has land to spare but has a shortage of people. To let a small population be sacrificed in order to fight for an excess of land, cannot be taken as wise. If despite Song's innocence, one still attacks it, it cannot be taken as benevolent.

長木，此猶錦繡之與短褐也。臣以三事之攻宋也，為與此同類，臣見大王之必傷義而不得。」王曰：「善哉！雖然，公輸盤為我為雲梯，必取宋。」於是見公輸盤，子墨子解帶為城，以牒為械，公輸盤九設攻城之機變，子墨子九距之，公輸盤之攻械盡，子墨子之守圉有餘。公輸盤詘，而曰：「吾知所以距子矣，吾不言。」子墨子亦曰：「吾知子之所以距我，吾不言。」楚王問其故，子墨子曰：「公輸子之意，不過欲殺臣。殺臣，宋莫能守，可攻也。然臣之弟子禽滑厘等三百人，已持臣守圉之器，在宋城上而待楚寇矣。雖殺臣，不能絕也。」楚王曰：「善哉！吾請無攻宋矣。」子墨子歸，過宋，天雨，庇其閭中，守閭者不內也。故曰：「治於神者，眾人不知其功，爭於明者，眾人知之。」（《公輸》）

【今譯】

　　公輸盤為楚國造雲梯這種器械，完成了，將用它攻打宋國。墨子聽說了，就從齊國起身，走

Knowing these things and still choosing not to advise against them, it cannot be taken as loyal. Having advised against them and still unable achieve anything, it cannot be taken as powerful. In order to uphold righteousness, if one chooses not to kill a few, and yet still chooses to kill a lot, it cannot be taken as logical."

Gongshu Pan was convinced [by these words].

Master Mozi said, "In that case, why not call off the attack?"

Gongshu Pan said, "No, I can't. I have already proposed it to the king.

Master Mozi said, "Why not take me to see the king?"

Gongshu Pan said, "Alright."

Master Mozi went to the king of Chu and said, "Suppose there is such a man: he discards his well-decorated carriage and wants to steal his neighbor's broken cart; he discards his well-embroidered clothes and wants to steal his neighbor's rough-woven clothes; he discards his epicurean food and wants to steal his neighbor's coarse food. What kind of man is this?"

The king said, "He must be a kleptomaniac."

了十天十夜，到了楚國國都郢，會見公輸盤。

公輸盤說：「先生對我有甚麼吩咐嗎？」墨子說：「北方有一個欺侮我的人，我願借助你殺了他。」公輸盤不高興。墨子說：「我願意獻給你十鎰黃金。」公輸盤說：「我講義，決不殺人。」

墨子站起來，再一次對公輸盤行了拜禮，說：「請聽我說。我在北方聽說你造雲梯，將用它攻打宋國。宋國有甚麼罪過？楚國土地有餘，人口卻不足。現在犧牲不足的人口，掠奪有餘的土地，不能說是智慧。宋國沒有罪卻攻打它，不能說是仁。知道這些卻不去爭諫，不能稱作忠。爭諫卻沒有結果，不能算是強。依你的道義不殺個別的人，卻殺眾多的百姓，不可說你懂得類推之理。」公輸盤服了。

墨子又問他：「那麼，為甚麼不停止攻宋呢？」公輸盤說：「不能。我已經跟楚王說好了。」墨子說：「為甚麼不將我引見給楚王？」公輸盤說：「好吧。」

Master Mozi said, "The territory of Chu (Jing) covers an area of five thousand *li*, the territory of Song covers an area of five hundred *li*; this is like comparing the well-decorated carriage with the broken cart. In Chu (Jing), there is the lake of Yun Meng, which is filled with rhinoceroses and deer; there is the Yangtze River and the Han River, which have the most fish, turtles and crocodiles in the whole world. Song is said to have not even pheasants, rabbits, or foxes. This is like comparing the fine food with the coarse food. In Chu (Jing), there are tall pines, catalpas, cedars and camphor trees; in Song, there are hardly any tall trees. This is like comparing the well-embroidered clothes with rough-woven clothes.

"I consider these three kinds of behavior as equivalent to the attack of Song. In my opinion, if your Majesty chooses to do it, it will unavoidably harm righteousness and thus fail."

The king of Chu said, "Well said! Nonetheless, Gongshu Pan has built the scaling ladder for me; I must conquer Song."

So, turning to Gongshu Pan, Master Mozi untied his belt and used it to represent the city wall, with the writing sticks as the defensive weapons. Gongshu Pan attempted nine rounds of attacks with various strategies; Master Mozi repelled him nine times. Gongshu Pan used up all his machines for the attacks, while Master Mozi still had plenty of means of defense.

　　墨子見到楚王，說：「現在這裏有一個人，丟棄他華麗的彩車，鄰居有破車，卻想去偷；丟棄自己的錦繡衣裳，鄰居有粗布褂子，卻想去偷；丟棄他的美食佳餚，鄰居有糟糠，卻想去偷。這是甚麼人呢？」楚王回答說：「這人一定是患了偷竊病。」

　　墨子說：「楚國的地方，方圓五千里，宋國的地方，方圓五百里，這就像彩車與破車相比；楚國有雲夢大澤，犀、兕、麋鹿充滿其中，長江、漢水中的魚、鱉、黿、鼉富甲天下，宋國卻連野雞、兔子、狐狸都沒有，這就像美食佳餚與糟糠相比；楚國有巨松、梓樹、楠、樟等名貴木材，宋國連棵大樹都沒有，這就像錦繡衣裳與粗布褂子相比。從這三方面看，我認為楚國進攻宋國，與患了偷竊病的人同屬一種類型。我認為大王您如果這樣做，一定會傷害道義而不能成功。」

　　楚王說：「說得好！雖然這樣，公輸盤已經為我造好了雲梯，我一定要攻取宋國！」

　　於是又見公輸盤。墨子解下腰帶，圍作一座

Gongshu Pan was crushed, yet he said, "Now I know how to beat you, but I will not say it."

Master Mozi said, "I know how you can beat me, but I will not say it."

The king of Chu asked for their reasons.

Master Mozi said, "What Master Gongshu has in mind is simply to kill me. If I were killed, there would be no one to guard the city, and you could launch the attack. However, my disciples, Qin Huali and three hundred others, all have defensive weapons in their hands and are getting ready up on the city walls of Song to wait for the invaders from Chu. Even if I were killed, there would be endless others to fight against you."

The king of Chu said, "Well said! I now make the decision not to attack Song."

When Master Mozi was on his way back [to Qi], he passed through Song. It was raining, so he sought shelter at a gate, yet the gate keeper did not let him in. Hence, it is said, "For those who manage with wonderful foresight, people do not know their contribution; for those who argue endlessly in public, people are familiar with them." ("Gong Shu")

城的樣子，用小木片作為守備的器械。公輸盤九次運用機巧多變的攻城器械，墨子九次擋住了。公輸盤攻城的器械用盡了，墨子守城的辦法還是綽綽有餘。公輸盤無奈，卻說：「我知道怎麼對付你了。我不說。」墨子也說：「我知道你想怎麼對付我了。我不說。」楚王問他們原因。

墨子回答說：「公輸盤的意思，不過是殺了我。殺了我，宋國就沒有人能防守，就可以攻打了。但是，我的弟子禽滑厘等三百人，已經手持我守禦用的器械，在宋國的都城上等待楚寇呢。即使殺了我，守禦的人卻是殺不盡的。」楚王說：「好吧，我就不攻打宋國了。」

墨子從楚國歸來，經過宋國，天下着雨，他到閭門去避雨，守閭門的人卻不接納他。所以說：「運用神機的人，眾人不知道他的功勞；而於明處爭辯不休的人，眾人卻都知道他。」

【時析】

這篇文章是中國歷史上的名著之一，早被列入了內地中學課本。墨子出於正義救宋，他不費

Contemporary interpretation:

This passage is one of the masterpieces in Chinese history and has been included in the textbooks used in secondary schools in China.

For the sake of righteousness, Mozi wanted to save Song. He made the king of Chu give up his plan to attack Song without sending any troops, which matches well with what *The Art of War* stated: "To allow the opponent to withdraw its troops without fighting any battles." Through sand table exercises about attacks, Mozi defeated Gongshu Pan nine times, and Gongshu Pan was in the end lost for words. Even if the king of Chu had killed Mozi, his three hundred "volunteers" were already guarding the city walls of Song so that Chu would not be able to prevail in its attack of Song.

The passage shows vividly that Mozi was a person who possessed righteousness, courage and wisdom.

The last scene is also informative.

Mozi rescued Song, and yet when he passed through Song on his way back home and wanted to shelter from the rain, permission was declined at the gate. This reveals that Mozi did not seek to rescue Song in a loud and visible manner so that he would be known to everyone. Instead, he did it discreetly,

一兵一卒就打消了楚王攻宋的念頭，很符合《孫子兵法》中所說的「不戰而屈人之兵」。通過有關攻城的沙盤演習，他九次勝了公輸盤，弄得公輸盤無話可說。即使楚王殺了他，在墨子的三百「義勇軍」早已赴宋守衛的情況下，楚國攻宋也佔不到任何便宜。文章活現了一個有義、有勇、有智的墨子。

耐人尋味的是最後一個鏡頭。墨子救了宋國，但在經過宋國遇雨時，卻不得城門而入。可見墨子之救宋，並沒有大張旗鼓，弄得人人皆知，只是運作於無形之中，這倒是頗符合道家的聖人理想。老子說，聖人「生而不有，為而不恃，功成而弗居」（《老子》第 2 章），莊子則說，「至人無己，神人無功，聖人無名」（《逍遙遊》）。墨子正是這樣的「聖人」、「至人」、「神人」。

which matches well with the Daoist ideal of the sage. Laozi said, the sage should "be and does not possess, act and does not proclaim, contribute and does not lay claim to it." (*Lao Tzu* Chapter 2)

Zhuangzi said, "The perfect man has no self; the godly man has no merit; the sage has no fame." ("Xiao Yao You")

Mozi is exactly such a "sage," a "perfect man" and a "godly man."

墨子今譯時析
Mozi — A Modern Translation and Contemporary Interpretation

編撰 Authors
周偉馳 Zhou Weichi   鄭偉鳴 Terry Cheng   呂子德 Troy Lui
英文翻譯 English Translation   伍美蓮 Ng Mei-lin

中文責任編輯 Chinese Editor   黃為國 Wong Wai-kwok
英文責任編輯 English Editor   鄭偉鳴 Terry Cheng

中文校對 Chinese Proofreading   苗淑敏 Miao Shumin
英文審校 English Copyediting   Carol Dyer

裝幀設計 Graphic Designer   方子聰 Paul Fong

策劃 Planning	保華生活教育集團文化委員會 Culture Committee, B & P Group
顧問 Advisor	葉國華教授，保華生活教育集團主席 Prof. Paul Yip, Chairman, B & P Group
督印人 Supervisor	陳保琼博士，保華生活教育集團行政總裁 Dr Betty Chan, Chief Executive Officer, B & P Group

出版 Publishing	耀中出版社 Yew Chung Publishing House
地址 Address	香港九龍新蒲崗大有街一號勤達中心１６樓 16/F, Midas Plaza, No.1 Tai Yau Street, San Po Kong, Kowloon, Hong Kong
電話 Tel	852-39239711
傳真 Fax	852-26351607
網址 Website	www.llce.com.hk
電郵 Email	contact@llce.com.hk

初版 First Edition	2021.10
承印 Printing	香港志忠彩印有限公司 HK Zhizhong Colour Printing Co., Limited
書號 ISBN	978-988-78352-7-1